The American
Criminal Justice
System

A Concise Guide to Cops, Courts,
Corrections, and Victims

By James Windell

cognella™
San Diego, CA

Bassim Hamadeh, CEO and Publisher
Christopher Foster, General Vice President
Michael Simpson, Vice President of Acquisitions
Jessica Knott, Managing Editor
Kevin Fahey, Cognella Marketing Manager
Jess Busch, Senior Graphic Designer
John Remington, Acquisitions Editor
Jamie Giganti, Project Editor
Brian Fahey, Licensing Associate
Kate McKellar, Interior Designer

First published in the United States of America in 2013 by Cognella, Inc.

Printed in the United States of America

ISBN: 978-1-60927-605-8 (pbk) / 978-1-60927-606-5 (br)

cognella™

www.cognella.com 800.200.3908

Contents

Introduction

When I agreed to write a textbook for introductory classes in criminal justice classes, I had been teaching criminal justice for more than 12 years. In addition, I have worked in the criminal justice field in one capacity or another for nearly 40 years of my career. The combination of teaching and work in the criminal justice system has given me an opportunity to develop my own particular viewpoints and biases.

As a student who is about to read this textbook, you should be aware of some aspects of my background which have helped to shape my perspectives, views, and prejudices, which I am sure will be evident in this book. Although I have endeavored to be impartial, fair, and unbiased in this textbook, I know this is not really possible given my experiences, the life lessons I've learned, the research I have done, and the reading I've been doing for many years. My way of viewing the criminal justice field will seep into various parts of a book like this.

What you should know about me and my background is that I have been teaching criminal justice classes at Wayne State University in Detroit. As a teacher on an urban campus, I recognize that the students who take Introduction to Criminal Justice classes are very diverse, coming from many different racial and cultural backgrounds. However, after they take an introductory class, I believe they want to learn more about the American system of justice. Although, obviously, all other countries have criminal justice systems, I have opted to avoid talking about other countries and how they go about handling law enforcement and criminal justice. I could not possibly do justice to every country students might want to know about. Consequently, in this book, as in my classes, my goal is to provide students with an overview of the American version of justice.

Furthermore, while students want to know more about the American criminal justice system, they start out learning about criminal justice against the backdrop of their own beliefs and prejudices. Like the public in general, new students in criminal justice have false beliefs and misconceptions about how the justice system in this country works. One of my other goals, besides giving an overview of our justice system, is to dispel some of the myths that students bring with them, while at the same time reporting what I believe is more truthful and accurate.

My experience in the field of criminal justice has allowed me to work closely with law enforcement, lawyers, prosecutors, probation officers, and judges. I have come to have high respect for many people in all parts of the criminal justice system. I know that most police officers, prosecutors, probation officers, corrections officers, prison psychologists, and judges are hard-working and that they want to make a difference, assist people in need, and live up to high ideals in their field. Most of them, in fact, do exactly that.

However, I have also seen the other side of the justice system—the side of the system where there are the problems, flaws, corruption, and the distasteful. I have seen—and sometimes worked with—the people who lack integrity, misuse their authority, and give the justice system, and some of the players in that system, a bad name. As a result, I have set out in this book to give an overview of the problems and challenges faced by the criminal justice system. Some of these problems and challenges are very serious and lead not only to criticism and mistrust of the system, but worse, they lead to imprisonment or death for some who are undeserving of such fates. I hope that students who read this book and go on to work in the criminal justice field will do so with a realistic view of the challenges before them but with a determination to take advantage of the opportunities they will have to make the criminal justice field much better than it is now.

This textbook is intended to go along with class lectures and class assignments. Since it is a concise introduction to criminal justice, there is no intent to cover everything you will need to know to excel in the field. Instead, the goal is to open up a new world of learning for you. I hope you will develop an interest in the field of criminal justice and that you will want to pursue more knowledge in the parts of the field that most interest you.

The sections at the end of each chapter, entitled For Your Consideration, will give you more areas you can flag for future pursuit. These areas include important events in criminal justice history, court cases, movies, television shows, websites, and books. My hope is that you will find something so intriguing that you will want to do further investigation on your own.

By reading this book, listening to class lectures, completing a research paper or term paper, and by doing more reading on your own, I trust that you will leave the class that uses this textbook with considerably more information, knowledge, and fascination with the field of criminal justice. Criminal justice is a critical field of study and it will touch your life—perhaps in many ways—in the future. Therefore, I sincerely hope that what you learn from this book and your first criminal justice class will make your encounters with the criminal justice system more meaningful and highly successful. But first, enjoy reading and learning.

Part One

Myths and Realities in the
Criminal Justice System

Chapter One

Myths and the Criminal Justice System

INTRODUCTION

Neither crime nor the criminal justice system is exactly the way it is portrayed on television or in the movies. In fact, watching cop shows or legal shows on TV—even the very well-done television dramas—is likely to perpetuate various myths about crime and criminal justice. Some of the best shows, such as *Law & Order* and *Southland*, have touches of realism about them, but that is all you can expect. Too often, those cop shows and legal shows are unrealistic in several ways.

For example, here are the major ways TV crime dramas (seen weekly by millions of viewers) are myth makers or myth perpetuators:

- Most cop shows and many legal shows feature a murder that must be solved; this reinforces the belief of many Americans that murder rates are high and are continually climbing.
- Most TV shows that emphasize crime also strongly suggest that detectives, uniformed police officers, forensic technicians, coroners, and even prosecutors solve crimes within an hour; the reality is that many, if not most, crimes go unsolved.
- Detectives are portrayed as having almost unlimited time and resources to pursue leads and follow up clues; in real life, there is a very limited amount of time that detectives can devote to a single case before they have to move on to other, more pressing cases.

Crime is a sociopolitical artifact, not a natural phenomenon. We can have as much or as little crime as we please, depending on what we choose to count as criminal.

—*Herbert L. Packer,* The Limits of the Criminal Sanction, *1968*

- Forensic laboratories and the forensic technicians who work in those laboratories in TV shows are not only highly skilled and efficient, but have the latest equipment and the finest technology to aid their processing of crime scene data; the truth is quite the opposite in most cities.
- Forensic tests and examinations of evidence can be completed immediately with results passed on to the detectives for help in solving cases; in real life, it often takes weeks, months, or even years for crime scene analysis to be completed.

This book is designed to give a more realistic introduction to crime and criminal justice. By studying this book, you should have a more realistic and practical view of the criminal justice system. Although there may be some underlying cynicism in this book because it does not glamorize the criminal justice system, still it is well to keep in mind that any student who studies criminal justice and criminology and goes on to pursue a career in the vast criminal justice system should have a healthy sense of the frustrations and challenges of working in criminal justice.

The author's viewpoint shows that, despite the challenges of work in the criminal justice field, a career in criminal justice offers exciting and important employment choices that require well-trained individuals who will accept the work in this field as necessary for the smooth functioning of our society.

What Is Criminal Justice?

Criminal justice, according to *Black's Law Dictionary* (Garner, 2000), represents the methods by which a society deals with those who are accused of committing crimes. Other authorities in the field of criminal justice see criminal justice as an institution of social control, similar to the family, schools, organized religion, the media, and the law.

The study of criminal justice, though, concerns a field of study that looks at how our society provides citizens with services related to crime.

The Criminal Justice System

During the administration of United States president Lyndon Baines Johnson, President Johnson appointed a commission to study crime. When Johnson was running against Barry Goldwater for the presidency, Goldwater—a conservative Republican—accused Johnson of being "soft on crime." Smarting from this criticism, even though Johnson thoroughly trounced Goldwater in the election, Johnson appointed a commission to study crime in the United States. Known as the President's Commission on Law Enforcement and the Administration of Justice, this commission issued a ground-breaking report in 1967, which was entitled "The Challenge of Crime in a Free Society."

In the lengthy report of the Commission on Law Enforcement and the Administration of Justice (1968), the commission defined the criminal justice system as an apparatus that society uses to "enforce the standards of conduct necessary to protect individuals and the community." While other experts in the field might quibble with this definition, its meaning helps us to better understand the nature of the criminal justice system.

> **Myth:** *The criminal justice system in America is a tightly knit and well-structured group of organizations that share a common goal.*
>
> **Reality:** *According to Bohm & Haley, authors of a criminal justice textbook (2002), the United States criminal justice system is a loose confederation of more than 50,000 agencies of federal, state, and local governments. Other authorities have pointed out that with so many agencies comprising the criminal justice system, there is just no way that the agencies that represent the criminal justice system can have similar goals.*

Typically, the criminal justice system is made up of three main components: law enforcement, the judicial system, and corrections. This book will, in fact, devote much of its chapters to those three areas, which are often referred to simply as cops, courts, and corrections. However, these days it is important to consider that the criminal justice system also includes victims and the community. Both victims and citizens play an ever increasing role in the criminal justice system.

The Difference between Criminal Justice and Criminology

Criminology is the study of the causes of crime as well as the criminal justice system, including corrections. In that sense, there is little difference between the study of criminal justice and criminology. Some experts in the field might contend that criminology is more of an academic discipline, although there is little that distinguishes criminal justice classes and criminology classes.

What Is a Crime?

As was quickly learned by President Johnson during his campaign for the presidency, crime is one of America's most enduring and important social problems. If a legislator or a politician talks about crime, he or she is likely to get people to sit up and listen. Crime typically ranks consistently alongside such other social issues as the economy, poverty, and war. These are issues that concern the public.

Everybody in America seems to be concerned about crime, but what is crime? Simply put, a crime is a social harm that is punishable under the law. In a more formal sense, Dean Champion, in *The American Dictionary of Criminal Justice* (2001), defines crime as any act or omission prohibited by law by anyone who is held accountable by that law. The important part of Champion's or any other definition is that the act or omission must be in violation of criminal law. And criminal laws are laws or ordinances passed by elected officials and representatives who decide which behaviors and acts will be punished. When a law is passed by a governmental body, it becomes part of the criminal code of the respective city, state, or federal government.

What Is Justice?

We know what a crime is, we know a little bit about the criminal justice system, but what exactly is justice?

Justice is first of all an ideal concerning the maintenance of rights and the correction of wrong in our society. But to many people, particularly victims, justice has a more important meaning. It can mean the proper and appropriate administration of the laws. To some, that might mean that criminal offenders get their just deserts. To law enforcement, justice may mean that criminal offenders receive their appropriate punishment. But to many, justice may simply mean that there is a fair and proper administration of criminal law.

Given such issues as racial bias, racial profiling, discrepancies in the sentencing of Caucasians and African Americans, as well as other issues in our criminal justice system, it may be argued that our criminal justice system fails to live up to the ideal standard of fair and impartial use of the law in criminal proceedings.

Is There an Ideal Model of the Administration of the Criminal Justice System?

In his 1968 book, *The Limits of the Criminal Sanction*, Herbert L. Packer wrote that there are two competing models of criminal justice administration. One of those models is the crime control model; the other is the due process model. These models are two very different ways of looking at the goals and procedures of the criminal justice system. These models should not be viewed as exactly defining the way any particular official or law enforcement agency handles suspects, criminal offenders, or convicted felons. Rather, elements of both models appear in different ways and at different times in the criminal justice system.

The crime control model:

The crime control model tends to emphasize:

- Efficiency in the processing of criminal defendants
- The goal of controlling crime
- Less concern about protecting an individual's rights
- Applying sanctions to those convicted of crimes
- Punishment to prevent and control crime

The due process model:

- Assumes that freedom and rights are of great importance to every individual
- Believes that every effort should be made to ensure that due process procedures are followed
- Stresses the rights of defendants
- Emphasizes that every individual accused of a crime is presumed innocent until proven guilty
- Implies that it is better to let a guilty person go free than to convict the innocent

Questions Raised about Criminal Justice and Crime

In the quote given at the beginning of this chapter, Herbert L. Packer states that crime is a sociopolitical artifact, not a natural phenomenon. He goes on to say that we can have as much or as little crime as we choose. But what does this mean? Based on what you've read in this chapter, how can we have as much or as little crime as we choose?

What do you now understand to be the criminal justice system? How is it different from what you thought before you read this chapter?

It is important that students of criminal justice think about such critical questions. This book will raise many more questions in future chapters. In Chapter Two, there will be more discussion about crime and what citizens fear when it comes to crime.

FOR FURTHER CONSIDERATION

Historical Events Relevant to Chapter One

January 15, 1981: The crime show *Hill Street Blues* debuts on the NBC television network. A police drama, it depicts the lives of the officers in a precinct in an unknown American city. It runs until May 1987, winning many awards along the way.

September 22, 1997: The police show *Brooklyn South*, created by Steven Bochco, debuts on CBS . It only lasts a year, but is a realistic and gritty show portraying life in a run-down Brooklyn police precinct and focusing on the work of uniformed officers. It is available on DVD.

September 24, 1789: The United States Congress passes the First Judiciary Act. This act provides for an attorney general, the Supreme Court, and creates the U.S. Marshals.

October 4, 1636: The first code of law was created in what would become America. The men still onboard a ship passed the code of law for the Plymouth Colony; it became known as the Plymouth Compact.

Significant Court Decisions

Gitlow v. New York, **268 U.S. 652 (1925):** In Chapter One, we addressed the question, What is a crime? The U.S. Supreme Court has had to tackle this question several times. In *Gitlow v. New York*, the Supreme Court was faced with trying to decide if the actions of Benjamin Gitlow, a left-wing member of the Socialist Party, were criminal actions or whether he was protected under the free-speech clause of the First Amendment. What Gitlow had done was to write, publish, and distribute 16,000 pamphlets that urged the establishment of socialism by strikes and "class action ... in any form" (Hall and Ely, 2009, 123). After being arrested and charged with violation of the New York Criminal Anarchy Law of 1902, Gitlow was convicted. But he appealed his case and it eventually went before the U.S. Supreme Court. In a split decision, the majority upheld his conviction and the majority opinion stated that "[A] state may punish utterances endangering the foundations of organized government and threatening its overthrow by unlawful means" (Hall and Ely, 2009). In a dissenting opinion, Justices Oliver Wendell Holmes and Louis D. Brandeis wrote that only actions, not expressions, should be punished.

Websites to Check Out

- What is a crime? *About.com.* Available at:*http://crime.about.com/od/Crime_101/a/What-Is-A-Crime.htm*
- What is a crime? *Oxford Journal of Legal Studies.* Available at: *http://ojls.oxfordjournals.org/content/27/4/609. abstract*
- Crime in the media. *Political Research Associates* Available at: *http://www.publiceye.org/defendingjustice/ overview/beckett_media.html*

Books

- Kappeler, V. E., and Potter, G. W. (2005). *The Mythology of Crime and Criminal Justice.* 4th ed. Long Grove, IL: Waveland Press, Inc. In this book, the authors challenge many popular notions in the field of criminal justice.
- Masters, R., et al. (2013). *CJ: Realities and Challenges.* New York: McGraw Hill. This textbook attempts to dispel many myths about the criminal justice system.

Movies

Dirty Harry (1971). In this movie (as well as other *Dirty Harry* sequels), Clint Eastwood plays a San Francisco Detective who argues—more by action than by dialogue—that crime control is a more important approach to dealing with crime than is the due process approach.

TV Shows

- *Law & Order: Law & Order* is an American police procedural and legal drama television series created by Dick Wolf. It premiered on September 13, 1990, and completed its 20th and final season in May 2010. It was the longest-running police show. Based in New York City, the series follows a two-part approach, in which the first half hour is focused on the investigation of a crime (usually murder) and the apprehension of a suspect. The second half hour features the prosecution of the defendant by the Manhattan District Attorney's office. Plots are often based on real cases that recently made headlines. Available on DVD.
- *NYPD Blue*: A television police drama set in New York City featuring the daily lives of officers of the fictional 15th Precinct of Manhattan. Created by Steven Bochco and David Milch, it ran on ABC from September 1993 until March 2005. Like *Hill Street Blues*, there was a real-life sense of what police work in a New York precinct is really like.
- *Hill Street Blues:* Another one-hour show based in an unknown American city, it aired from 1981 to 1987 on NBC. This was one of the originators of the gritty police drama.
- *Brooklyn South:* Brooklyn South was a police drama that aired in only one year during the 1997–1998 television season. The series, created by Steven Bochco, Bill Clark, David Milch, and William M. Finkel-

stein, portrays a gritty, realistic police station similar to that of *NYPD Blue*, but differed by focusing on the uniformed police officers rather than the detectives.

- *Dragnet:* Originally running for eight years starting in 1951, this cop show features a detective (Sgt. Joe Friday) and his partner who investigated various kinds of cases. *Dragnet* was perhaps the most famous and influential police procedural drama in television history. The series gave millions of audience members a feel for the boredom and drudgery, as well as the danger and heroism, of real-life police work. *Dragnet* earned praise for improving the public's perception of police officers. Actor and producer Jack Webb's aims in *Dragnet* were for realism and unpretentious acting. He achieved both goals, and *Dragnet* remains a key influence on subsequent police dramas in many media.

Review for Chapter One

Research Paper or Term Paper Topics:

- How does the media influence people's opinions about crime?
- What are the differences between the crime control approach to dealing with crime and the due process approach?

Important Terms to Know

Crime:	A crime is a social harm that is punishable under the law. More formally, it can be defined as any act or omission prohibited by law by anyone who is held accountable by that law.
Crime control model:	A model of criminal justice administration that emphasizes efficiency in the processing of criminal defendants and punishment to prevent and control crime.
Criminal justice:	Criminal justice represents the methods by which a society deals with those who are accused of having committed crimes.
Due process model:	A model of criminal justice administration that emphasizes the rights of individuals and the assurance that due process procedures are followed.
Justice:	Justice is an ideal concerning the maintenance of rights and the correction of wrong in our society. But justice can also mean the proper and appropriate administration of the laws.

The President's Commission on Law Enforcement and the Administration of Justice:

A commission appointed by President Lyndon Johnson to study crime in America. This commission issued its report in 1967 entitled "The Challenge of Crime in a Free Society."

Study Guide Questions

1. What is criminal justice?
    a. The methods by which a society deals with the accused
    b. The methods by which society seeks justice
    c. The methods by which society deals with those convicted of crime
    d. All of the above

2. What is a crime?
    a. A crime is any action that bothers another person
    b. A crime is any opinion or expression that is offensive
    c. A crime is a social harm that is punishable under the law
    d. A crime is any behavior some people consider morally wrong

3. What are the two models of criminal justice administration?
    a. Crime control and free speech
    b. Due process and "get tough on crime"
    c. Crime control and the death penalty
    d. Crime control and due process

4. In which criminal justice model would punishment be viewed as essential?
    a. The due process model
    b. The crime control model
    c. The restorative justice model
    d. The freedom of speech model

5. Rather than being a tightly knit and structured group of organizations with a common goal, the criminal justice system is
    a. an organization of completely separate entities
    b. an organization of 50,000 agencies that often have different goals.
    c. a loose conglomeration of police departments
    d. a great many agencies and programs that subscribe to the priorities established by the FBI

References

Bohm, R. M., and Haley, K. N. (2002). *Introduction to Criminal Justice*. 3rd ed. New York: Glencoe/McGraw-Hill Co.

Champion, D. (2001). *The American Dictionary of Criminal Justice*. Los Angeles: Roxbury Publishing Co.

Garner, B. A. (Ed.) (2000). *Black's Law Dictionary.* 7th ed. St. Paul, MN: West Publishing Co.

Packer, H. L. (1968). *The Limits of the Criminal Sanction*. Stanford, CA: Stanford University Press.

The President's Commission on Law Enforcement and the Administration of Justice (1967). *The Challenge of Crime in a Free Society.* Washington, DC: U.S. Government Printing Office.

Chapter Two

It All Starts with Crime

Jane Bashara, a 56-year-old woman and mother of two who lived in Grosse Pointe, an upscale suburb of Detroit, Michigan, was found strangled in her SUV in an alley in downtown Detroit in February 2012. Her husband, Bob, a Grosse Pointe Park businessman, allegedly ran a dominatrix studio in Detroit. He had reported his wife missing the day before her body was found.

The day after her body was located, Joseph Gentz, a 48-year-old man who did work for Bob Bashara, went to the police station and said he had been hired to kill Jane Bashara. Then he said at a later time that Bob Bashara had forced him at gunpoint to kill his wife. Gentz was questioned and let go. Bob Bashara was also questioned by the police, but maintained his innocence of the murder, which the police indicated likely occurred in the Bashara's garage.

On Sunday, March 4, 2012, Gentz was arrested and on March 6 was arraigned and charged with both first degree murder and conspiracy to commit murder. However, he was referred to the state forensics center for a competency evaluation, as both the prosecutor and Gentz's defense attorney were not sure he was competent to stand trial. Bob Bashara was still said to be a "person of interest" in the murder.

Bernard Madoff, a wealthy New York businessman and founder of Bernard L. Madoff Investment Securities LLC, was arrested by the FBI on December 11, 2008. In March 2009, he was charged with securities fraud for running an elaborate Ponzi scheme that bilked thousands of investors out of billions of dollars. Federal investigators believed he had been running a fraudulent investment company since the 1970s and court-appointed trustees estimated that his clients lost as much as $18 billion.

It is commonly assumed that these three components—law enforcement ... the judicial process ... and corrections ... add up to a "system" of criminal justice. A system implies some unity of purpose and organized interrelationship among component parts ... no such relationship exists ...

—National Commission on the Causes and Prevention of Violence: To Establish Justice, to Insure Domestic Tranquility, 1969

In cases like the Bernard L. Madoff case, the criminal justice system responds to a complaint of wrongdoing. In this instance, there was a complaint lodged about financial wrongdoing. When stocks or bonds are involved, as in a Ponzi scheme, the Securities and Exchange Commission (SEC), a regulatory agency, may receive an initial complaint and they may look into the complaint. After an investigation, the Securities and Exchange Commission may notify the FBI, since federal laws were likely violated. The FBI and their financial fraud division would then launch an investigation which could take months or even years, as very often financial crimes involve many people and often millions of dollars. However, in this instance, the SEC had actually audited and investigated Madoff's firm many times beginning in the 1990s, but could apparently find no evidence of wrongdoing (Scannell, 2009). But a financial analyst again contacted the SEC in 2000 strongly suggesting another investigation of the firm because the numbers just didn't add up (Stewart, 2011).

When the FBI has gathered enough evidence, the case will go to a United States District Court, a federal prosecutorial agency, for charges. When an arrest is made, it would be FBI agents who make the arrest. The FBI did, in fact, arrest Madoff on December 11, 2008, on a criminal charge of securities fraud (U.S. Department of Justice, 2012).

When Flight 253 landed in Detroit's Metro Airport, federal agents were on hand to arrest Umar Farouk Abdulmutallab. He was arraigned in a U.S. District Court, and after pleading guilty, he was sentenced by a U.S. District Court judge and incarcerated in a federal correctional facility.

What We Expect of the American Criminal Justice System

Our three crime stories involved three different people and three very different kinds of crime. But in each instance, law enforcement agencies responded to complaints about a crime, investigated the crimes, and in all three cases made an arrest. Although only two of these three cases have been concluded by sentencing of an offender, we expect the justice system to respond quickly and appropriately to each and every crime that occurs. When arrests are made and offenders are sentenced, the public can feel a sense of satisfaction that the justice system did its job.

That's what we expect of our criminal justice system. We expect that when an individual commits a crime, there will be an investigation and an arrest of the guilty parties. Then, if those parties don't plead guilty, we fully expect a fair trial and hopefully, a conviction of the guilty offender.

Finally, we expect that the offender will receive an appropriate sentence in which that convicted person will be forced to pay his or her debt to society.

The Criminal Justice System

That is why we have a criminal justice system. If there were no crime, we would have no need of a criminal justice system. However, the history of mankind demonstrates that when people live together in societies and communities, there is a need for rules and laws. And those are needed because inevitably there are those individuals who will violate the rules, the laws, and the norms of their society. Because there will always be violators of the established norms of a community, there must be a system in place to deal with these offenders.

A Brief History of Criminal Justice Systems

We know that criminal justice systems were in place in societies several thousand years ago. For instance, one of the earliest known set of laws was enacted in the time of Hammurabi, the ruler of Mesopotamia, in what is now modern-day Iraq, about 2100 B.C. (Oliver & Hilgenberg, 2006). The Code of Hammurabi, a set of laws that the god Bel gave to Hammurabi, was carved in rock columns and preserved in a temple. Hammurabi's code indicated what behaviors were violations of laws and the corresponding punishment for breaking those laws (Oliver & Hilgenberg, 2006).

Hammurabi's code was based on the concept of *lex talionis*, or in the words of the Bible's Old Testament, "an eye for an eye." This means that punishment should be in direct proportion to the crime committed. Thus, if one caused another to lose an arm, for instance, the offender should lose the same arm. If an individual caused the death of another person, then they should be put to death. Hammurabi's code listed more than 200 laws, but the death penalty was authorized for 25 different crimes, such as this one: "If any one steal the property of a temple or of the court, he shall be put to death, and also the one who receives the stolen thing from him shall be put to death" (Oliver & Hilgenberg, 2006).

A few hundred years later, Athenian law in Athens, Greece, developed the concept that a "private harm" could also be a harm against all society (Gargarin, 2002). In the sixth century B.C., the Athenians created a system of "popular courts" in order to ensure that every citizen was granted certain rights and had the ability to appeal decisions (Selden, 2001). Although Athenian law became quite complex, it was not actually written down until around 403 or 404 B.C.

The Romans codified their laws in 452 A.D. when the Roman Tribune requested that the laws of Rome be codified and written into ten tables. Later, two additional tables were added and these became known as the "Roman Twelve Tables." These tables spell out various types of crimes such as murder, bribery, sorcery, and theft. These particular crimes were all punishable by execution, which could be by crucifixion, drowning, beating to death, burning alive, or impaling (Farrington, 2000).

Since these early attempts to codify laws, there have been attempts to inform citizens of the laws and to bring about fair and impartial punishments. Of course, when we look back at the criminal justice systems of European countries from the Middle Ages until the middle of the 19th century, we would have to conclude that their systems were rather crude. For example, England did not have any police until watchmen and later constables were employed beginning around the reign of King Edward I in the 12th century A.D. Aside from watchmen and constables, who patrolled streets and watched for fires, England had no police department until Sir Robert Peel organized the London Metropolitan Police in 1829.

Also, prior to the 19th century, the court system in England was handled by circuit court judges who traveled around circuits going from to town to town holding court. In addition, when it came to punishment for crimes, England again provides an example of the lack of general and differentiated sentencing guidelines. By English law, by the early 1700s, there were over 200 crimes which were punishable by hanging (Friedman, 1993). If a person, for instance, were caught shoplifting silk from a shop, the thief could be hanged. And often the hanging took place within one day after the sentence was handed down.

Criminal Justice Today

Most countries today, including the United States, have an evolved criminal justice system that is multilayered and sophisticated compared to the justice systems in Europe prior to the 19th century. As you will note by the various chapters of this book, the American system of justice is made up of ordinances and laws that define what constitutes crime, of law enforcement agencies, of prosecutors, of judges and courts, and of corrections. In addition, more and more victims are being recognized as an important part of administering justice.

How Has Crime Changed over Time?

In some ways crime hasn't changed at all over the past several hundred years. A small percentage of people in every city, county, and state will violate the established norms. That is, some people will steal, rob, rape, or murder. However, with changes in society, more laws are placed on the books—whether in a city's ordinances, a state's criminal code, or the federal government's criminal code.

If you think back to Hammurabi's Code or to the Roman Twelve Tablets, there were only a few dozen or a couple of hundred criminal laws. Now, the federal government and each state has a criminal code with laws that take up hundreds of pages. Furthermore, with changes in citizen's concerns (think about current concerns about cyber-bullying or acts of terrorism) and because of changes in our technology (consider online theft, identity fraud, and hacking), there are new laws that have been brought into existence to try to prevent new forms of criminal behavior and to punish those who commit those new crimes.

What Do We Know about Crime?

In the next chapter, we will discuss what we know about crime and how much crime takes place in our country.

FOR FURTHER CONSIDERATION

Historical Events Relevant to Chapter Two

January 21, 1908:   The Sullivan Ordinance, enacted in New York City, makes it illegal for women to smoke. Even though it is against the law, some women continue to smoke!

October 10, 1973:   The vice president of the United States, Spiro Agnew, pleads no contest to a charge of federal income tax evasion and resigns.

November 10, 1992:   Financier Charles Keating Jr. was sentenced in Los Angeles to nine years in prison for swindling investors when his Lincoln Savings & Loan company collapsed. Later, the conviction was overturned on technicalities (such as Judge Lance Ito giving the jury incorrect instructions). The swindle cost the taxpayers $3.4 billion.

November 21, 1990:   Former Drexel Burnham Lambert junk bond "king" Michael Milken is sentenced to 10 years in prison for securities violations.

Websites to Check Out

- *Code of Hammurabi.* Available at: *http://www.commonlaw.com/Hammurabi.html*
- *Roman Twelve Tables.* Available at: *http://www.csun.edu/~hcfll004/12tables.html*
- *Common Law.* Available at: *http://www.luminarium.org/encyclopedia/commonlaw.htm*

Books

- Albanese, J. S. (2013). *Criminal Justice.* 5th ed. Upper Saddle River, NJ: Pearson Education, Inc.
- Oliver, W. M., and Hilgenberg, J. F. (2006). *A History of Crime and Criminal Justice in America.* Boston: Allyn & Bacon. This book provides an overview of the history and development of the criminal justice system in America.
- Scheingold, S. A. (1991). *The Politics of Street Crime: Criminal Process and Cultural Obsession.* Philadelphia: Temple University Press.

TV Shows

- *Southland*: A television show created by Ann Biderman and airing weekly on TNT, it focuses on patrol officers and their duties and responsibilities.
- *The Rookies*: A crime drama series that was broadcast on ABC from 1972 until 1976. The series, available on DVD, follows the exploits of three rookie police officers.
- *Rookie Blue:* A police series that debuted on June 24, 2010, on ABC. The series follows the lives of five rookie cops from 15 Division in Toronto who have just graduated from the academy. They must learn not only to deal with their duties as police officers, but also deal with the problems and expectations of their families and friends.

Review for Chapter Two

Research Paper or Term Paper Topics:

- The history and development of criminal codes from ancient times to the present
- The American public's fear of street crime

Important Terms to Know

Street crime: Small-scale, personal offenses such as single-victim homicide, rape, robbery, assault, burglary, and vandalism.

The Criminal Justice System:
A loose amalgamation of governmental agencies and departments that include law enforcement, courts, corrections, and victims.

Hammurabi's Code: Hammurabi was the ruler of Mesopotamia in what is now modern-day Iraq. About 2100 B.C. he enacted a set of laws spelling out what were crimes and what were the appropriate punishments for those crimes.

Lex talionis: A concept that is often referred to as "an eye for an eye." The concept refers to punishment that is in direct proportion to the crime committed.

Study Guide Questions

True or False:

1. In order for a behavior to be considered a crime it must be defined by society as a crime.

2. Behaviors that society considers deviant are consistent across time and location.

3. The criminal justice system is set into motion when a legal norm is violated.

4. According to the contemporary view, the main parts of the criminal justice system are law enforcement, judiciary, corrections, and victim services.

Multiple Choice Items:

1. Which group is the most fearful of crime?
   a. elderly women
   b. young men
   c. middle-aged men
   d. residents of rural communities

5. Media reports on violent crimes such as murder give viewers the impression that
   a. These crimes are more common than they actually are
   b. These crimes are less common than they actually are
   c. Media coverage is accurate regarding the frequency of these crimes
   d. These crimes never occur

References

Barkan, S. J., and Bryjak, G. J. (2004). *Fundamentals of Criminal Justice*. Boston: Allyn and Bacon.

Catalano, S. (2004). *Criminal Victimization, 2003*. Washington, DC: Bureau of Justice Statistics.

Farrington, K. (2000). *History of Punishment & Torture: A Journey through the Dark Side of Justice*. London, England: Hamlyn.

Friedman, L. (1993). *Crime and Punishment in American History*. New York: Basic Books.

Fuller, J. R. (2010). *Criminal Justice: Mainstream and Crosscurrents*. Upper Saddle River, NJ: Prentice Hall.

Gargarin, M. (2002). *Antiphon the Athenian: Oratory, Law, and Justice in the Age of the Sophists*. Austin: University of Texas Press.

National Commission on the Causes and Prevention of Violence. (1969). *To Establish Justice, to Insure Domestic Tranquility*. Washington, DC: U.S. Government Printing Office.

Oliver, W. M., and Hilgenberg, J. F. (2006). *A History of Crime and Criminal Justice in America*. Boston: Allyn & Bacon.

Roper Center for Public Opinion Research, (2011), "Topics at a glance: iPoll Questions," University of Connecticut, (USGALLUP.11MCH3.RO6B), Available: http://www.ropercenter.uconn.edu/cgi-bin/hsrun.exe/Roperweb/pom/StateId/QfmkTuGm2nA4EIWou4Z8xQ3VZXqt3-3pLd/.

Scannell, K. (2009). Madoff chasers dug for years, to no avail. *Wall Street Journal.* http://online.wsj.com/article/SB123111743915052731.html?mod=googlenews_wsj.

Shelden, R. G. (2001). *Controlling the Dangerous Classes: A Critical Introduction to the History of Criminal Justice.* Boston: Allyn & Bacon.

Smith, S. K., Steadman, G. W., Minton, T. D., and Townsend, M. (1999). *Criminal Victimization and Perception of Community Safety in 12 Cities.* Washington, DC: U.S. Department of Justice, Office of Justice Programs, Bureau of Justice Statistics, & Office of Community Oriented Police Services.

Sourcebook of criminal justice statistics online, (1997), "Attitudes toward crime in the United States," Available at: http//:www.albany.edu/sourcebook/pdf/t2332011.pdf.

Stewart, J. B. (2011). *Tangled Webs.* New York: Penguin Press.

United States Department of Justice–United States Attorney's Office, Available at: Usdoj.gov. http://www.usdoj.gov/usao/nys/madoff.html.

Chapter Three

What Do We Know about Crime?

As America has suffered through a very sour economy since December 2007, it wasn't just trends forecaster Gerald Celente who predicted crime rates would soar. Celente was joined by various public officials and even criminologists who said that a serious recession would lead to sharp increases in crime.

For example, R. T. Rybak, the mayor of Minneapolis, Minnesota, said in 2009 that the trend toward less crime in his city might not continue: "When the economy is bad, people do desperate things they wouldn't otherwise do" (fedgazette, 2009).

University of Montana criminologist Dan Doyle stated, "Domestic violence can go up when times are hard just because the level of tension within families and communities rises" (fedgazette, 2009).

And University of Missouri–St. Louis sociologist Richard Rosenfeld predicted on several occasions that as the economy worsened, so would the crime rate. Writing an opinion piece in the *Los Angeles Times* in March 2008, Rosenfeld wrote that "crime rates are likely to increase as the economy worsens." In the same article he added, "Crime is a national problem—and one that is sure to get worse in the months ahead" (Rosenfeld, 2008).

But was there an increase in crime in 2008, 2009, 2010, or 2011? Surprisingly, the answer is that there was not.

We're going to start seeing huge vacant real estate and squatters living in them as well. It's going to be a picture the likes of which Americans are not going to be used to ... and with it, there's going to be a lot of crime. And the crime is going to be a lot worse than it was before because in the last 1929 Depression, people's minds weren't wrecked on all these modern drugs ... So, you have a huge underclass of very desperate people ...

—*Gerald Celente, the well-known trends forecaster, predicting disaster in America by 2012 because of the economic downturn, November 2008*

WHAT DOES THE PUBLIC THINK ABOUT CRIME?

As we observed in Chapter Two, there is considerable fear about crime among Americans. However, there is a phenomenon that accompanies that fear. And that is that adults in the United States consistently overestimate the amount of crime that takes place in this country. For instance, survey results show the following:

- In 2009, a Gallup Poll found that 74 percent of Americans said there was more crime in the United States than there was the year before (Jones, 2009).
- In a 1995 public opinion poll, 80 percent of Americans reported a general fear of crime (Sourcebook of Criminal Justice Statistics, 1997).
- In March 2008, one third of Americans said crime had increased in their neighborhoods over the past year (Willingham, 2009).

Almost every year since 1972, the Gallup Company has asked the following question of a random sample of American adults: Is there more crime in your area than there was a year ago, or less crime? The results of this poll show that in a majority of years, not only since 1990, but going back to 1972, there have been more than 50 percent who answered there is more crime today than there was a year ago (Sourcebook of Criminal Justice Statistics Online, 2011). However, in every section of the country since 1993, crime has been steadily and consistently decreasing.

Myth:	*Americans have a realistic concern about crime in their communities.*
Reality:	*The reality is that adults in the United States have no accurate knowledge as to whether crime is going up or down in their community.*

If people in this country don't have a good grasp of the statistics regarding crime, what exactly are the facts concerning the amount of crime in this country?

WHAT ARE THE FACTS?

- There is no crime wave in the United States.
- Criminal victimization has been steadily declining for more than 30 years.
- In 2010, there was a 5.5 percent decrease in the number of violent crimes over 2009.
- Murder and non-negligent manslaughter offenses dropped 4.4 percent from 2009 to 2010.
- There was a 13 percent drop in violent victimization from 2009 to 2010.

How Much Crime Is There in the United States?

That's an interesting and tricky question. Crime statistics must be treated with great caution and not a little bit of skepticism. First, in order to be both cautious and skeptical, you must ask two questions about crime:

1. Are crime measurements measuring what they purport to be measuring?

2. Does the source of crime statistics have something to gain from the way crime measurements are presented to the public?

By asking these two important questions, you will be less likely to simply accept the crime statistics you are reviewing at face value. But where does information about crime come from?

Reporting on the Amount of Crime

Information about crime comes from agencies, private groups, and scholars. But the four most frequently used data sources for estimating crime come from:

-   The Uniform Crime Report
-   The National Crime Victimization Survey
-   The National Incident-Based Reports System
-   Self-Report studies

Each has advantages and disadvantages, and each can be biased or slanted. But if you put them all together, you are likely to get a fair idea of the amount of crime that takes place in America.

The Uniform Crime Report

In the 1920s, the International Association of Chiefs of Police (IACP) saw the need for national crime statistics. The IACP formed a committee on Uniform Crime Reports to bring about a system for uniformly measuring crime (Masters et al., 2013). In 1930, the Bureau of Investigation (which would later be officially named the Federal Bureau of Investigation) was given the task of annually collecting and publishing crime statistics for all the states' law enforcement agencies. This annual report became known as the Uniform Crime Report (UCR).

The UCR comes from the voluntary national collection of crime statistics from around 17,000 state and federal law enforcement agencies. Crimes are categorized and published in two broad categories: violent crimes

The advantages of NIBRS over UCR is that NIBRS provides more data on each crime, making it possible to examine crimes in much more detail. The FBI hopes that eventually NIBRS will replace UCR as the source of official FBI crime information. However, not all police departments have the resources necessary to collect, process, and report the wide array of data. As of 2009, only 44 percent of the nation's law enforcement agencies were participating in NIBRS (Masters et al., 2013). According to the FBI, as of 2007, 6,444 law enforcement agencies contributed NIBRS data to the UCR program, representing 25 percent of the U.S. population and 25 percent of the crime statistics collected by the UCR program—thus rendering it impractical to make generalizations about crime nationwide (FBI, 2012).

SELF-REPORT DATA

Self-report studies are an important source of information about offenders and their offenses. Self-report surveys ask people to reveal information about themselves and their own law violations. The basic assumption of self-report studies is that the assurance of anonymity and confidentiality will encourage people to be honest about their illegal activities.

Self-report surveys are a way to learn more about the "dark figures of crime"—the individuals who don't show up in official statistics. Self-report studies were first used in the 1940s (Thornberry & Krone, 2000). The first self-report survey studies found that there was an enormous amount of hidden crime in the United States. In fact, those early self-report crime surveys indicated that more than 90 percent of all Americans had committed crimes for which they could have been arrested and even imprisoned (Bohm & Haley, 2012).

Although self-report surveys have established validity and reliability, they are sometimes criticized because not everyone may be candid about their illegal activities and some may exaggerate their criminal acts. There is also a "missing cases" phenomenon, which is a concern. Since surveys are often given to groups of individuals such as high school students, some of the people who do not participate or are absent may skew the results.

WHO COMMITS CRIMES?

Jeffrey Reiman, in his book *The Rich Get Richer and the Poor Get Prison* (2004), describes the stereotypical image of the individual who commits a crime:

> Think of a crime, any crime ... What do you see? The odds are you are not imagining a mining company executive sitting at his desk, calculating the costs of proper safety precautions and deciding not to invest in them. Probably what you see with your mind's eye is one person attacking another physically or robbing something from another via the threat of a physical attack. Look more closely. What does the attacker look like? It's a safe bet he (and it is a *he*, of course) is not wearing a suit and tie. In fact,

my hunch is that you—like me, like almost anyone else in America—picture a young, tough, lower-class male when the thought of crime first pops into your head (p. 65).

We think as Jeffrey Reiman suggests because traditionally we imagine crime as a lower-class phenomenon. And we can back this up with logic: The people who have less wealth, power, or status are the people with the greatest incentive to commit crime. If lower-class individuals are unable to obtain goods and services through conventional means, then they are more likely to resort to theft and other illegal activities (such as selling drugs or being involved in prostitution) to obtain what they want or need.

But is there a relationship between social class and crime?

According to some researchers using self-report surveys, there is no relationship between social class and commission of crime (Dunaway et al., 2000). However, it may be that official processing by police, courts, and correctional agencies may be related to socioeconomic class (Siegel, 2002). Using self-report surveys, researchers have found that there is no difference in the amount of crime committed by lower-class and middle-class youth. Yet, lower-class youth are much more likely to be arrested, convicted, and incarcerated (Siegel, 2002). The consensus is that there is no evidence of a relationship between lower-class individuals and criminal offending. It's been argued that official statistics probably reflect social class in processing lower-class offenders (Tittle, Villemez, & Smith, 1978).

If criminal offending is not related to social class, what is it related to?

We do know that there are other factors that are related to crime. For instance, it is generally agreed that age is inversely related to criminality. That is, young people are more likely to commit crimes than are older individuals, and young people are more likely to get arrested. Youth ages 13 to 17 make up about six percent of the U.S. population, but they account for about 25 percent of serious crimes and about 17 percent of all crimes (Siegel, 2002).

The peak age for property crimes is about 16 and for violence the peak age is about 18. In contrast, adults who are 45 and older make up more than 30 percent of the population but account for less than 10 percent of serious crimes (Siegel, 2002). According to the UCR, 16 percent of all persons arrested nationally are under the age of 18 and 44 percent are under age 25. It doesn't matter what type of crime, the age patterns are similar. Forty-eight percent of violent crime arrests, including homicide, involve persons under 25 years of age. Fifty-six percent of property crime arrests involve people under 25 as well (Albanese, 2013).

In addition to age, gender is important in determining who commits crime. Men make up 81 percent of individuals arrested for violent crimes and 63 percent of those arrested for property crimes (Albanese, 2013). Women, on the other hand, make up 25 percent of all persons arrested in the United States. They are most frequently arrested for larceny, but they account for only 44 percent of all larceny arrests. For the 10-year period from 2000 to 2009, female arrests rose 11 percent, compared to a five percent decrease for males (FBI, 2011).

increasing. Another study (Romer, Jamieson & Aday, 2003) found that TV viewers who watched local news reports on TV were more likely to have an increased fear of crime and to have greater concerns about crime in general.

WHY DO PEOPLE COMMIT CRIMES?

Now that we know more about how crime is measured and the amount of crime in the United States, it is important to discuss why people engage in criminal activities. The theories of crime behavior will be explored in the next chapter.

FOR FURTHER CONSIDERATION

Historical Events Relevant to Chapter Three

March 14, 1950:   The FBI debuts its "10 Most Wanted" list.

June 11, 1930:   Congress authorizes the Federal Bureau of Investigation (FBI) to collect, compile, and distribute crime records, with its first report due in September (compiling August stats). One newspaper declared that "Uncle Sam ... is going to put his finger on the pulse of crime in America." This data collection of uniform crime statistics is authorized under Public Law 337, Title 28, §554. Since that time, the FBI has collected crime statistics nationally from police agencies on a voluntary basis, releasing a report each year.

September, 1930:   The FBI issues its first Uniform Crime Report. This report is for August 1930 and is based on responses from 400 police departments.

Websites to Check Out

- *The Bureau of Justice Statistics.* Available at: *http://bjs.ojp.usdoj.gov/.* The mission of the Bureau of Justice Statistics is to collect, analyze, publish, and disseminate information on crime, criminal offenders, victims of crime, and the operation of justice systems at all levels of government. Included are National Crime Victimization Surveys.
- *The FBI.* Available at: *http://www.fbi.gov/stats-services/crimestats.* Uniform Crime Reports dating back to 1960 can be found at the FBI's website.

Book

- Holden, H. M. (2008). *FBI: 100 Years: An Unofficial History.* Minneapolis, MN: Zenith Press. This book provides an overview of the history of the FBI. As with almost every other book about the FBI, little attention is paid to the development of the Uniform Crime Report.

References

Albanese, J. S. (2013). *Criminal Justice*. 5th ed. Upper Saddle River, NJ: Pearson Educational, Inc.

Bohm, R. H., and Haley, K. N. (2012). *Introduction to Criminal Justice*. 7th ed. New York: McGraw-Hill.

Dunaway, R. G., Cullen, F., Burton, V., and Evans, T. D. (2000). The myth of social class and crime revisited: An examination of class and adult criminality. *Criminology* 38, 589–632.

FBI, (2010), "Uniform crime report" [online], Available at: http://www.fbi.gov/about-us/cjis/ucr/crime-in-the-u.s/2010/crime-in-the-u.s.-2010/tables/table-43/10tbl43a.xls.

FBI, (2011), "Uniform crime report" [online], Available at: http://www.fbi.gov/about-us/cjis/ucr/crime-in-the-u.s/2011/preliminary-annual-ucr-jan-dec-2011.

FBI, (2012), "NIBRS General FAQs" [online], Available at: http://www.fbi.gov/about-us/cjis/ucr/frequently-asked-questions/nibrs_faqs/.

Fedgazette, (March 1, 2009), "The mystery of crime" [online], Available at: www.minneapolisfed.org/publications_papers/pub_display.cfm?id+4137.

Huizinga, D., and Elliott, D. (1987). Juvenile offenders: Prevalence, offender incidence, and arrest rates by race. *Crime and Delinquency*, 33, 206–223.

Jones, J. M. (October 14, 2009), "Americans perceive increased crime in U.S. Gallup Poll" [online], Available at: http://www.gallup.com/poll/123644/americans-perceive-increased-crime.aspx.

Kort-Butler, L. A., and Hartshorn, K. J. S. (2011). Watching the detectives: Crime programming, fear of crime, and attitudes about the criminal justice system. *Sociological Quarterly* 52 (1), 36–55.

Masters, R. E., Way, L. B., Gerstenfeld, P. B., Muscat, B. T., Hooper, M., Dussich, J. P. J., Pincu, L., and Skrapec, C. A. (2013). *CJ: Realities and Challenges*. 2nd ed. New York: McGraw-Hill.

Menard, S., and Huizinga, D. (2001). Repeat victimization in a high-risk neighborhood sample of adolescents. *Youth & Society* 32(4), 447–472.

Reiman, J. (2004). *The Rich Get Richer and the Poor Get Prison*. Boston: Allyn & Bacon .

Romer, D., Jamieson, K. H, and Aday, S. (2003). Television news and the cultivation of fear of crime. *Journal of Communication* 88–104.

Rosenfeld, R. (2008). The economics of crime. *Los Angeles Times* March 20, 2008.

Sample, B., and Philip, M. (1984). "Perspectives on race and crime in research and planning." In *The Criminal Justice System and Blacks* by D. Georges-Abeyie, ed. New York: Clark Boardman.

Sourcebook of Criminal Justice Statistics Online, (1997), "Attitudes toward Crime in the United States," Available at: http//:www.albany.edu/sourcebook/pdf/t2332011.pdf.

Sourcebook of Criminal Justice Statistics Online, (2011), "Perceptions of Crime and Safety in Neighborhoods," Available at: http://www.albany.edu/sourcebook/tost_2.html#2_n.

Siegel, L. J. (2002). *Criminology: The Core*. Belmont, CA: Wadsworth.

Thornberry, T. P., and Krone, M. D. (2000). "The self-report method for measuring delinquency and crime." Pp. 33–83 in David Duffee, Robert D. Crutchfield, Steven Mastrofski, Lorraine Mazerolle, David McDowell, and Brian Ostrom, eds. *CJ 2000: Innovations in Measurement and Analysis*. Washington, DC: National Institute of Justice.

Tittle, C., Villemez, W., and Smith, D. (1978). The myth of social class and criminality: An empirical assessment of the empirical evidence. *American Sociological Review* 45, 643–656.

Truman, J., (2010), "Criminal Victimization, 2010," (NCJ 235508), Bureau of Justice Statistics, [online], Available at: http://www.bjs.gov/index.cfm?ty=pbdetail&iid=2224.

UCR Study Task Force, (1985), "Blueprint for the future of the uniform crime reporting program," U.S. Department of Justice [online], Available at: www.ncjrs.gov/pdffiles1/bjs/98348.pdf.

Watson, P. J., (2008), "Celente Predicts Revolution, Food Riots, Tax Rebellion by 2012" [online], Available at: www.infowars.com/cvelente-predicts-reviolutikin-food-riots-tax-rebellions-by-2012/.

Willingham, K., (2009), "Crime rates on rise? 80 percent of Americans think so" [online], *Examiner.com,* Available at: http://www.examiner.com/article/crime-rates-on-rise-80-percent-of-americans-think-so.

Wolfgang, M., Figlio, R., and Sellin, T. (1972). *Delinquency in a Birth Cohort.* Chicago: University of Chicago Press.

EARLY THEORIES

Hundreds of years ago, philosophers and criminologists developed theories of deviant behavior based on social and religious morals. There was no use of scientific observations, nor was there empirical research to determine why some people were deviant. When people behaved in deviant or immoral ways, it led those who were in positions of authority to theorize about the nature of good and evil.

In the Middle Ages, there seemed little differentiation between sin and crime (Fagin, 2007). If an individual was deviant, it was because he or she was evil, morally weak, or had the devil inside him or her.

Given these kinds of explanations, the religiously-based criminal justice system of the time took what was seen as appropriate action to deal with the morally deficient. Which is why law-violators were frequently tortured, burned at the stake, or subjected to trial by ordeal. Trial by ordeal referred to various methods of torture that usually featured magical or superstitious ways of determining moral guilt (Siegel, 2006).

CLASSICAL THEORIES

Cesare Beccaria is known as the founder of classical criminology. Beccaria was an Italian nobleman and jurist who was dissatisfied with the justice system of his time.

Born in 1738, Beccaria viewed the Italian justice system as using extreme punishment in a legal system in which laws were arbitrary and unfair. In his efforts to make changes, Beccaria wrote a book entitled *On Crimes and Punishment* in 1764. In this book, Beccaria explained his belief that people are rational and they do things that bring them pleasure and avoid doing things which bring them pain. Furthermore, he was of the opinion that people are responsible for their actions. He advocated certain and swift punishment of appropriate intensity and duration for the offense committed. If this kind of response was used consistently, he theorized, then it would deter people from committing crimes.

The English philosopher Jeremy Bentham lived at about the same time as Beccaria. Bentham is credited with the formation of the neoclassical school of criminology. The neoclassical school of criminology is very similar to the classical school of thought, in that both believe criminal offending is a matter of free-will choice.

The difference between them, though, is that Bentham's view holds that sometimes there are mitigating circumstances. For instance, children, according to Bentham, shouldn't be held to the same degree of accountability as an adult. Furthermore, Bentham argued that someone suffering from mental illness should be exempt from criminal liability.

In short, both the classical and neoclassical schools of criminology believed people are rational and that they make free-will choices about committing crimes.

Biological Theories

Dissatisfaction with the classical approach to explaining crime first appeared toward the end of the 19th century. At that time, crime was viewed by many as a growing problem and that the harsh punishments of the time seemed to have little effect on criminal offending.

At about the same time, the emerging use of the scientific method along with the development of social science began to change how people viewed social problems and how those problems might be solved. The naturalist Charles Darwin described his theory of evolution through natural selection in his book *The Origin of Species*. Émile Durkheim, a sociologist, noted differences in rates of suicide in different regions of France. Durkheim employed observations to develop a social theory of suicide in his book *Suicide*. Both Darwin and Durkheim were pioneers in the scientific method, which was based on observation. Rather than just thinking about problems, both believed that scientific questions were best answered when scientists first gathered facts and data.

This scientific approach gave rise to the positivist school of criminology. The positivist school saw human behavior as based on a combination of internal and external influences, such as biology, psychology, and/or social factors. While the classical school still saw crime as emanating from free will and choice, positivism believed it was a combination of internal and external forces that shaped behavior.

The Positivists

The early positivists such as Cesare Lombroso (1836–1909) considered biological attributes to be the real roots of crime. Lombroso took body measurements of offenders in Italian prisons and concluded that there were "born criminals." These born criminals had distinctive body measurements and skull sizes.

Positivism, following Lombroso and others, continued to be influential as it played a major role in explaining criminal behavior. But with the development of psychoanalysis in the late 19th century and the growth of psychology in the late 19th and 20th centuries, the theories of the mind became much more prominent in offering explanations for the causes of crime.

Psychoanalysis and Psychology

While Sigmund Freud's psychoanalytic theory was used to offer explanations as to why some people might commit crimes, biological theories became much more refined as increasingly sophisticated research in the areas of genetics, chromosomal abnormalities, glandular dysfunction, chemical imbalances, and nutritional deficiencies helped offer other biological theories.

In general, all psychological explanations look inside the human mind for the causes of criminal offending. The oldest, and perhaps one of the most influential theories, was Freud's psychoanalytic theory. Although Freud did not set out to explain criminal behavior, some of his followers offered explanations based on psychoanalytic theories.

Basically, psychoanalytic theory views behavior as resulting from the interactions of the three components of personality: the id, the ego, and the superego. Freud saw the id as the instinctual, primitive part of the personality. The ego was that part that mediated between the self-centered desires of the id and the learned values of the superego. The superego acts as a person's conscience, but develops from the values an individual learns early in life. When there is a faulty ego or superego, then these two parts of the personality fail to control the id. This results in personality imbalances and the result is likely to be deviant behavior.

Although psychoanalysis was influential in the early part of the 20th century, it gave way to other psychologically based theories. For instance, a cognitive theory of crime hypothesized that criminal offending results from habits of thought and interpretations of reality. More recent refinements of cognitive theory suggest that criminals interpret situations differently than non-criminals. For example, criminal offenders might tend to view situations in more hostile ways and then are most likely to respond with aggressive behavior.

OTHER PSYCHOLOGICAL THEORIES

Psychological theories about the causes of crime go back to the 19th century. In addition to Freud's psychoanalytic theory, Charles Goring studied the mental characteristics of English convicts. By studying more than 3,000 convicts, he found that there was a relationship between crime and a condition he called defective intelligence, which included such traits as feeblemindedness, epilepsy, and insanity.

Other psychoanalysts who followed Freud or studied with him were seemingly more interested in criminal behavior than was Freud. August Aichhorn, for instance, examined many delinquent youth and concluded that social stress alone could not account for delinquent or criminal behavior. Aichhorn said there had to be a predisposition for antisocial acts (Siegel, 2006). Such predispositions, according to Aichhorn, include impulsivity, a tendency to consider satisfying their own needs more important than the needs of others, and a lack of guilt.

More recently, psychologists have linked criminal behavior to a psychological condition called disruptive behavior disorder (Siegel, 2006). Children and teens can experience either of two forms of disruptive behavior disorder. One is oppositional defiant disorder, in which young people show an ongoing pattern of uncooperative, defiant, and hostile behavior toward authority figures. Adolescents with oppositional defiant disorder may frequently lose their temper, may argue with adults, may be easily frustrated and moody, and they may abuse drugs as a form of self-medication (Siegel, 2006).

The other form of disruptive behavior disorder is conduct disorder, which is a much more serious behavioral and emotional disorder. Young people who are diagnosed as having a conduct disorder have difficulty following rules and are usually viewed as being antisocial. They may be involved in such behaviors as fighting, bullying others, committing sexual assaults, robbery, and cruelty to animals. Although it is not precisely known what causes conduct disorders, research has implicated brain dysfunction, neurotransmitter (the chemicals that send messages in the brain) irregularities, and genetics (Siegel & Welsh, 2009).

There is growing research in recent years to show that there is a link between mental illness and criminal behavior. That is, when people have such serious mental illness as schizophrenia, bipolar disorder, and severe depression, there appears to be an increased risk for serious, violent crimes. Studies in recent years have found a positive relationship between psychotic disorders and criminal violence (Siegel, 2006).

SOCIOLOGICAL EXPLANATIONS

Sociological explanations of crime look at criminal behaviors as emanating from environmental influences. Early and influential sociological theories were proposed beginning in the 1930s. For example, Edwin Sutherland suggested that delinquent behavior is learned in much the same way that people learn other things—by observation, role modeling, and reinforcement.

Sutherland called his learning process theory differential association, and he proposed that an individual becomes a criminal by associating with people who condone violation of the law. In effect, criminal attitudes are learned from others (Cole & Smith, 2007).

While Sutherland's differential association was an early sociological explanation of crime, there are several others, including:

- Blocked opportunity: Criminal behavior results from lack of access to legitimate means for achieving goals.
- Labeling theory: When society reacts negatively toward an individual or labels him or her, the person acquires a negative self-image and acts accordingly.
- Social bonding: If an individual has weak bonds to society, then that person is less likely to respect the customary social rules or laws.
- Social strain: These theories focus on social disorganization, anomie (a state of normlessness in society), and on subcultures that focus on negative social structure and relationships. Developed most completely by Robert Agnew, it is believed that in some individuals, crime may provide an effective short-term solution to strain (Siegel, 2006).
- Subculture theories: These theories focus on an identifiable segment or group characterized by specific patterns of behavior. These identifiable segments could include gangs and some lower social class neighborhoods.
- Conflict theories: These views of the causation of crime look at how powerful groups in society make the laws that confer criminal status on the least powerful members of society.
- Critical or radical criminology: The emphasis in these theories is on social class inequality and economic conditions rather than on the characteristics of the individual criminal.
- Gender-based: These theories focus on why women are not represented in crime statistics—or even in theories about crime causation. The gender-based theories support the idea that it is how the justice system responds to women's criminal offending that explains why there are fewer arrests and less incarceration for women.

There are also social process theories within the broad category of sociological theories. These theories concern themselves with the process by which people become criminals. The social process theories include:

- Learning theory: While learning theory can be viewed as a psychological theory where people learn by using other people as models, learning theory is also a social process theory. As a social process theory, criminologists look at how individuals might become criminal by learning from the media, including—and perhaps most importantly—television. Whether the process is learning or imitation, the end result is the same: What people see on TV, or in the movies, or in video games may influence how they behave (Reid, 2009).

- Control theories: In these approaches, the focus is on explaining why people obey the law. People who follow the law are said, by these theories, to do so because they respond to appropriate social controls. For instance, Travis Hirschi's control theory emphasizes social bonds. The basic concept of control theory is the individual's bonds to the family and other social institutions.

Finally, there are a number of so-called integrated theories. These theories of the causation of crime attempt to explain delinquent and criminal behavior from several points of view. The integrated approaches try to combine various schools of thought regarding crime causation to explain criminal offending. The major integrated theories are:

- Developmental and life-course theories: These approaches take the position that age-related variables explain the changes in delinquent and criminal behavior best. The life course approach is based on the premise that development is an ongoing process that unfolds over the entire lifespan.
- Age-graded theory: Sampson and Laub developed a theory which contends that people are inhibited from offending by their social bonds to the age-graded institutions (such as school, work, and marriage) at various stages of their lives (Siegel & Welsh, 2009).
- General theory: Robert Agnew contributed a general theory (in addition to his strain theory) which argues that such factors as personality traits, types of social support, and peer relationships, for example, must all be taken into account to determine why people offend. In addition, Gottfredson and Hirschi proposed a general theory of crime, which suggests that it is a lack of self-control caused by inadequate child-rearing practices by parents along with various inborn traits that lead to impulsiveness and risk-taking behavior (Siegel & Welsh, 2009).

Is It Nature or Nurture?

The survey of the leading explanations of criminal offending does not really address the central questions related to nature versus nurture. That question is: Are criminals born or made?

Some biological explanations—especially those showing that genetics seem to play a critical role in some criminal offending—make a strong argument for a "nature" explanation of crime. Some research, for instance, shows that a strong indicator of a person's tendency to commit crimes is related to the criminal behavior of fathers, thus suggesting that criminals are born (Siegel & Welsh, 2009).

On the other hand, various sociological explanations demonstrating that poverty, social organization, and social environment are related to criminal behavior make an equally strong case for a "nurture" explanation of crime (Masters et al., 2013).

Although it may be fun to debate the nature versus nurture question, the bottom line is that there is currently no clear and convincing research for either side. The best answer that can be proposed at this time is that both biological and inherited traits, as well as psychological traits and social influences, play important roles in explaining criminal offending. It is still too early to say that we can predict with any great certainty which young children will and which young children will not grow up to be future criminals.

Criminological Theory Summaries Theory	Main Points	Theorists/Researchers
Classical	Crime occurs when the individual sees the benefits outweighing the costs. Crime is a free-willed choice by a rational individual.	Beccaria
Positivist	Crime is caused or determined. Lombroso placed more emphasis on biological deficiencies, whereas later scholars would emphasize psychological and sociological factors. Uses science to determine the factors associated with crime.	Lombroso Guerry Quetelet
Individual Trait	Criminals differ from non-criminals on a number of biological and psychological traits. These traits cause crime in interaction with the social environment.	Glueck & Glueck Mednick Caspi Moffitt
Social Disorganization	Disorganized communities cause crime because informal social controls break down and criminal cultures emerge. They lack collective efficacy to fight crime and disorder.	Shaw & McKay Sampson Bursik & Grasmick
Differential Association Social Learning Subcultural	Crime is learned through associations with criminal definitions. These definitions might be generally approving of criminal conduct or be neutralizations that justify crime only under certain circumstances. Interacting with antisocial peers is a major cause of crime. Criminal behavior will be repeated and become chronic if reinforced. When criminal subcultures exist, then many individuals can learn to commit crime in one location and crime rates—including violence—may become very high.	Sutherland & Cressey Sykes & Matza Akers Wolfgang & Ferracuti Anderson
Anomie Institutional/Anomie	The gap between the American Dream's goal of economic success and the opportunity to obtain this goal creates structural strain. Norms weaken and "anomie" ensues, thus creating high crime rates. When other social institutions (such as the family) are weak to begin with or are also weakened by the American Dream, the economic institution is dominant. When such an institutional imbalance exists—as in the United States—then crime rates are very high.	Merton Messner & Rosenfeld

Adapted from: Cullen & Agnew. (2002). *Criminological Theory: Past to Present* (Essential Readings). Los Angeles, CA: Roxbury.

FOR FURTHER CONSIDERATION

Historical Events Relevant to Chapter Four

March 15, 1738: Birthday of Cesare Beccaria in Milan, Italy. Beccaria's short treatise entitled *On Crimes and Punishments* becomes the foundation of criminological theory and continues to guide criminal justice today.

April 15, 1967: Richard Speck is found guilty of murdering eight student nurses in Chicago. Initially sentenced to death, the Supreme Court ruled that the death penalty was unconstitutional in the *Furman v. Georgia* decision in 1972. He was then resentenced to consecutive life terms totaling 400 years. Speck grew up in an abusive home and became a drifter and alcoholic.

May 6, 1856: Sigmund Freud, the founder of psychoanalytic theory, is born in Austria.

May 22, 1924: The discovery of the body of Bobby Franks, 13, of Chicago led to the arrest of Nathan Leopold and Richard Loeb. The two college students, who both came from wealthy families, kidnapped and murdered Franks in a so-called "thrill killing."

May 20 and May 21, 1998: Kipland "Kip" Kinkel, born in 1982, at the age of 15 murders his parents on May 20. Kinkel then goes to school at Thurston High School in Springfield, Oregon, the next morning where he shoots two students and wounds 22 others. The documentary *Killer at Thurston High* details his life, showing that, although he was brought up in a loving home, he had learning disabilities and a mental disorder that led to his shooting rampage.

June 7, 2002: Michael Skakel, who grew up in a wealthy family in Greenwich, Connecticut, is found guilty of the 1975 murder of 15-year-old Martha Moxley. Various movies, books, and documentaries about Michael Skakel and his family suggest that he grew up without much guidance or supervision.

November 5, 1835: Cesare Lombroso was born in Italy. As an Italian criminologist, he rejected the classical theory of crime and developed a theory that proposed that criminality was inherited, and criminals were born offenders and that they could be identified by physical defects.

November, 24, 1859: Charles Darwin's book *On the Origin of Species by Means of Natural Selection*, a groundbreaking scientific work, is published in England. Darwin's theory of natural selection was developed through his use of observation as a scientific method of data collection.

Websites to Check Out

- *Criminological theory.* Available at*: https://www.criminology.fsu.edu/crimtheory/.* This website features lecture notes and course materials from Cecil E. Greek, PhD, who teaches a course in criminological theory at Florida State University.
- *Criminological theory on the web.* Available at: *www.umsl.edu/~keelr/200/Diane_Demelo/diane.pdf.* This website gives information about most criminological theories.

Books

- Barkan, S. E., and Bryjak, G. J. (2004). *Fundamentals of Criminal Justice.* Boston: Allyn & Bacon. This textbook features succinct explanations of the important theories of criminal behavior.
- Beccaria, C. (1986). *On Crimes and Punishments.* Indianapolis, IN: Hackett Publishing Co. Beccaria's book from the 18th century advocates for reform in the criminal justice of his time, but is still worth reading today.

Movies and Videos

- *Killer at Thurston High*: Kirk, M. (director). Frontline. PBS. WGBH Educational Foundation. 1999.
- *When a Child Kills: Nathaniel Abraham.* Kurtis, B. (director). American Justice. A&E Television Network. 2000.
- *Born Killers: Leopold and Loeb.* Meindl, C. (director). In Search of History. A&E Television Network. 2002.
- *Monster.* Jenkins, P. (director). Film & Entertainment. DEJ Productions, Inc. 2004.
- *Aileen Wuornos: The Selling of a Serial Killer.* Broomfield, N. (director). DEJ Productions. 2004.
- *Mind of a Serial Killer.* Klein, L. (director). NOVA. Mercury Productions with WGBH Educational Foundation. 2005.
- *Serial Killers: Profiling the Criminal Mind.* Unknown directors. Biography and Investigative Reports. A&E Television Networks. 2000.

Review for Chapter Four

Research Paper or Term Paper Topics:

- Psychological theories that explain why people commit crimes
- The relationship between poverty and crime
- Family factors related to criminal offending

Important Terms to Know

Classical criminology: A theory holding that decisions to violate the law are weighed against possible punishments. The theory suggests that people have free will to choose either criminal or conventional behavior.

Conduct disorder: A serious group of emotional and behavior disorders in childhood and adolescence. Youth diagnosed with conduct disorder are antisocial and unable to follow rules and laws. They often have run-ins with law enforcement as they get older.

Differential association theory:
Edwin Sutherland's view that criminal offending results from negative peer influences and more specifically, from an excess of definitions favorable to violations of the law.

Disruptive behavior disorder:
Children who are frequently uncooperative, hostile and much more difficult to handle may develop more severe behavior disorders that can lead to delinquency and criminal offending. It has two components: oppositional defiant disorder and conduct disorder.

General theory: A developmental theory that modifies social control theory by integrating concepts from biosocial, psychological, and routine activities and rational choice theories.

Labeling theory: The view that labeling a person as a criminal or a delinquent will influence future behavior and likely will cause more criminal behavior.

Life course theory: A theory that focuses on changes in criminality over the life course.

Positivist school of criminology:
This is a view of criminal offending that uses the scientific method and suggests that human behavior is a product of social, biological, psychological, and other forces.

Psychoanalytic theory: A branch of psychology developed by Sigmund Freud that maintains that the human personality is controlled by unconscious mental processes developed early in childhood.

Scientific method: The scientific method is a method or procedure that has characterized science since the 17th century and consists of systematic observation, measurement, and experiment and the formulation, testing, and modification of hypotheses in order to arrive at conclusions.

Social bond:	Social bonds tie an individual to the institutions and processes of society. Elements of social bonds include attachment, commitment, involvement, and belief.
Social control theory:	Travis Hirschi's view that social bonds to family, school, and other conventional social institutions inhibit the development of criminal behavior.
Trial by ordeal:	Judicial practices, generally in the Middle Ages, by which the guilt or innocence of the accused is determined by subjecting him to an ordeal, that was not only unpleasant, but could be a test of life or death. The proof of innocence was often whether the person survived, if he escaped injury, or if his injuries healed.

Study Guide Questions

True or False:

1. Classical theories of criminology propose that people are rational and choose to commit crime.

2. All psychological theories related to the causation of crime look inside the human mind to find the causes of offending.

3. There is no link between mental illness and criminal behavior.

4. Life course theories of criminal offending believe that the entire life span of an individual is important.

Multiple Choice Items:

5. The positivist school of criminality views crime as caused by
   a. a combination of internal and external forces
   b. free will
   c. criminal minds
   d. psychological forces alone

6. Sociological explanations of crime include
   a. blocked opportunity
   b. labeling theory
   c. social bonding
   d. all of the above

7. Integrated theories of criminal offending
    a. make sure philosophical views are not segregated
    b. combine various schools of thought
    c. omit psychological views
    d. fail to mention development theories

8. It is still not clear whether
    a. crime is a disease
    b. criminals are people who just like being bad
    c. biology or learning is the prime determinant of criminal offending
    d. criminal offending can be traced to any influences.

References

Cole, G. F., and Smith, C. E. (2007). *The American System of Criminal Justice*. 11th ed. Belmont, CA: Thomson Wadsworth.

Fagin, J. A. (2007). *Criminal Justice: A Brief Introduction*. Boston: Allyn & Bacon.

Masters, R. E., Way, L. B., Gerstenfeld, P. B., Muscat, B. T., Hooper, M., Dussich, J. P. J., Pincu, L., and Skrapec, C. A. (2013). *CJ: Realities and Challenges*. 2nd ed. New York: McGraw-Hill.

Reid, S. T. (2009). *Crime and Criminology*. 12th ed. New York: Oxford University Press.

Siegel, L. J. (2002). *Criminology: The Core*. Belmont, CA: Wadsworth.

Siegel, L. J. (2006). *Criminology*. 9th ed. Belmont, CA: Thomson Wadsworth.

Siegel, L. J., and Walsh, B. C. (2009). *Juvenile Delinquency: Theory, Practice, and Law*. 10th ed. Belmont, CA: Wadsworth.

Part Two

The Law Enforcement
Response to Crime

Chapter Five

How Does the Criminal Justice System Respond to Crime?

When most people think of the criminal justice system, they think first of the police. Law enforcement is—at least to many citizens—the face of the criminal justice system. It is the one part of the justice system most people have contact with, and it is the agency most people expect will deal with crime. In fact, very few people have dealings with prosecuting attorneys, or judges, or any aspect of the correctional system. But everyone has had an encounter with a police officer—either through a request for help or by being stopped for a traffic violation.

But it is the police who Americans expect will respond to crime, and we anticipate that the police will do their job by investigating a crime and ultimately solving that crime.

It is commonly assumed that these three components—law enforcement, the judicial process, and corrections—add up to a "system" of criminal justice.

—National Commission on the Causes and Prevention of Violence: To Establish Justice, to Insure Domestic Tranquility, 1969

LAW ENFORCEMENT RESPONSE TO CRIMES

Remember the criminal events used as an example of three different crimes in Chapter One. The first was the murder of Jane Bashara in Grosse Pointe, Michigan, in 2011. When Jane Bashara's body was found in her car in Detroit, the police were summoned, and patrol officers arrived on the scene first.

When a government agency—the Securities and Exchange Commission (SEC)—was alerted to possible irregularities related to Bernard Madoff's investment company, they began an investigation. When the SEC found evidence of possible criminal wrongdoing, they notified the FBI. The FBI then conducted its own investigation into Madoff and his company's financial transactions.

When the FBI's investigation was concluded, charges were brought before the Department of Justice. Federal prosecutors levied charges, and Bernard Madoff was indicted. Plea bargaining then began between the federal government and Madoff and his attorneys. Eventually, a plea deal was reached and Madoff accepted a guilty plea.

Then there was the case of the Underwear Bomber. When Umar Farouk Abdulmutallab was subdued by fellow passengers on that flight into Detroit, the pilot of the Northwest Airlines plane carrying Abdulmutallab and 289 passengers notified authorities that law enforcement was needed when they landed at Detroit's Metro Airport. Federal authorities met the plane, and Abdulmutallab was arrested. He was detained until he was arraigned before a federal judge in Federal District Court in Detroit. Although the accusations against Abdulmutallab were completely different than those brought against Bernard Madoff, they were both charged with violating federal statutes.

The federal judge bound Abdulmutallab over for trial and a trial date was set. In the meantime, federal law enforcement conducted an investigation in preparation for a trial. However, before that trial could be completed, Abdulmutallab pleaded guilty.

As we can see in all three cases, when a crime has been committed, or at least alleged to have been committed, law enforcement responds. The law enforcement response will depend on the crime—whether it is a federal crime or a state crime—and where the crime occurred.

DO STATE OR FEDERAL LAW ENFORCEMENT OFFICERS RESPOND?

If the crime represents a violation of a state law, then the local police respond. We saw this in the Jane Bashara case. She was murdered in Detroit (or at least her body was found in Detroit); thus, the police department in that area—in this instance, Detroit—responded and took jurisdiction of the case. However, since Mrs. Bashara was also a Grosse Pointe resident, the Grosse Pointe police also became involved. While the two police departments worked together, eventually the Detroit police department took over the investigation.

On the other hand, if the crime is a violation of a federal law, then—as we saw in the Madoff crime and in the Abdulmutallab crime—the federal government responded to the crime.

HOW DID THIS DUAL SYSTEM OF POLICING EVOLVE?

When the first United States Congress met in 1789, they adopted a law called the United States Judiciary Act of 1789. This act established the U.S. federal judiciary. Along with the federal judiciary, the U.S. Marshals was also created by this act. This first law enforcement agency was formed to be the enforcement arm of the federal courts. However, since no other mention was made in the Constitution about law enforcement or the police, it was up to the new country to develop a system of policing.

Since America was colonized by the English, it is no surprise that early citizens of the fledgling country were people who were familiar with the systems previously developed in England. The major system developed in the new country was the constable-watch system. The watch system employed in the cities and urban areas developed in the middle years of the 19th century.

The watch system as it developed in England's towns and villages generally meant that men—usually ordinary citizens—would be responsible for patrolling the streets watching for any kind of criminal activity. Constables—again, based on the system that had been used in England prior to the 19th century—were mostly supervisors of watchmen.

In America, Boston developed a watch system as early as 1634 (Haley & Bohm, 2002). Essentially, that was the predominant policing system in America for the succeeding 200 years. Citizens were expected to serve as the watch, but some of the citizens who could afford to do so could pay to have a watch replacement. As a consequence, often the worst kind of men ended up protecting the community (Haley & Bohm, 2002).

Much later, particularly in rural and southern areas of the United States, the office of sheriff was established, and the power of the posse was used to maintain order and apprehend offenders (Haley & Bohm, 2002). This meant that two forms of law enforcement (in addition to the U.S. Marshals, who helped bring law and order to the Western frontier) began to evolve. There was the watch in villages, towns, and cities, and the sheriff in rural areas and counties. Some areas in the northern parts of the United States often had both systems.

Although England organized its London Metropolitan Police in 1829, America didn't imitate the English model for several years. It was in the 1840s that New York City combined its day watch and night watch to form the first paid, unified police force (Haley & Bohm, 2002). Then, in 1853, the New York state legislature created the Municipal Police Department. However, it was found to be so corrupt that it was abolished by the legislature four years later (Haley & Bohm, 2002). The legislature replaced it with the Metropolitan Police. Other big-city police departments were created later on in the 1850s and 1860s. For instance, Boston combined its day and night watches in 1855 to bring about its own police department.

The First Police Departments

The duties of the first police officers in those early years were very similar to what the watchmen were doing. But after the Civil War, city police departments began to establish a unique identity as they began to wear uniforms, carry nightsticks, and arm themselves with firearms.

Another form of early policing was established in what were becoming the key slave states of the South. These states were Virginia, North Carolina, and South Carolina. And the form of policing evolving in these states was the slave patrols (Oliver & Hilgenberg, 2006). Although the slave patrols actually began in the 17th century, they were organized to prevent slaves from escaping from their owners. As time went on, the slave patrols would develop into more formal, government-sanctioned entities as they were legislated into existence (Oliver & Hilgenberg, 2006). For example, the code of 1705 in Virginia allowed the patrols to check blacks who were not on plantation property to ensure they had appropriate documentation and were not escaped slaves.

The slave patrols were often made up of hired hands from plantations and frequently they treated blacks with suspicion and hostility. Sometimes blacks were mistreated, tortured, or even murdered (Oliver & Hilgenberg, 2006).

TRANSITIONAL POLICING

There was little change in policing from the time of the early formation of police departments in the 1850s until the 1930s. It was apparent to many that changes were needed because, according to Oliver and Hilgenberg in *The History of Crime and Criminal Justice in America* (2006), the reality of American policing was that the police were corrupt, tied into politics, and very brutal in their approach to dealing with citizens.

As the country headed into the 1920s and the grand social experiment known as Prohibition created a new series of crimes and law enforcement challenges, police departments were unable to cope with the demands brought about by the attempt to ban the manufacture, distribution, transportation, sale, or consumption of alcohol. However, the status of police officers did not make their jobs any easier. Police officers in the 1930s were generally underpaid, poorly trained, and ill equipped (Oliver & Hilgenberg, 2006). It was a low-status job often given to political cronies or brutish men without an education (Walker, 1992). In addition, corruption was rampant. Often, police officers worked with politicians who themselves worked with gangsters and the whole system ensured that gangsters could make sure that thirsty Americans could get booze—no matter what the federal law said.

Many cities, as well as the federal government, were concerned about the rise in crime and the flourishing bootlegging business. More than 100 surveys and studies were conducted during the 1920s to study the police problem, crime, and the criminal justice system (Oliver & Hilgenberg, 2006).

The most significant of these studies was the one initiated by President Herbert Hoover in 1929. Named the National Commission on Law Observance and Enforcement, this commission was under the direction of George W. Wickersham, the U.S. attorney general. In 1931, the National Commission on Law Observance and Enforcement, most commonly known simply as the Wickersham Commission, gave its report and recommendations. The Wickersham Commission's report concluded that Prohibition was unenforceable, but the report condemned the police and said that the police by and large were corrupt, that brutality by the police was widespread, and that police officers at all levels were ill equipped, ill trained, and ill prepared to perform the duties of law enforcement (Oliver & Hilgenberg, 2006).

Following the Wickersham Commission's report and the number of recommendations given in the report (for instance, one recommendation was for more extensive training for new police recruits as well as for officers already on the job), it might be expected that changes would be forthcoming. That was not the case, however. There was no immediate response, but over the next few decades gradual changes would come about.

Police chiefs and police organizations, with such forward-thinking men as August Vollmer and O. W. Wilson leading the way, brought about improved standards for hiring police officers, improved education and training, and better equipment for the police (Dempsey, 1999).

THE ROLE OF POLICE OFFICERS

In the second half of the 19th century, policing in big cities took on the role of providing public health services as well as other social welfare functions. For example, in Boston, police officers often served soup to the indigent, and the homeless were housed at night in police stations (Oliver & Hilgenberg, 2006). These welfare services tended to disappear in the 20th century, and policing began to focus more on maintaining order and enforcing the laws (Walker, 1992). As the 20th century proceeded, certain police roles emerged. For instance, patrol officers took on a readily identifiable role in terms of their traffic functions and responding to crime scenes.

What Do the Police Do Today?

In a typical police department of today, the job of police officers involves a wide variety of functions. But the major roles played by the police are patrol, traffic enforcement, peacekeeping and order maintenance, and investigating crimes.

The Patrol Function

Uniformed police officers do a number of very different jobs on a daily basis. Whether they are providing patrol services in a car, on horseback, on a bicycle, or on a motorcycle, the primary goals of police patrol are to deter crime, enhance feelings of public safety, and to be available for public service.

In regard to making officers available for service, the response of uniformed patrol officers, typically the first responders when a call is received at a police station, can be important in making an arrest or helping to secure a crime scene. However, in many instances, response time has no effect on clearing a crime. But this has little to do with patrol officers themselves. Many times a crime is not detected immediately after it occurs, so response by the police may not be critical. In addition, people often delay calling the police. And although patrol officers may be available to respond to a call, there may be administrative details that result in delays in information given to the officers on the street (Dempsey, 1999).

But it is the police dispatcher who notifies patrol officers in the vicinity to go to the scene. When uniformed officers arrive at the crime scene, they have an important set of tasks to carry out. They must:

- Secure and preserve the crime scene
- Determine if a crime, indeed, has been committed
- Identify witnesses and potential suspects
- Ask for emergency medical assistance if there is an injury
- Report back to their supervisor as to whether a crime has occurred and indicate whether detectives or crime scene technicians should be dispatched to the scene

Given this set of responsibilities, their effective and efficient handling of the crime scene can be essential, and it can even be said that is the most crucial aspect among the steps that will be taken leading to the gathering of evidence and the eventual solution of the crime (Walker, 1992).

Patrol officers play other roles in addition to being first on the scene of a crime. They have an important role in providing what Bayley (1994) calls a symbolic presence. In Bayley's view, the police—especially uniformed officers—are a symbol of police presence; they validate for citizens that law enforcement is doing its job and making citizens feel safe. Whether uniformed officers are directing traffic when a traffic light has malfunctioned or when sports fans are leaving the parking areas after a football game, their mere presence helps to reassure citizens that law and order exists (Bayley, 1994).

Additionally, patrol officers serve the public in many other ways: For instance, by answering questions or coming out to a neighborhood to deal with domestic violence incidents, responding to a security alarm that has signaled a possible break-in, or responding to complaints of noise from a neighbor's party.

Myth: *Putting more uniformed officers out on the street helps to reduce crime.*

Reality: *Bayley refers to this as one of the biggest myths related to the police. "Everyone knows," Bayley says, "that the number of police officers on the street has no effect on crime" (p. 3). That is, he says, everyone knows this—except the public (Bayley, 1994).*

THE RESEARCH ON POLICING AND THE PREVENTION OF CRIME

Myth: *Police presence reduces crime.*

Reality: *The mere presence of police officers alone has little or no effect on crime.*

The assumption is that by putting more officers on the street, this will lead to reduced crime. This strategy is referred to as preventive patrol. However, this assumption has been tested to see if it works.

The first such research project was conducted in 1974 and was called the Kansas City Preventive Patrol Project. Conducted to test the degree to which preventive patrol affected such things as offense rates and the level of public fear, the experiment was relatively simple (Walker, 1992).

The southern part of Kansas City, Missouri, was divided into 15 areas. Five of these areas were patrolled in the usual fashion; five others featured doubled patrols; and the last five saw patrols eliminated altogether (no officers were assigned to these five areas and officers only went into those areas when they were called).

The results? Surprisingly, in the three sections of the city, there were no significant differences in the rate of offending in terms of burglaries, robberies, auto thefts, larcenies, and vandalisms. Furthermore, citizens didn't seem to realize any changes in the patrol patterns, and there seemed no difference in citizens' fear of crime during the study (Schmalleger, 2012).

This study called into question the wisdom of random preventive patrol. However, the Kansas City experiment did usher in an era of more evidence-based policing, in which police practices have been put to the test to see which are effective and which ones are not.

Traffic Enforcement Functions

Local police agencies and state highway patrols are responsible for ensuring safety on the streets and highways. In some states, state police officers patrol freeways, expressways, and interstate highways, while local police patrol provides traffic enforcement services on lesser streets and roadways. The major responsibilities of highway patrol officers are to respond to traffic accidents, set up roadblocks to detect drunken drivers, and to generally enforce traffic laws.

Peacekeeping and Order Maintenance

Although patrol officers and traffic patrol officers make up the bulk of policing (Fuller, 2010), the police do a great variety of other things, all of which can fall under the heading of peacekeeping and order maintenance. For example, duties that are included in this category are:

- Responding to domestic dispute situations
- Controlling crowds at various public events, such as concerts, baseball games, and parades
- Working vice as an undercover officer
- Dealing with the mentally ill
- Working with juveniles
- Responding to emergencies, such as natural disasters, terrorist attacks, and blackouts

TV Series

- *Highway Patrol: Highway Patrol* starred Broderick Crawford as Dan Mathews, a gruff and dedicated head of a police force in an unidentified Western state. It made its debut in October 1955, and ran until 1959. It was actually created in response to the California Highway Patrol, which wanted a TV show to feature the California Highway Patrol. Episodes were usually fast paced, with a greater interest in chasing criminals than enforcing driving laws.
- *Adam-12:* This TV series about a couple of patrol officers ran from 1968 to 1975. *Adam-12* was the first TV series to more realistically portray the satisfactions and frustrations of being a police officer in the late 1960s through mid 1970s.
- *Southland:* This cop show, featuring patrol officers on the streets of South Los Angeles, debuted on NBC on April 9, 2009. It takes a rather raw and authentic look at the work and the daily lives of the police officers patrolling the streets of Los Angeles. It also tends to focus more on the experiences and interactions of patrol officers and detectives than it does on police procedure.

Review for Chapter Five

Research Paper or Term paper Topics:

- The history of policing in America
- Patrol officers and their responses to the mentally ill
- The unique duties and roles of patrol officers.

Important Terms to Know

Kansas City Preventive Patrol Project:
A research project conducted in Kansas City in 1974 to determine if police presence in the form of patrol officers had an effect on crime rates. It was found that the presence—or absence—of patrol officers had almost no effect on crime rates.

National Commission on Law Observance and Enforcement:
A commission, also known as the Wickersham Commission, appointed by President Herbert Hoover in 1929 to study crime in the United States.

Patrol officers:
Patrol officers are uniformed police officers who perform a variety of functions, including responding first to calls to the police department and handling traffic duties.

Slave patrols:
Organized groups of men who captured escaped slaves from Southern states.

Watch system: A system whereby ordinary citizens would be responsible for patrolling the streets to watch out for fires or crime.

Study Guide Questions

True or False:

1. The oldest law enforcement agency in the United States. is the FBI.

2. Federal law enforcement officers are involved when a federal law is violated.

3. The London Metropolitan Police was established in 1829.

4. The conclusion of the National Commission on Law Observance and Enforcement was that Prohibition was enforceable.

5. Patrol officers are typically first responders when a call comes in to the police station.

Multiple Choice Items:

6. Slave patrols were organized in the south in the United States to
    a. defeat the Ku Klux Klan
    b. protect slaves from abuse
    c. prevent slaves from escaping from their owners
    d. investigate crimes on plantations

7. The Wickersham Commission was the more informal name for
    a. The International Association of Chiefs of Police
    b. The National Commission on Law Observance and Enforcement
    c. The Knapp Commission
    d. none of the above

8. The outcome of the Kansas City Preventive Patrol Project was that
    a. crime went up in areas with decreased patrol officers
    b. citizens realized that there were fewer officers in some areas
    c. there were no differences in the rate of crime in most crime categories
    d. citizens' fear of crime went up

9. Patrol officers do various tasks including
    a. solving crimes
    b. investigating police corruption
    c. performing forensic work and detecting crime
    d. responding to domestic disputes, controlling crowds, and responding to emergencies

References

Bayley, D. H. (1994). *Police for the Future.* New York: Oxford University Press, Inc.

Bohm, R. H., and Haley, K. N. (2002). *Introduction to Criminal Justice.* 3rd ed. New York: Glencoe/McGraw-Hill.

Dantzker, M. L. (2000). *Understanding Today's Police.* 2nd ed. Upper Saddle River, NJ: Prentice Hall.

Dempsey, J. S. (1999). *An Introduction to Policing.* 2nd ed. Belmont, CA: Wadsworth Publishing Co.

Fuller, J. R. (2010). *Criminal Justice: Mainstream and Crosscurrents.* 2nd ed. Upper Saddle River, NJ: Prentice Hall.

Oliver, W. M., and Hilgenberg, J. F. (2006). *A History of Crime and Criminal Justice in America.* Boston: Allyn & Bacon.

Schmalleger, F. (2012). *Criminal Justice: A Brief Introduction.* 9th ed. Upper Saddle River, NJ: Prentice Hall.

Walker, S. (1992). *The Police in America: An Introduction.* 2nd ed. New York: McGraw Hill.

Chapter Six

Investigating Crime and the Rule of Law

There are very specifically defined rules of procedure that must be followed so that any evidence collected by the police can be later used in court. The Fourth Amendment to the U.S. Constitution is a brief amendment, but it has an important function in preserving the rights of citizens. The Fourth Amendment reads:

The right of the people to be secure in their persons, houses, papers, and effects, against unreasonable searches and seizures, shall not be violated, and no Warrants shall issue, but upon probable cause, supported by Oath or affirmation, and particularly describing the place to be searched, and the persons or things to be seized (Hall & Ely, 2009, p. 413).

SEARCH AND SEIZURE

The Fourth Amendment governs the search and seizure of evidence in a criminal case. There are three important elements of this amendment which control the activities of law enforcement when it comes to searching for and collecting evidence. These critical elements define:

- When suspects and their property can be searched
- When a search warrant is needed
- How a search warrant is obtained

The conclusion is inescapable that but one remedy exists to deter violations of the search and seizure clause. That is the rule which excludes illegally obtained evidence. Only by exclusion can we impress upon the zealous prosecutor that violation of the Constitution will do him no good. And only when that point is driven home can the prosecutor be expected to emphasize the importance of observing constitutional demands in his instructions to the police.

—*Frank Murphy*, Wolf v. Colorado, *338 U.S. 25 44 (1949) (Dissenting opinion)*

Stop and Frisk

A police officer can search a suspect if the officer has a search warrant or if the search is incident to a lawful arrest. But what if the officer wants to stop and frisk a suspect?

Although it has been common practice over the decades—virtually since police departments were established—for officers to stop and frisk suspicious people, it has not always been exactly clear whether the police actually had the right to stop a suspicious individual and whether they could conduct a frisk looking for weapons or contraband. However, in the court case of *Terry v. Ohio* (1968), the U.S. Supreme Court defined this right and the parameters of what constitutes a "stop and frisk."

The *Terry v. Ohio* case involved an officer who observed three men walking slowly back and forth in front of a store. The officer thought the men were acting in a suspicious manner and he concluded they might be casing the store for a robbery. The officer confronted the three men, and after asking some questions, patted them down. In the process of patting them down, he discovered that two of the men were carrying revolvers. He arrested the men and they were subsequently charged with carrying concealed weapons.

Later, in court, the men claimed that the officer did not have probable cause to search them. Therefore, they argued that the search was illegal and the guns should not be admitted into evidence. The case was appealed up to the U.S. Supreme Court. The Supreme Court agreed the officer did not have probable cause, but the Court made a distinction between a search without a warrant (which would require probable cause) and a stop and frisk. The Court held that a frisk (or a pat-down of the outer clothing of an individual) is essential to the proper performance of a police officer's investigative duties (Albanese, 2013).

Myth: *An aggressive stop-and-frisk policy by a police department can result in recovering large amounts of illegal guns.*

Reality: *Guns are recovered in less than one percent of stop and frisks.*

Procedural Law and Search and Seizure

Law enforcement—and indeed the entire criminal justice system—is governed by procedural law. Procedural law is a body of laws for how things should be done at each step of the criminal justice process. Procedural law includes court procedures such as rules of evidence and police procedures, which involve such things as search and seizure, arrest, and interrogation (Fagin, 2007).

Rules of Evidence

Rules of evidence stipulate the requirements for introducing evidence and define the qualifications of an expert witness and the nature of the testimony he or she may give (Fagin, 2012). Rules of evidence affect police officers' conduct because collecting evidence is part of their job. The rules state that evidence gathered through immoral, illegal, or unconstitutional means should not be used as evidence in a trial.

The Exclusionary Rule

Evidence is declared inadmissible under the exclusionary rule, and the rule prohibits the use of evidence or testimony obtained in violation of the Constitution.

The origins of the exclusionary rule can be traced back to a 1914 case heard by the U.S. Supreme Court. The case was *Weeks v. United States* (1914), and the Court ruled that evidence against Fremont Weeks, who was accused of transporting lottery tickets through the mail, was obtained without a search warrant. Weeks took action against the police and petitioned for the return of his private possessions. The conclusion of the Supreme Court was unanimous. The Court held that the seizure of items from Weeks's residence directly violated his constitutional rights. The Court also held that the government's refusal to return Weeks's possessions violated the Fourth Amendment. To allow private documents to be seized and then held as evidence against citizens would mean that the protection of the Fourth Amendment declaring the right to be secure against such searches and seizures would be of no value whatsoever. This was the first application of what eventually became known as the exclusionary rule (Bohm & Haley, 2012).

In 1961, the Supreme Court in *Mapp v. Ohio* extended the exclusionary rule by requiring that state courts use the rule—just as it was used in federal court proceedings.

Mapp v. Ohio (1961) was a case involving a woman by the name of Dollree Mapp. The police received a tip from an informant that there was evidence at her home related to a bombing suspect. The police arrived at Ms. Mapp's house and asked for permission to search her house. Ms. Mapp refused them permission and they left. Later, they returned, and this time they said they had a search warrant. They waved a blank piece of paper at her.

The police proceeded to search her home. They did not find any evidence of a bombing suspect. But they did find some obscene material. Ms. Mapp was arrested and was convicted in state court of possession of obscene materials (Fagin, 2007). Ms. Mapp appealed her conviction on the basis that her Fourth Amendment rights had been violated. The Supreme Court ruled that the same standards as in *Weeks v. United States* applied to defendants in state courts. That is, illegally obtained evidence would be inadmissible. As a result, Ms. Mapp's conviction was reversed.

> **Myth:** *Many criminal offenders get away with crime because of the exclusionary rule.*
>
> **Reality:** *Very few defendants get a free pass because of the exclusionary rule. In point of fact, it is used in less than three percent of felony cases.*

FRUIT OF THE POISONOUS TREE DOCTRINE

The exclusionary rule, as established in 1914 by *Weeks v. United States*, applies to primary evidence. That means that direct evidence (say, for example, a photo album containing photos of missing and presumed dead individuals) obtained by illegal means would be excluded, but that any other evidence (perhaps the burial sites of some of those bodies, which were discovered based on those photos) would still be permitted. However, this was further clarified a few years after the *Weeks v. United States* decision.

In *Silverthorne Lumber Co. v. United States* (1920), the U.S. Supreme Court added another rule of evidence—the fruit of the poisonous tree doctrine. In this decision, the Court declared that the rules of evidence applied not only to evidence directly obtained by illegal means but also to any other evidence garnered indirectly. For instance, if the police obtained the financial records from the residence of a suspect but gathered this evidence without a search warrant, they could not use those records to determine what bank accounts the suspect had and then get a judge to sign a legal search warrant in order to seize those bank accounts.

Although the *Silverthorne Lumber Co. v. United States* case only applied to federal courts, this doctrine was expanded to state courts in the 1949 case of *Wolf v. Colorado*. In effect, the Supreme Court in *Wolf v. Colorado* (1949) held that state courts had to enact procedures to protect the rights of citizens against police abuses of search and seizure.

EXCEPTIONS TO THE SEARCH WARRANT RULE

The Fourth Amendment's intent is that search warrants be secured by the police in order for a search and seizure to take place. In order for the police to obtain a search warrant, there must be probable cause. Probable cause means that there is a likelihood of a direct link between a suspect and a crime (Fagin, 2007).

However, over the years, the U.S. Supreme Court has authorized a number of circumstances in which the police can conduct a search or seizure without a search warrant. The most important of these search warrant exceptions are:

- Search incident to a lawful arrest
- Plain view searches
- Consent to search
- Exigent circumstances
- Search of automobiles
- Search of persons: Stop and frisk
- Public safety exceptions
- Good faith exceptions

SEARCH INCIDENT TO A LAWFUL ARREST

When the police are making a lawful arrest, they are entitled to a search of the person arrested without a search warrant. This right was articulated by the Supreme Court in the case of *Chimel v. United States* (1969). In this case, the court ruled that the police can not only search the person, but they can search the area within the immediate control of the individual. They cannot extend this search beyond the person's reach or to other rooms (Fagin, 2007).

PLAIN-VIEW SEARCHES

Evidence that is within plain view of a police officer is subject to confiscation. The court declared in *Harris v. United States* in 1968 that if a police officer has the legal right to be somewhere, any contraband that is in his view can be seized.

If, for instance, a police officer has been invited into a suspect's house and the officer sees stacks of money, along with weapons and plastic bags that could contain heroin on a nearby table, such evidence can be seized. However, the police cannot look in closets, in covered containers, or under a table cloth (for example). On the other hand, the Court has ruled that the police do not have to act blind or stupid. What this means is that the police do not have to be careless or inattentive. If an officer sees a stack of wooden boxes with the words "Rifles—Property of the U.S. Army" stenciled on the sides, the officer has probable cause to believe that there are guns in the boxes and that they very likely are not the legal property of the individual.

CONSENT TO SEARCH

A warrentless search can also be conducted if a person gives consent to search. For example, according to the Supreme Court, if an individual allows an officer to come into her home and then consents to the request "Do you mind if I look around?" she has given consent to a search and any evidence located can be seized by the officer. That includes looking in closed containers in a car (*Florida v. Jimeno* [1991]).

EXIGENT CIRCUMSTANCES

Officers can make an arrest or conduct a search without a warrant under exigent circumstances. An exigent circumstance refers to a situation in which a police officer must act swiftly and the officer determines that they do not have time to go to a court to seek a warrant (Cole & Smith, 2007). For instance, if officers are in hot pursuit of a fleeing suspected felon or if there are sounds of a struggle coming from within a house and it is possible someone might be in danger, officers need not stop to obtain a warrant and thereby risk losing evidence or allowing a suspect to get away.

To justify a warrantless search, officers do not need to prove that there was a potential threat to public safety (Cole & Smith, 2007). Officers often have to make on-the-spot decisions to apprehend a suspect or seek evidence when it is thought that delay might result in evidence being lost or destroyed. Practically speaking, judges are often reluctant to second guess a police officer who has had to make a split-second decision when the urgency of a situation required—in the officer's judgment—a warrantless search (Cole & Smith, 2007).

SEARCH OF AN AUTOMOBILE

If the police have probable cause, they can search an automobile without first obtaining a search warrant. The courts have taken note of the special circumstances of cars and motorized vehicles as long ago as 1925 and established the Carroll doctrine.

The Carroll doctrine came out of the case of *Carroll v. United States* (1925). The special circumstances of a car or automobile, of course, is that cars and other motorized means of transportation are readily mobile and they can be moved if there is a delay while an officer is attempting to get a search warrant. In the Carroll doctrine, the Supreme Court stated that evidence obtained in the search of an automobile without a warrant is permissible if the police have probable cause to believe a crime has occurred.

> **Myth:** *People always have to consent to a search of their automobile if they are stopped by the police.*
>
> **Reality:** *The police need probable cause to search an automobile. And if stopped, a motorist does not have to consent to a search.*

The exclusionary rule applies to automobile searches if the officer does not have the right to stop a car and driver in the first place. Lacking a reason to make a traffic stop makes any evidence confiscated inadmissible.

One other aspect of an auto search is the searching of a vehicle that has been impounded. If, for instance, a car has been illegally parked in a street's no parking zone and is towed to an impound lot, a search and inventory of the belongings of the car can be conducted. Any contraband found in an inventory search can be used as evidence (Cole & Smith, 2007).

SEARCH OF A PERSON: THE PAT-DOWN SEARCH

We have already discussed the pat-down search or the "stop and frisk." This is essentially a warrantless search because as indicated previously, it is a limited search, as only the outer clothing of the individual can be patted down. And the primary purpose of a stop and frisk is to ensure the safety of the police officer.

PUBLIC SAFETY EXCEPTIONS

There are many circumstances encountered by law enforcement when the public good is paramount. For example, the police can pursue a fleeing felon into an apartment building and search for the individual. Likewise, if an armed suspect who just robbed a bank and shot a bank employee flees into a nearby neighborhood, the police could search houses and other places where the suspect or his weapon could be found.

Furthermore, public safety concerns allow for the search of airline passengers and travelers (and their vehicles) who are crossing a border into another country. Evidence seized in these types of searches could legally justify an arrest and could be used as evidence in court (*Florida v. Bostick* [1991]).

The Good Faith Exception

Another search authorized by the Court to not require a search warrant is when the initial warrant has an error, thus rendering it invalid. For example, if during the filling out of a search warrant the wrong address is entered on the warrant and the police carry out a search at that incorrect address, evidence found at the "wrong" address can be seized. In effect, the court has said that there is no misconduct by the police and it was a "good faith" mistake on the part of law enforcement.

Interrogation of Suspects

After an arrest has been made and a search has been carried out, the police have the authority to question the individual. There is no place in the Constitution where the word interrogation is mentioned. However, it is implied in the Fifth Amendment:

No person shall be held to answer for a capital, or otherwise infamous crime, unless on a presentment or indict-ment of a Grand Jury, except in cases arising in the land or naval forces, or in the Militia, when in actual service in time of War or public danger; Nor shall any person be subject for the same offense to be twice put in jeopardy of life or limb; nor shall be compelled in any criminal case to be a witness against himself, nor be deprived of life, liberty, or property, without due process of law; nor shall private property be taken for public use, without just compensation (Hall & Ely, 2009, p. 413).

The implication of an interrogation occurs in the section of the Fifth Amendment "nor shall be compelled in any criminal case to be a witness against himself." The writers of the Bill of Rights were well aware of historical precedence in England as well as other countries where individuals were forced to testify against themselves because they were subjected to torture in order to exact a confession from them.

The U.S. Supreme Court, in the landmark 1966 case of *Miranda v. Arizona*, established that the Fifth Amendment pertained to police interrogations and confessions obtained by law enforcement.

This important case involved Ernesto Miranda, who was arrested at his home in Phoenix, Arizona, for suspicion of rape and was taken to the Phoenix police station. He was identified by a rape victim as her assailant. He was placed in a police interrogation room and questioned by two police officers. After two hours, the officers left the room and had a written confession signed by Miranda. A typed paragraph at the top of the confession indicated that it had been made voluntarily "with the full knowledge of my legal rights, understanding any statement I made may be used against me" (Albanese, 2005, p. 174).

Ernesto Miranda subsequently went to trial and was convicted of kidnapping and rape. He was sentenced to 20 to 30 years in prison. But he appealed his conviction on the grounds that he did not have legal representation during interrogation.

When this appeal reached the U.S. Supreme Court, the court noted that Ernesto Miranda was uneducated, indigent, and "a seriously disturbed individual with pronounced sexual fantasies" (Albanese, 2005, p. 174). Since only the police were present during interrogation and since the police officers admitted that they did not inform him that he had the right to an attorney during interrogation, the court had reason to doubt as to whether the confession was truly voluntary.

The Supreme Court overturned Miranda's confession, stating that his confession was inadmissible as evidence. To safeguard the rights of individuals in future cases, in the opinion throwing out Miranda's confession, the Court provided a five-point warning, which is now well known as the Miranda warning. We all can recite the Miranda warning because it has been used so frequently in movies, cop shows on TV, and in police procedural novels:

> *"You have the right to remain silent. You have the right to an attorney. If you cannot afford an attorney, one will be provided for you. Any statements made by you can and will be used against you in a court of law."*

In addition, the Supreme Court's decision stated that:

- The suspect must be warned prior to any questioning that he has the right to remain silent.
- Any statements made by the person can be used in a court of law.
- The suspect has the right to the presence of an attorney.
- If the person cannot afford an attorney, one will be appointed prior to any questioning.
- Opportunity to exercise these rights must be afforded to the suspect throughout the interrogation. After such warnings have been given, the individual may knowingly waive these rights and agree to answer questions or make a statement (Albanese, 2005).

The right to legal counsel did not originate with the Miranda decision. It had actually been established by the Supreme Court as early as 1931 in the case of *Powell v. Alabama*. In that case, the conviction of the so-called Scottsboro Boys, nine young black men accused of raping two white women, was overturned by the Court because the men were never provided the opportunity for legal counsel. Other cases since *Powell v. Alabama* have further established other rights regarding legal counsel.

For example, the Court ruled that indigent defendants have the right to counsel, and that there is the right to have an attorney present during interrogation (*Escobedo v. Illinois* [1964]). Prior to the Escobedo case, in which a suspect, Danny Escobedo, was denied an opportunity to see his attorney (who was present in the police station during questioning), the police routinely blocked the suspect's ability to be represented by counsel during interrogation. The Court's decision in Miranda added specific warnings required at police interrogations to stop this kind of police conduct.

Since the Miranda decision, the Supreme Court has decided other cases in which the definition of an interrogation has been given and the Court has addressed exactly what police questioning actually is. In general, the interpretation by the courts is that any words or questions by the police that are reasonably likely to elicit an incriminating response by a suspect qualifies as an interrogation (Siegel & Worrall, 2012).

In order to ensure that the rights of suspects have been protected, most police departments use forms to show that suspects have signed off to guarantee they were given their Miranda warnings. In addition, a majority of police departments videotape interrogations and confessions. One study found that more than 60 percent of large police departments in the United States now videotape interrogations and confessions (Albanese, 2005). In a study conducted by the National Institute of Justice (Gelber, 1993), it was found that about 85 percent of police departments believed that videotaping improves the quality of interrogations. Such procedures help to ensure that suspects are given the Miranda warning, that they have not been coerced into giving false confessions, and that questioning has been done appropriately following proper procedures.

Both the Fourth Amendment and the Fifth Amendment have protected the rights of suspects. Furthermore, the interpretations of these amendments by the courts have done much to deter police misconduct, which helps to avoid false confessions and wrongful convictions. Although abiding by these Court rules has provided special challenges to the police, there are other challenges and problems related to law enforcement. These will be addressed in the next chapter.

FOR FURTHER CONSIDERATION

Historical Events Relevant to Chapter Six

June 10, 1968:   The U.S. Supreme Court decides the case of *Terry v. Ohio*, which holds that a stop and frisk only requires reasonable suspicion.

June 13, 1966:   The Supreme Court hands down its opinion in *Miranda v. Arizona*. The Miranda warnings were articulated in this famous opinion.

June 19, 1961:   The Supreme Court issues its opinion in the case of *Mapp v. Ohio*. This case finding requires state law enforcement officers to comply with Fourth Amendment standards when conducting searches.

November 7, 1932:   The Supreme Court announces its decision in *Powell v. Alabama*. The Court rules that the conviction of the Scottsboro youths must be overturned because the defendants were not provided with counsel, and thus were denied a fair trial.

Important Court Cases

- *Carroll v. United States* (1925): The Supreme Court recognized the car search exception to the warrant requirements of the Fourth Amendment for the first time.
- *Chimel v. United States* (1969): This case provides the standards for establishing the limits of a warrantless search pursuant to a lawful arrest.
- *Mapp v. Ohio* (1961): This court decision required state law enforcement officers to comply with Fourth Amendment standards when making searches.
- *Terry v. Ohio* (1968): This case was the first in a now substantial line of Supreme Court cases recognizing stop and frisk as a valid practice by the police.
- *Weeks v. United States* (1914): This case marked the establishment of the exclusionary rule. The Court said that federal courts and officers had to guarantee the rights of the Fourth Amendment.
- *Wolf v. Colorado* (1949): The majority of the U.S. Supreme Court ruled that protection from arbitrary intrusion by law enforcement is implied in the concept of ordered liberty and thereby incorporated by the Fourteenth Amendment and applicable to the states.

Websites to Check Out

- *Search and seizure.* Available at: *http://criminal.findlaw.com/criminal-rights/search-seizure/.* Sponsored by *Findlaw.com,* this website features reliable information on all aspects of criminal law.
- *Articles about search and seizure in the New York Times.* Available at: *http://topics.nytimes.com/topics/reference/timestopics/subjects/s/search_and_seizure/index.html.* This *New York Times* website allows easy access to previous articles in the *New York Times* related to search and seizure.

Books

- Scheb, J. M., and Scheb, J. M. II. (1999). *Criminal Law and Procedure.* 3rd ed. Belmont, CA: West/Wadsworth.
- Schmalleger, F. (2006). *Criminal Law Today.* 3rd ed. Upper Saddle River, NJ: Prentice Hall.
- Thomson/West Editorial Staff (2007). *Search and Seizure Checklists.* 2007–2008 ed. Eagan, MN: Thomson/West.
- White, W. S., and Tomkovicz, J. J. (2004). *Criminal Procedure: Constitutional Constraints upon Investigation and Proof.* 5th ed. Newark, NJ: Matthew Bender & Co.

TV Series

- *Without a Trace:* This TV series, that ran on CBS from 2002 to 2009, was a police procedural show that followed a fictitious missing persons department in the New York office of the FBI. Many episodes over the years featured the agents' awareness of the Fourth Amendment rights of suspects.
- *Law & Order: Law & Order* was a police procedural and legal drama TV series that ran from 1990 until 2010. The detectives in the first half hour of each episode often have few good clues and must usually chase several dead ends before finding a likely suspect. Toward the middle of the episode, the police begin working with the prosecutors to make the arrest. Sometimes this means the prosecutors will indicate to the detectives that they do not have enough evidence for a search warrant or an arrest warrant. Many episodes include legal proceedings to suppress evidence. And most of these scenes end with evidence or statements being suppressed, often on a technicality.
- *The Closer:* A TNT cable show, *The Closer* ran for seven years until its end in 2012. It featured a Los Angeles police department deputy chief of police (Brenda Leigh Johnson) who came to head the department with a reputation as a "closer"—the nickname given to interrogators who not only solve a case, but obtain confessions that lead to convictions. Deputy Chief Johnson sometimes uses deceit and intimidation to persuade a suspect to confess, but usually just narrowly avoids crossing the line of violating a suspect's Fourth Amendment rights.

Review for Chapter Six

Research Paper or Term Paper Topics:

- How to obtain and use a search warrant
- Warrantless searches
- Interrogation and the Miranda warning

Important Terms to Know

Evidence:	Evidence consists of legal proofs presented to the court in the form of witnesses, records, documents, objects, and other means for the purpose of influencing the opinions of the judge or the jury toward the case of the prosecution or the defense.
Exigent circumstances:	Emergency or urgent circumstances.
Procedural law:	That aspect of the law that specifies the methods to be used in enforcing criminal law.
Substantive law:	That part of the law that creates and defines what conduct is criminal and which punishments should be imposed for violations of criminal laws.
Stop and frisk:	A frisk or a pat-down search of the outer garments of the suspect is permissible if the officer has reasonable suspicion that the suspect is engaging in criminal activity and may be dangerous.
Exclusionary rule:	According to the exclusionary rule, evidence obtained as a result of an unreasonable or illegal search is not admissible in a criminal prosecution.
Fruit of the poisonous tree doctrine:	This rule prohibits the admission of evidence obtained as a result of an illegal or initially tainted admission, confession, or search.
Plain-view searches:	Plain-view searches occur when the police are conducting a search pursuant to a search warrant and come across contraband or evidence they can plainly see but which they did not expect to find.
Good faith exception:	The United States Supreme Court ruled that the exclusionary rule does not apply when the police in good faith relied on case law that was later changed by another judicial opinion or on a valid law or statute later declared

unconstitutional, or on a search warrant that was later declared invalid even though originally signed by a judge.

Study Guide Questions

True or False:

1. The Fourth Amendment governs search and seizure evidence in a criminal case.

2. Procedural law has to do with a body of laws governing how courts proceed with appointing judges.

3. The importance of the Supreme Court's decision in *Mapp v. Ohio* is that illegally obtained evidence is inadmissible.

4. A search does not require a search warrant if it is made incident to a lawful arrest.

Multiple Choice Items:

5. A stop and frisk, or pat-down search, of a suspect requires
   a. probable cause
   b. a search warrant
   c. reasonable suspicion
   d. a judge's approval

6. The exclusionary rule prohibits the use of evidence that is
   a. discovered in plain view
   b. of little value
   c. not obtained by crime scene investigators
   d. in violation of the Fourth Amendment

7. Evidence obtained by illegal means may result in further evidence found using that illegally obtained evidence would fall under the
   a. Fruit of the poisonous tree doctrine
   b. Miranda warnings
   c. Stop and frisk rule
   d. Misconduct rule

8. A search and seizure is legal if
    a. the officer means well
    b. an individual gives the officer permission to search
    c. the police are trying to get evidence to prosecute a serial killer
    d. the police follow the rule of cutting corners in order to ensure a conviction

References

Albanese, J. S. (2013). *Criminal Justice.* 5th ed. Upper Saddle River, NJ: Pearson.

Bohm, R. H., and Haley, K. N. (2012). *Introduction to Criminal Justice.* 7th ed. New York: Glencoe/McGraw-Hill.

Carroll v. United States, 267 U.S. 132 (1925).

Chimel v. United States, 395 U.S. 752 (1969).

Cole, G. F., and Smith, C. E. (2007). *The American System of Criminal Justice.* 11th ed. Belmont, CA: Thomson Wadsworth.

Escobedo v. Illinois, 378 U.S. 438 (1964).

Fagin, J. A. (2007). *Criminal Justice: A Brief Introduction.* Boston: Allyn & Bacon.

Florida v. Bostick, 501 U.S. 429 (1991).

Florida v. Jimeno, 500 U.S. 248 (1991).

Gelber, W. A. (1993), "Videotaping interrogations and confessions," National Institute of Justice, Available at: https://www.ncjrs.gov/App/Publications/abstract.aspx?ID=139962.

Hall, K. L., and Ely, J. W. (2009). *The Oxford Guide to United States Supreme Court Decisions.* 2nd ed. New York: Oxford University Press.

Harris v. United States, 390 U.S. 234 (1968).

Mapp v. Ohio, 367 U.S. 643 (1961).

Powell v. Alabama, 287 U.S. 45 (1931).

Siegel, L. J., and Worrall, J. L. (2012). *Introduction to Criminal Justice.* 13th ed. Belmont, CA: Wadsworth.

Silverthorne Lumber Co. v. United States, 251 U.S. 385 (1920).

Terry v. Ohio, 392 U.S. 1 (1968).

Weeks v. United States, 232 U.S. 383 (1914).

Wolf v. Colorado, 338 U.S. 25 (1949).

Chapter Seven

Problems and Challenges in Policing

Like most professions and careers, the job of being a police officer involves various problems and challenges. However, unlike most other professions, policing is not only a public service, but it involves a great deal of public visibility and scrutiny. The work of police officers is subject to media attention, and it is frequently controversial.

Although as citizens we depend on the police for many services, we also have high expectations for law enforcement. We want them to be available to handle our grievances and problems—no matter how petty and trite those problems might be. At the same time, we want them to be polite, courteous, sensitive, and well trained. We want them to catch dangerous criminals, but we also expect them to be respectful of our rights and our privacy.

As a result of these sometimes conflicting expectations and needs, the role of a police officer may be very stressful.

There's a lot of law at the end of a nightstick.

—Grover A. Whalen, Courtroom, 1950

STRESS AND THE POLICE

Is the job of a police officer more or less stressful than other jobs?

Certainly there are aspects of policing that are stressful. Performing dangerous undercover duties, apprehending violent criminals, arresting fugitives, responding to volatile domestic disputes, intervening in a riot, or investigating a multiple murder may all be extremely stressful situations that are likely to tax the emotional resources of almost any officer. However, there are aspects of the job that are also very routine and even boring. Conducting surveillance or writing reports in the police station may be some of the least desirable aspects of policing for many officers.

Studies related to what constitutes the usual work of the police bear out the fact that the police are involved in many activities that are rather mundane compared to what the public might think makes up the bulk of a police officer's job. Most often, though, it is police dramas and cop shows on television that demonstrate to the public what *typically* happens during an officer's shift. However, in order for television shows to stay on the air and generate revenue for the network, those shows must be exciting and they must portray police work as glamorous, violent, thrilling, and dangerous.

Studies beginning in the 1960s found that police officers spend a majority of their time in non-law enforcement-related activities. Bayley, a noted expert on policing, has found that as little as seven to ten percent of calls to police departments have anything to do with crime (Bayley, 1994). Scott (1981) found that only about three percent of calls to the police involve violent crimes.

What these findings strongly suggest is that calls to police departments—and the resulting activities of officers—are related to requests for information, requests for assistance, requests for straightening out traffic problems, and requests for help with a variety of other citizen concerns and problems. Also, with the increase of home and business security devices and alarms, some police departments find that a great deal of time is spent each day by officers responding to false alarms. False burglar alarms are a major issue facing police departments, as estimates from agencies across the country suggest that between eight to 25 percent of calls for service are for false alarms (Gaines, Famega, & Bichler, 2007). It is estimated that annually there are 36 million false alarms in the United States, costing about $1.8 billion (Blackstone, Hakim, & Spiegel, 2002).

Myth:	*Police work is exciting because most police officers spend most of their time arresting criminals.*
Reality:	*Very little time is spent by the average police officer dealing with offenders or making arrests. The average police officer may make less than 25 arrests in a year.*

Other research finds that the average police officer makes one to two arrests per month, and that an officer may expect to arrest a violent criminal about once every two to three months (Bayley, 1994).

Thus, while there may be stress on the job at times for police officers, the stress is likely to be internal as many police officers go into law enforcement expecting an exciting and risky career. On the other hand, they may be faced with the reality that the role of police officer could be more accurately described as problem solver or service provider. This will produce stress for the officer who would like to consider himself or herself a crime fighter.

Domestic Violence

One of the services that police officers provide is responding to conflicts and disputes. This can include disputes between neighbors, but it can—and often does—include disputes between family members. Frequently, this may mean physical conflicts between spouses, but with greater attention being paid to abuse and aggression in general, these calls to residences may include conflicts or violence between parents and children—or even between siblings. The average yearly rate of intimate partner violence is 4.2 per 1,000 for females and 0.9 per 1,000 for males (Bureau of Justice, 2011).

It has long been said—at least as part of police lore—that the most dangerous calls for the police are those in which domestic violence is alleged (Hess, Orthman, & Chao, 2010). These situations are often described as volatile and risky for police officers because of the unpredictability of the situation when an officer is entering someone else's home. Many officers believe such incidents pose the greatest risks to their safety. However, there is little evidence to support this belief (Masters et al., 2013). There is research indicating that traffic stops and pursuits pose the greatest threats to officers' safety (Law Enforcement Officers Killed, 2010).

With increasing numbers of domestic violence calls, police officers are often given special training these days to better learn how to intervene and appropriately respond to these situations.

Some jurisdictions have instituted mandatory arrest policies in domestic violence cases (Reid, 2009). Under mandatory arrest policies, police officers must arrest the alleged perpetrator of domestic violence if there is sufficient evidence that violence has occurred. Some research has suggested that mandatory arrest policies result in reduced numbers of domestic violence incidents (Reid, 2009). However, there are other studies that dispute this finding (Dixon, 2008).

Myth: *Many police officers are killed responding to domestic violence calls.*

Reality: *Responding to domestic disturbances is not the most dangerous situation for police officers. Some research shows that only about five percent of officer fatalities occurred when they were responding to domestic disturbances.*

Nonetheless, the police have a duty to protect victims from domestic violence. In fact, police officers and police departments may be liable to lawsuits if they fail to protect a victim. Yet, many spouses and other family members may refuse to cooperate, request that the suspected perpetrator not be arrested, or ask that charges be dropped.

HIV and AIDS

Dangers other than violence also threaten police officers' safety. The increase in serious diseases that can be transmitted by blood and other body fluids, the possible planned release of active biological weapons such as anthrax or smallpox, and the fact that crime and accident scenes are often dangerous make caution and wariness important for officers responding to a crime scene (Schmalleger, 2012).

The spread of the HIV virus and the AIDS disease beginning in the 1980s has led to special problems for the police. As officers come into contact with the public and suspects, they have to be concerned about whether the person has HIV or AIDS. This requires officers to take greater precautions in making sure they do a thorough pat-down or search so that they are not likely to come into contact with the AIDS virus. However, the possibility of AIDS transmission by casual contact has been scientifically determined as extremely remote (Schmalleger, 2012).

Mental Illness

Among the specialized problems confronting police officers today are those related to mental illness. Officers are expected to be sensitive to the mentally ill, but mentally ill individuals may be suspects or they may be violent individuals posing risks for officers. Many police departments provide training for officers so they can be better versed in spotting mental illness and responding to it appropriately.

Volatile and sometimes deadly confrontations between the police and the mentally ill have been more common since state psychiatric hospitals began to discharge large numbers of patients in the 1960s and 1970s (Mental Illness and Violence, 2011).

Most police academies do not include specific training to identify those people with mental health problems or to respond appropriately to them (Masters et al., 2013). In response, police departments throughout the United States have launched "crisis intervention" training to have at least a few officers in each department with sufficient training to respond more effectively to mentally ill citizens (Mental Illness and Violence, 2011).

Racial Profiling

Racial profiling is the informal practice of some officers and the official policy of some law enforcement departments to target some ethnic and racial groups on the basis that certain characteristics of individuals and groups are indicative of criminal behavior (Barkan & Bryjak, 2004). In effect, racial profiling is the police practice of stopping, questioning, and searching a disproportionate number of racial and ethnic minorities, most often African Americans and Hispanics.

According to some experts (Barkan & Bryjak, 2004; Risse & Zeckhauser, 2004), the practice is predicated on the belief that certain minority or ethnic groups are involved in a significant amount of crime. Often, racial profiling is aimed at spotting and intercepting drivers, airline passengers, and others who might be users, smugglers, or distributors of illegal drugs.

> **Myth:** *Stopping drivers based on their race is good police work because stops of minorities frequently yield illegal drugs or other contraband.*
>
> **Reality:** *Minority drivers are less likely to be carrying contraband than are white drivers.*

Although many law enforcement officers have denied engaging in racial profiling, anecdotal and social science research has supported the presence of racial profiling as a fundamental aspect of policing throughout the United States (Barkan & Bryjak, 2004). Among the studies and research of the practice is the important study done by the American Civil Liberties Union in Maryland (Harris, 1999). Published as "Driving While Black: Racial Profiling on Our Nation's Highways," the findings of this research showed that 80.3 percent of the drivers pulled over were African Americans, Hispanics, and other minorities (Harris, 1999). This study confirmed in a dramatic way that racial profiling on I-95 in Maryland exists. The report indicated that there was a disparity between the number of minority and white drivers stopped by the police.

Another report, entitled "Racial Profiling: Texas Stops and Searches," found that, in addition to being pulled over more often, blacks were 1.6 times more likely to be searched after being stopped, and Hispanics were 1.4 times more likely to be searched than were whites (Inciardi, 2005).

While racial profiling on the nation's highways is not a new phenomenon, the terrorist attack on the World Trade Center on September 11, 2001 added a new dimension to racial profiling. That is, Muslims and Arab passengers on airlines have been targeted for searches, questioning, detention, and even interrogation by the FBI (Inciardi, 2005).

President George W. Bush, in his February 27, 2001, address to a Joint Session of Congress declared that racial profiling is "wrong and we will end it in America" (Department of Justice, Fact Sheet: Racial Profiling, 2003). The president directed the attorney general to review the use by federal law enforcement authorization of race as a factor in conducting stops, searches, and other law enforcement investigative procedures. The "End Racial Profiling Act of 2011," co-sponsored by Illinois senator Richard Durbin, was proposed to terminate existing programs at both the federal and state levels that openly use the tactic of racial profiling in their investigations. The bill has met with opposition by some members of Durbin's Senate Judiciary Committee, including a vice president of the Fraternal Order of Police. Calling the legislation "offensive" to law enforcement, Captain Frank Gale of the Denver police department told lawmakers that if enacted, the law would make it more difficult for officers and prosecutors to carry out otherwise sound arrests of minorities (Racial Profiling Bill Gets Heated, 2012).

Despite these efforts to eliminate racial profiling, several recent studies continue to document that racial profiling continues to be practiced by many law enforcement agencies (Persistence of Racial and Ethnic Profiling in the U.S., 2009).

POLICE MISCONDUCT

Police misconduct, including corruption, has been endemic to policing in the United States since the very beginning of police departments in the mid-19th century (Walker, 1992). Given the low standards used in recruiting police officers in the 19th and early 20th centuries, the lack of rigorous training of officers, and the power law enforcement officers held over citizens, you can begin to understand why cops took bribes or were on the payroll of organized crime syndicates.

Corruption has been defined as accepting "money or money's worth for doing something that [police are] under duty to do anyway ... under duty not to do, or to exercise a legitimate discretion for improper reasons" (Kappeler et al., 1998, p. 21). However, in recent years, a significant amount of both individual and systematic police corruption has been drug related. Of the 508 police convictions for criminal activity between 1994 and 1997, almost 45 percent were drug related (Masters et al., 2013). Just as every organization has some members who at least occasionally act in an inappropriate manner, all police departments experience some corruption (Barkan & Bryjak, 2004). In some police departments, there are only a few officers who violate regulations and criminal laws, whereas other departments or sections of departments are thoroughly corrupt (Barkan & Bryjak, 2004).

One area of misconduct that has received increasing attention in recent years is sexual misconduct (Reid, 2009). Most such reports involve allegations against male officers who take advantage of female citizens (Reid, 2009).

However, perhaps the area of police misconduct that has received the most attention is brutality and excessive use of force by the police. Although there were reports about police brutality in the early years of the 20th century (Reiss, 1980), concerns about police brutality resurfaced in the 1960s when student protests related to both the war in Vietnam and to civil rights were headline news all around the country. The police use of attack dogs, water hoses, night sticks, and even guns was prominently featured in television news broadcasts frequently during that turbulent decade.

But it was during the 1990s that several incidents of police brutality and excessive use of force caused shock waves throughout the nation. Starting with the beating of Rodney King in 1991 by Los Angeles police officers and caught on amateur video, there followed several other incidents that suggested to many that the police were out of control. For example, in Detroit, Malice Green was beaten to death by Detroit police department officers in 1992 during a traffic stop. Officers contended that he had drugs in his grasp that he wouldn't relinquish (Fleming, 2012). And in New York City, Amadou Diallo, a 23-year-old unarmed immigrant, was shot to death in 1999 by four city police officers who thought he could be a suspected serial rapist.

These incidents of force and violence not only resulted in injury and death to citizens, but in all such incidents, the end result was greater alienation between the police and minority groups. Furthermore, these cases, as well as many others in several cities in the United States, triggered lawsuits that cost cities and police departments millions of dollars (Masters et al., 2013). Officers who abuse their authority may face criminal prosecutions for violations of state and federal laws. However, civil lawsuits against the police for abuse of authority are more common than criminal prosecutions (Masters et al., 2013).

Research into excessive use of force has found that only about one percent of police-citizen encounters involves excessive use of force (Office of Justice Programs, 1999). Yet, these incidents generate considerable publicity and cause damage to the relationship the police must have with the community.

The use of deadly force by the police has been defined as "such force as under normal circumstances poses a high risk of death or serious injury to its human target, regardless of whether or not death, serious injury or any harm actually results" (Milton et al., 1977, p. 4). Police may use deadly force at some times and under some circumstances. Most rules for the use of deadly force come from federal statutes or administrative decisions. In 1995, the Department of Justice issued a uniform policy on the use of deadly force (Department of Justice Policy Statement, 1995). Many local police departments and state police agencies have developed policies based on a continuum of force, which describes the type of force acceptable in a variety of situations (Siegel & Worrall, 2012).

The Supreme Court has also ruled on deadly force. Historically, the shooting of fleeing felons has been allowed. However, as more efficient weapons were developed and as the use of more sophisticated forms of communication have been available to the police, deadly force has been less tolerated. In general, it is much easier to apprehend a suspect who flees and the police do not have to "shoot to kill." However, before 1985, the courts did not prohibit the use of force against fleeing felons.

But in 1985, the U.S. Supreme Court in *Tennessee v. Garner* ruled that the use of deadly force by police officers must be reasonable in order to be lawful. The Supreme Court stated that in order for deadly force to be reasonable, then it must be used only:

- to prevent an escape when the suspect has threatened the officer with a weapon.
- when there is a threat of death or injury to the officer or others.
- when there is probable cause to believe that the person has committed a crime involving the infliction or the threatened infliction of serious physical harm and, when practical, some warning has been given by the officer (Reid, 2009).

Following the *Tennessee v. Garner* ruling, the police are no longer allowed to shoot a fleeing suspect—particularly one who is unarmed and not posing an immediate threat to the officer or others. Although researchers have estimated that police use of force is relatively rare—about 1.7 percent of all contacts with citizens and 20 percent of all arrests—still, alternatives to deadly force have been steadily adopted by more police departments (Siegel & Worrall, 2012). For instance, many police departments are routinely using rubber bullets, stun guns, and Tasers, as well as pepper spray to subdue disorderly suspects.

What about High-speed Chases?

High-speed car chases are common occurrences in action movies, TV cop shows, and sometimes in real life when the police engage in high-speed pursuits with suspects in crimes. However, in recent years, with the alarming number of injuries and deaths to innocent bystanders, local police departments have developed policies to discourage and reduce the number of high-speed chases by police officers (Masters et al., 2013).

A final aspect of police misconduct to be covered in this chapter is related to wrongful convictions. That is, in recent years, especially since the advent of such projects and programs as the Innocence Project in New York and the Center for Wrongful Conviction at Northwestern University in Evanston, Illinois, it has become very apparent that not only do the innocent get arrested and convicted of crimes they didn't commit, but that police behavior contributes to this problem (Barkan & Bryjak, 2004).

There are a number of reasons why innocent people are convicted of crimes, but some of the most common reasons relating to the police are forced confessions, inappropriate interrogations, the manufacture of evidence, the failure to properly evaluate and use evidence, an overreliance on eye-witness identification, and the use of what is called "junk science" or faulty forensic science.

Part of the problem of wrongful conviction is related to media and police administration pressures, along with political pressures to solve crimes—particularly high-profile crimes. Another aspect of the problem is the desire of police officers and detectives to clear crimes and make arrests. Additionally, an important part of the problem is inadequate training of detectives and a lack of adequate supervision and oversight of the work of detectives. This failure to provide appropriate oversight can include police administrators who do not carefully review the work of detectives, as well as overzealous prosecutors who do not insist on the scrupulous and meticulous gathering of evidence.

POLICE REVIEW BOARDS AND COMMUNITY-ORIENTED POLICING

All in all, most police officers show a great deal of integrity and reflect professional attitudes. As standards for recruitment of officers and as training of law enforcement has improved, fewer problems of the types reviewed in this chapter occur. Unfortunately, when some of these problems and special types of police misconduct do appear in the media, the public trust of the police is eroded.

Two developments have helped to curb the problems of police misconduct. One is the use of civilian review boards and independent police review boards. When misconduct by police officers is alleged, many police de-partments—especially those in larger cities—turn the matter over to a civilian review board for investigation and recommendations. These boards allow for the citizens' role in determining whether police misconduct has occurred, and if so, these boards can make recommendations to an internal affairs department within the police department for sanctions.

The second development which has helped to counter negative perceptions of the police has to do with growing trends to bring about a closer working relationship between the police and the community.

Known as community-oriented policing, the intent of community-oriented policing (COP) or community-oriented policing services (COPS) is to respond to an emerging recognition that the police cannot be successful in fighting crime without a working relationship with the community that they serve. Promulgated since the 1980s, COP has brought about closer relationships between the police and the citizens in their jurisdiction. The primary features of most community-oriented policing programs are:

- Community-based crime prevention.
- Reorientation of patrol activities to emphasize the importance of non-emergency services.
- Increased police accountability to the public.
- Decentralization of command, including a greater use of civilians at all levels of police decision making (Schmalleger, 2012).

More and more police departments are incorporating community-oriented policing into their typical activities. The Bureau of Justice Statistics noted recently that in 1997 there were only about 21,000 officers nationwide who were classified as engaging in community-oriented policing activities. That number has jumped to about

100,000 more recently, with over 600,000 officers trained by the Community Oriented Policing Services of the Bureau of Justice (COPS, 2012).

Community-oriented policing and better training, which raise the standard of professionalism among police officers, has brought about more officers today who adhere to ethical codes and standards established by the police profession. By recruiting officers who are more highly educated and who subscribe to professional standards, the discretionary activities of police officers has been limited, but in exchange there is the gain of respect and regard of the public that many police officers receive today.

FOR FURTHER CONSIDERATION

Historical Events Relevant to Chapter Seven

January 24, 1985:   In Portland, Oregon, Penny Harrington, a woman who earned a degree in criminal justice from Michigan State University, becomes the first female police chief of a major American city.

February 4, 1999:   Amadou Diallo, an unarmed West African, was killed by four undercover New York City police officers, who fired 41 rounds at him in a case of mistaken identity. The four officers were indicted, but all were acquitted after having been charged with second degree murder.

March 3, 1991:   Rodney King is beaten by Los Angeles police officers; the beating is caught on videotape. Four officers were indicted by a grand jury and were charged with assault and excessive use of force. A trial for Theodore J. Briscoe, Stacy Koon, Laurence M. Powell, and Timothy E. Wind begins on March 4, 1992. With defense attorney Michael P. Stone defending them, they were found not guilty on April 29, 1992. A second trial was held beginning on February 3, 1993; the charges in this second trial were for violating Rodney King's civil rights. This time the jury found Koon and Powell guilty (they were sentenced to 30 months in prison) and Briscoe and Wind were found not guilty.

March 6, 2000:   Three white New York City police officers were convicted of a cover-up in a police station attack on Haitian immigrant Abner Louima. Louima was assaulted, brutalized, and forcibly sodomized with the handle of a bathroom plunger by several officers after being arrested outside a Brooklyn nightclub in 1997. On December 13, 1999, Officer Justin Volpe was sentenced to 30 years in prison without the possibility of parole, a $525 fine, and restitution in the amount of $277,495. Officer Charles Schwarz was convicted on June 27, 2000, for helping Volpe assault Louima in the bathroom and was sentenced to 15 years in prison. At the time of Schwarz's conviction, there were numerous questions raised about whether he could receive a fair trial in the highly charged atmosphere. Schwarz's conviction was overturned by the U.S. Court of Appeals for the Second Circuit, which found that Schwarz was denied a fair trial. However, in 2002, he pleaded guilty to a perjury charge for testifying that he did not lead Louima to the bathroom, and was sentenced to five years in prison. Louima's subsequent civil suit against the city of New York resulted in a settlement of $8.75 million on July 30, 2001, the largest police brutality settlement in New York City history.

April 29, 1992:	Rioting erupted in Los Angeles after a jury in Simi Valley, California, acquitted four white police officers of nearly all charges in the videotaped beating of black motorist Rodney King. During three days of civil unrest, 53 people eventually died.
June 5, 1978:	The first black chief of police is appointed in Chicago.
September 12, 1910:	Former social worker Alice Stebbins Wells was appointed the first woman police officer in the United States in Los Angeles.
October 2, 1996:	Mark Fuhrman pleaded "no contest" to perjury for lying under oath at the O. J. Simpson trial. He received three years' probation and a $200 fine.
November 3, 2003:	Ella Bully-Cummings was appointed by Mayor Kwaime Kilpatrick as Detroit's first female chief of police. She succeeded Jerry Oliver, who had resigned on October 31, 2003, after having violated the law by having an unregistered handgun in his checked luggage on an air flight.

Important Court Cases

- ***Chambers v. Florida*, 309 U.S. 227 (1940):** The U.S. Supreme Court ruled in *Chambers v. Florida* that, based on facts in a murder case that were admitted by the police and sheriff's officers in Florida, the confessions of four men had clearly been compelled and were therefore inadmissible. It marked one of the first times that the Supreme Court had accepted the contention that treatment short of physical violence should result in the suppression of evidence. Several of the features of this case, such as not allowing the defendants to contact anyone, holding them without formal charges or arraignment, and denying them counsel during questioning were common tactics in law enforcement at the time and were eventually rejected by the court in *Miranda v. Arizona* (1966).
- ***Tennessee v. Garner*, 471 U.S. 1 (1985):** A Tennessee statute provides that, if, after a police officer has given notice of an intent to arrest a criminal suspect, the suspect flees or forcibly resists, "the officer may use all the necessary means to effect the arrest." Acting under the authority of this statute, a Memphis police officer shot and killed 15-year-old Edward Garner, after he was told to halt. The boy fled over a fence at night in the backyard of a house he was suspected of burglarizing. The officer used deadly force despite being "reasonably sure" the suspect was unarmed, and thinking that he was older than he was. Edward's father subsequently brought an action in Federal District Court, seeking damages for violations of his son's constitutional rights. The U.S. Supreme Court held that the Tennessee statute was unconstitutional, insofar as it authorizes the use of deadly force against, as in this case, an apparently unarmed and not dangerous fleeing suspect. Such force, the Court said, may not be used unless necessary to prevent the escape, and unless the officer has probable cause to believe that the suspect poses a significant threat of death or serious physical injury to the officer or others.

Websites to Check Out

- *Department of Justice: Community Oriented Policing Services.* Available at: *http://www.usdoj.gov/cops/.* This website is the official website for COPS and features general information about community-oriented policing within the U.S. Department of Justice.
- *Policing.org: A community policing website: Community Policing Consortium.* Available at: *http://www.policing.com/about.html.* Created by Bonnie Bucqueroux, former associate director of the National Center for Community Policing at Michigan State University's School of Criminal Justice, this website is the self-proclaimed "headquarters" for community policing.
- *The Philosophy and Role of Community Policing. Michigan State University School of Criminal Justice.* Available at: *http://www.cj.msu.edu/~people/cp/cpphil.html.*
- *Racial Profiling Data Collection Resource Center. Northeastern University.* Available at: *http://www.racialprofilinganalysis.neu.edu/.* This website is designed to be a central clearinghouse for police agencies, legislators, community leaders, social scientists, legal researchers, and journalists to access information about current data collection efforts, legislation and model policies, police-community initiatives, and methodological tools that can be used to collect and analyze data regarding racial profiling.

Books

- Kennedy, R. (1997). *Race, Crime, and the Law.* New York: Pantheon Books.
- Langworthy, R. H., and Travis, L. F. (1999). *Policing in America: A Balance of Forces.* 2nd ed. Upper Saddle River, NJ: Prentice Hall.
- Meeks, K. (2000). *Driving While Black.* New York: Broadway Books.
- Skolnick, J. H., and Fyfe, J. J. (1993). *Above the Law: Police and the Excessive Use of Force.* New York: Free Press.
- Walker, S., Spohn, C., and DeLone, M. (1996). *The Color of Justice: Race, Ethnicity, and Crime in America.* Belmont, CA: Wadsworth Publishing Co.
- White, W. S., and Tomkovicz, J. J. (2004). *Criminal Procedure: Constitutional Constraints upon Investigation and Proof.* 5th ed. Newark, NJ: Matthew Bender & Co.
- Wilson, J. Q. (1970). *Varieties of Police Behavior: The Management of Law and Order in Eight Communities.* New York: Atheneum.

Movie

- *Fort Apache, the Bronx:* This 1981 crime drama portrays the many challenges police officers face in the out-of-date South Bronx region of New York City. The police station in the 41st precinct is nicknamed "Fort Apache" because to those who work there it feels like an army outpost in foreign territory. The precinct itself is one of the worst and most dilapidated in the entire department, approaching demolition and staffed mostly by officers who are unwanted and have been transferred out of other precincts. Additionally, the precinct is of little use to the large Puerto Rican community, as only a small percentage of the police officers are Hispanic in the largest non-English-speaking section of the Bronx. Some officers in the precinct attempt to maintain law and order but have conflicts with corrupt fellow officers, as well as with rioting due to police brutality and a hunt for the killer of two rookie cops at the film's beginning.

TV Series

- *Homicide: Life on the Streets:* This realistic cop drama debuted on NBC in 1993 and it ran until May 21, 1999. Based on David Simon's book, *Homicide: A Year on the Killing Streets*, it concerned life in the Baltimore homicide division. Basically a police procedural, the purpose of the show was to provide a no-nonsense glimpse into the lives of a squad of inner-city detectives. As opposed to many television shows and movies involving cops, *Homicide* initially opted for a bleak sort of realism in its depiction of the job of detective, portraying it as repetitive, spiritually draining, free of glamor and glory, but also a social necessity.
- *The Shield:* This Los Angeles cop drama debuted on the FX network in March 2002. *The Shield* is about an experimental division of the Los Angeles police department set in the fictional Farmington district of Los Angeles. The show features a group of detectives called the Strike Team who will stop at nothing to bring their version of justice to the streets. The Strike Team uses a variety of illegal and unethical methods to maintain peace on the streets, while making a profit through illegal drug protection schemes and robbery. The Strike Team is not above planting drugs on and coercing confessions out of gang members or framing them. Common themes in the series include the citizens' distrust of the police, the social impact of drugs and gang warfare, and the conflict between ethics and political expediency.
- *Cagney & Lacey:* This police series debuted on March 25, 1982, and ran for several years on CBS. The show was noteworthy not only for having two female detectives as lead characters, but also because it showed some of the problems faced by police officers, especially female police officers. One of the first episodes deals with a police shooting of a teenager who may have been unarmed. A detective who witnessed the shooting is pressured to change her account of what she witnessed. Other episodes dealt with such issues of police officers as alcoholism, date rape, the death of a fellow officer, and the harassment of women police officers.

Review for Chapter Seven:

Research Paper or Term Paper Topics:

- Stress and police officers
- Suicide and cops
- Excessive use of force by the police

Important Terms to Know

Community-oriented policing:
An approach to policing that emphasizes a collaborative relationship between the police and the community to reduce crime and enhance police-community relations.

Deadly force:
The intentional use of a firearm or other instrument that could result in a high probability of death.

Excessive use of force:
Police officers using more than the amount of force necessary to get control of suspects and protect themselves and others.

Mandatory arrest policies:
In some jurisdictions, the policy is that police officers arriving at a domestic violence scene must arrest the alleged perpetrator of domestic violence.

Police brutality:
Police officers using brutal and harsh tactics with a suspect or an arrestee.

Racial profiling:
The practices in many police departments to target some ethnic and social groups on the basis that certain characteristics of individuals and groups are indicators of criminal behaviors.

Study Guide Questions

True or False:

1. For the most part, police officers spend a majority of their time in activities unrelated to law enforcement.

2. The average police officer makes one to two arrests per month.

3. Domestic violence calls pose the greatest danger to police officers.

4. Some studies show that African Americans and other minorities are more likely to be pulled over in traffic stops.

Multiple Choice Items:

5. Research shows that this percentage of calls to police departments relates to crime:
    a. 7–10 percent
    b. 15–20 percent
    c. 25–30 percent
    d. 40–50 percent

6. The Rodney King beating in 1991 focused America's attention on this problem:
    a. police reviews
    b. police brutality
    c. police-community relations
    d. police evidence gathering

7. In *Tennessee v. Garner* in 1985, the U.S. Supreme Court ruled that the use of deadly force must be reasonable and that
    a. in order to shoot a fleeing suspect, that suspect must be over 21 years of age
    b. in order to shoot a fleeing suspect, that suspect must be running away from the officer
    c. in order to shoot a fleeing suspect, that suspect must be armed and pose a threat
    d. in order to shoot a fleeing suspect, that suspect must be a minority

8. Community-oriented policing has as one goal
    a. solving crimes
    b. keeping civilians out of policing
    c. maintaining traditional police approaches to fighting crime
    d. community-based crime prevention

References

Barkan, S. E., and Bryjak, G. J. (2004). *Fundamentals of Criminal Justice*. Boston: Pearson.

Bayley, D. H. (1994). *Police for the Future*. New York: Oxford University Press.

Blackstone, E. A., Hakim, S., and Spiegel, U. (2002, Spring). Not calling the police (first). *Regulation*, 16–19.

Bureau of Justice Statistics,(2011),"Intimate Partner Violence,"Available at:http://bjs.ojp.usdoj.gov/index.cfm?ty=tp&tid=971.

"COPS," U.S. Department of Justice [online], http://www.cops.usdoj.gov/Default.asp?Item=44.

Department of Justice, (2003), "Fact Sheet: Racial Profiling," Available at: www.usdoj.gov.

Department of Justice Policy Statement, (1995), "Use of deadly force," Available at: http://www.justice.gov/ag/readingroom/resolution14b.htm.

Dixon, J. (2009). Mandatory domestic violence arrest and prosecution policies: Recidivism and social governance. *Criminology & Public Policy*, 7 (4), 663–670.

FBI, (2010), "Law enforcement officers killed and assaulted," Available at: http://www.fbi.gov/about-us/cjis/ucr/leoka/leoka-2010.

Fleming, L. N., (June 17, 2012), "King case put spotlight on beating death of Detroiter Malice Green," *Detroit News* [online], Available at: http://www.detroitnews.com/article/20120617/METRO/206170337.

Gaines, L., Famega, C., and Bichler, G. (2007). *Police Response to Burglar Alarms Study: San Bernardino County.* San Bernardino, CA: Center for Criminal Justice Research.

Harris, D. A., (1999). "Driving while black: Racial profiling on our nation's highways," ACLU website [online], Available at: http://www.aclu.org/racial-justice/driving-while-black-racial-profiling-our-nations-highways.

Hess, K. M., Orthman, C. H., and Chao, H. L. (2010). *Police Operations: Theory and Practice.* 5th ed. Independence, KY: Cengage–Delmar.

Inciardi, J. A. (2005). *Criminal Justice.* 7th ed. New York: McGraw-Hill.

Kappeler, V. E., Sluder, R. D., and Alpert, G. P. (1998). *Forces of Deviance: Understanding the Dark Side of Policing.* Prospect Heights, IL: Waveland.

Masters, R. E., Way, L. B., Gerstenfeld, P. B., Muscat, B. T., Hooper, M., Dussich, J. P. J., Pincu, L., and Skrapec, C.A. (2013). *CJ: Realities and Challenges.* 2nd ed. New York: McGraw-Hill.

"Mental Illness and Violence," (January 2011), *Harvard Mental Health Letter* [online], Available at: http://www.health.harvard.edu/newsletters/Harvard_Mental_Health_Letter/2011/January/mental-illness-and-violence.

Milton, C. H., Halleck, J. W., Lerner, J., and Abrecht, G. L. (1977). *Police Use of Deadly Force.* Washington, DC: Police Foundation.

Office of Justice Programs, (1999), "Use of force by police: Overview of national and local data" [online], Available at: www.ncjrs.gov/pdffiles1/nij/176330-1.pdf.

"Persistence of racial and ethnic profiling in the U.S.," (2009), ACLU [online], Available at: https://www.aclu.org/pdfs/human-rights/cerd_finalreport.pdf.

"Racial Profiling bill gets heated," (April 17, 2012), The Root [online], Available at: http://www.theroot.com/blogs/end-racial-profiling-act/racial-profiling-hearing-gets-heated.

Reid, S. T. (2009). *Crime and Criminology.* 12th ed. New York: Oxford University Press.

Reiss, A. J. Jr. (1980). "Police Brutality." In R. J. Lundman, ed. *Police Behavior: A Sociological Perspective* (pp. 274–296). New York: Oxford University Press.

Risse, M., and Zeckhauser, R. (2004). Racial profiling. *Philosophy and Public Affairs*, 32, 131–170.

Schmalleger, F. (2012). *Criminal Justice.* 9th ed. Upper Saddle River, NJ: Prentice Hall.

Scott, E. J. (1981). *Calls for Service: Citizen Demand and Initial Police Response.* National Institute of Justice publication. NCJ 078362. Washington, DC: U.S. Government Printing Office.

Siegel, L. J., and Worrall, J. L. (2012). *Introduction to Criminal Justice.* 13th ed. Belmont, CA: Wadsworth.

Walker, S. (1992). *The Police in America.* 2nd ed. New York: McGraw Hill.

Part Three

The Prosecution and the Defense

Chapter Eight

Prosecutors and Charging Decisions

At one time in the history of the world, conflicts were settled by physical fighting and by wars (Dues, 2010). But it was the Greeks, more than two thousand years ago, who began to handle conflicts in different ways.

This new approach to conflict involved having opposing parties engage in debate. Those who could argue most persuasively and who could convince others of the merits of their side were declared the winners (Dues, 2010). This was the beginning of the adversary system.

Other countries adopted the adversary system, and it has come to characterize the American criminal justice system. In our system, the opposing advocates for each side are the attorneys. Arguing for the prosecution in a criminal trial are prosecutors, who are also known in various jurisdictions and states as district attorneys, state attorneys, or assistant attorneys general. On the opposite side are the defense attorneys, who represent the criminal defendant. In this chapter, prosecutors and the role they play will be described. In the next chapter, the focus will be on the defense.

He [the prosecutor] may prosecute with earnestness and vigor—indeed, he should do so. But, while he may strike hard blows, he is not at liberty to strike foul ones. It is as much his duty to refrain from improper methods calculated to produce a wrongful conviction as it is to use every legitimate means to bring about a just one.

—George Sutherland Berger v. United States, *295 U.S. 78, 88 (1935)*

THE PROSECUTOR'S ROLE BEFORE TRIAL

After the police investigate a criminal offense and after they have gathered evidence, the case—in the form of a complaint—is presented to the prosecutor. The complaint is assigned to an assistant prosecuting attorney (at least in most counties, where there is a prosecutor and one or more assistant prosecutors). The assistant prosecutor then decides if formal charges are to be brought against the defendant and what those formal charges will be.

Prosecutors, however, have a great deal of discretion and can decide to drop charges, to delay a charging decision, or to proffer charges against an individual. In addition—and very importantly—it is the prosecutor who will decide exactly what those charges should be.

As an example of this kind of charging decision and the discretion a prosecutor possesses, consider the controversial case related to the shooting death of Trayvon Martin in Florida in February 2012 by George Zimmerman, a designated neighborhood watch coordinator in a Sanford, Florida, condominium complex. Mr. Zimmerman claimed he was assaulted by unarmed teenager Trayvon Martin. Mr. Zimmerman said he shot the adolescent in self-defense.

In cases such as the Martin-Zimmerman case, the prosecutor (in Florida, the prosecutor is called a state attorney) in the county in which the crime takes place must sift through the evidence given him or her by the police to decide whether to bring charges against the defendant. In this specific case, however, Seminole County state attorney Norm Wolfinger was the state attorney initially responsible for the case. Wolfinger is responsible for prosecutions in Brevard and Seminole counties, where the shooting occurred. On March 22, 2012, Wolfinger removed himself from the case and requested that the case be assigned to another state prosecutor.

"This request is being made in light of the public good with the intent of toning down the rhetoric and preserving the integrity of this investigation," Wolfinger is quoted as saying (Lee, 2012, p. 1). On March 22, 2012, Florida governor Rick Scott announced his appointment of Angela Corey as the special prosecutor in the Martin investigation. She is the state attorney for Duval, Clay, and Nassau counties. After several weeks of investigation, on April 11, 2012, Corey charged Zimmerman with second degree murder in Martin's death (Horwitz, 2012).

In these kinds of situations, when charges are handed down, they are contained in an information, which is a charging document (see document examples in For Your Consideration at the end of this chapter).

Myth:	*Grand juries are used in every felony case.*
Reality:	*Only 22 states use grand juries regularly. Most charges against accused felons are not based on grand jury indictments.*

GRAND JURIES

Sometimes prosecutors call for a grand jury, which is composed of citizens drawn at random (just like those drawn to be jury members in a criminal trial), who are presented with the evidence possessed by the prosecution. In a grand jury proceeding, which is secret, only the prosecutor presents evidence, including witnesses, and the defendant and his or her attorney play no role in the hearing.

The grand jury considers the evidence and if they believe the evidence is sufficient they can issue an indictment. An indictment, much like an information, is a document announcing formal charges against the defendant. A grand jury can also decide not to indict—in which case the charges are dropped and the suspect is released.

What Factors Go into Charging Decisions?

Perhaps the most critical factor in a prosecutor's decision to bring formal charges against a defendant may be the amount of evidence given to him or her by the police. If the police have enough solid evidence linking a defendant to a crime and if the evidence appears to be sufficient for the prosecution to be successful if the case goes to trial before a jury, then the prosecutor is likely to file an information.

Other factors that can go into prosecutorial decision making include such things as race, ethnicity, and gender. If this happens, the accused may have legal recourse, although it is usually difficult to prove that bias actually played a part in a prosecutor's decision to charge or not charge (Reid, 2009).

There may be other factors, though, that are very practical. For instance, a lack of resources may lead to a refusal to prosecute. Bringing a case to trial may cost the prosecutor's office or the county hundreds of thousands of dollars. In the Casey Anthony case in Florida, where it was alleged that Casey Anthony had killed her daughter, it cost the county upwards of a million dollars for this trial—and Casey Anthony was acquitted by the jury (Liston, 2011). These kinds of cases may make prosecutors very wary of bringing charges against an individual if the trial is likely to be lengthy and expensive.

A tactical reason to drop charges may be related to gathering information. For example, a prosecutor may decide not to bring charges against an individual if that person can provide valuable information about more serious crimes. Similarly, bringing charges against a petty offender or a first-time offender may bring about more harm than good. For instance, attaching a criminal label to a one-time petty offender could possibly set that person on a course of a criminal career (Inciardi, 2005).

Sometimes the time and resources of the justice system must be considered when the prosecutor is deciding whether to bring charges. Cases involving drunkenness, vagrancy, or disorderly conduct, although annoying, are not dangerous crimes. If the prosecutor brought charges and elected to prosecute these minor kinds of offenses it could cause undue hardship not only for the defendant, but also for the criminal justice system. The courts could not handle in any efficient way all the cases for which charges could be filed.

A final factor for prosecutors to consider is the attitude of the victim and the willingness of the victim to testify. Some victims do not want the accused to be prosecuted. For instance, if a husband is accused of assault against a child, that child may not want to see his or her parent prosecuted. Furthermore, family members—even though they are victims—may be reluctant to testify or may refuse to testify altogether. This can also happen in other kinds of cases, in which witnesses—whether the victim or not—fear retaliation by the accused or his or her friends or family. If a prosecutor does not have solid evidence, including cooperative witnesses, there may be little or no chance of winning a case if it proceeds to trial.

Nolle Prosequi

Once the prosecutor has brought formal charges and the case is a matter of court record, the prosecutor can still terminate any further processing through a *nolle prosequi*. The *nolle prosequi* is a formal entry in the record, by which the prosecutor declares that he or she will not further prosecute the case. This can be related to some or all of the charges or to some or all of the defendants (Inciardi, 2005).

As was seen in the above discussion about charging decisions, prosecutors have a great deal of discretion. The *nolle prosequi*, however, is one of the most powerful examples of discretionary authority, literally in the entire criminal justice system.

There are several reasons why a prosecutor may decide on a *nolle prosequi*. One reason is that once the charges have been brought, the prosecutor decides that the evidence after all is just not sufficient for conviction. Or, the prosecutor may discover or decide that one or more key pieces of evidence are inadmissible in court. Finally, the *nolle prosequi* may rest on a plea bargain or the plea negotiation process.

Myth: *A plea bargain with a prosecutor is a simple act on the part of the accused of accepting or rejecting a plea deal.*

Reality: *It is not quite that simple. Prosecutors have many ways of forcing a defendant into accepting a plea bargain. For instance, they can threaten to add more charges or threaten to ask for a harsher sentence.*

Although this aspect of a prosecutor's authority has been criticized, it has repeatedly been upheld in appellate court decisions (Inciardi, 2005). In *United States v. Cowan* (1975), a United States attorney negotiated a plea agreement in which the defendant would plead guilty to one count of bribery and would cooperate with the Watergate investigation. In exchange, another indictment pending against the defendant in Texas would be dismissed through a *nolle prosequi*. In this case, the Fifth Circuit Court of the U.S. Court of Appeals upheld the prosecutor's "absolute power" to dismiss proceedings (Inciardi, 2005).

The major criticism, in addition to the absolute discretionary power the *nolle prosequi* affords prosecutors, is that its use can lead to corruption, favoritism, nepotism, and discrimination. Advocates of its use, however, point out that it is necessary to screen out trivial cases, eliminate false accusations, and get rid of cases in which the prosecution is almost certain to lose (Inciardi, 2005).

Plea Bargaining

Watching legal shows on television, you might get the idea that all criminal cases go to trial. Even shows like *Law & Order*, in which plea bargaining does take place, almost always end with a trial in which the prosecutors are pitted against the defense. Real life is different, though. Ninety-five percent—or sometimes even more—of all criminal cases end with a plea bargain (Covey, 2008). In other words, plea bargaining dominates the American criminal justice process.

Plea bargaining is the process by which a defendant agrees to plead guilty in exchange for some consideration from the prosecutor or the government. There are three types of plea bargains, and each could play a part in the process of a guilty plea.

The first type of plea bargain is the *charge bargain*. In this type of plea, the defendant pleads guilty to a less serious charge than the one listed in the information or indictment. For example, instead of a murder charge, the accused might accept a charge of manslaughter. The second type is *count bargaining*. In this plea negotiation, the person charged with multiple offenses will plead guilty to some of the charges, with the others being dropped. And the last type of plea is *sentence bargaining*. This occurs when a defendant pleads guilty to the crime but does so in exchange for a lesser sentence than would likely have been imposed if he or she were convicted in a trial (Owen et al., 2012).

As indicated previously, it would be impossible for our court system to handle the work volume if every criminal case went to trial. Therefore, the use of plea bargains helps to determine the outcomes of cases quickly and efficiently. This quick resolution of cases through negotiated guilty pleas was first used in the 19th century in America, but became commonplace starting in the 1960s and 1970s. While the practice of negotiated guilty pleas has experienced heavy criticism, plea bargains were upheld by the U.S. Supreme Court in the 1971 case of *Santobello v. New York* (Cole & Smith, 2008).

In the *Santobello v. New York* decision, written by Chief Justice Warren Burger, the majority opinion described plea bargaining in favorable terms. Furthermore, in this opinion, Burger wrote that prosecutors were obliged to fulfill promises made during plea negotiations. Burger went on to write that plea bargaining is an essential component of the administration of justice. He noted that properly administered, plea bargains save time and criminal justice resources while also protecting the community (Cole & Smith, 2008).

Critics have charged that prosecutors who engage in plea negotiations are soft on crime. However, given the high rate of plea bargaining, it seems reasonable to conclude that the prosecutor, the defense, and the defendant all have strong motivations to engage in the practice. In most instances, a prosecutor has a single goal after charging a defendant—to obtain a conviction. If a case goes to trial, no matter how certain the prosecutor might be that they have a rock-solid case that will end with the defendant being convicted, there is always the chance that a jury might see things a different way. Plea bargaining removes this risk. The prosecutor can secure a conviction without risking an acquittal.

Prosecutorial Misconduct

The job of the prosecutor is broader than simply representing the government in criminal cases. As a public servant and chief law enforcement officer for the state, the prosecutor is also charged with the responsibility of upholding the interests of justice in the name of the whole community—which is usually the county in which he or she is elected. As an elected official, state prosecutors or chief prosecutors are ethically sworn to administer justice for all. When they take office after election, prosecutors take an oath that requires them to seek justice (Boyes-Watson, 2003).

The American Bar Association's Standards Relating to the Administration of Criminal Justice states that the duty of the prosecutor is to seek justice, "not merely to convict" (Dzienkowski, 2005, p. 914). Furthermore, these same standards indicate that a prosecutor should not "[k]nowingly use illegal means to obtain evidence or to employ or instruct or encourage others to use such means" (Dzienkowski, 2005, p. 918). Also, the American Bar Association points out that a prosecutor should not intentionally avoid pursuit of evidence because he or she believes it will damage the prosecution's case or aid the accused (Dzienkowski, 2005).

> **Myth:** *Prosecutors are more interested in justice than in winning cases.*
>
> **Reality:** *There are many pressures on prosecutors to do everything possible to win cases: the pressure to secure a conviction for the victim; the pressure to earn the praise of fellow prosecutors; the pressure to convict someone for a crime.*

As the above standards note, prosecutors are not free to use any means possible to convict a defendant. Serious problems are caused by overzealous or unscrupulous prosecutors (Reid, 2009). This was evident in the case of three white Duke University lacrosse players in the spring of 2006. Despite weak evidence against the players, Michael Nifong, the prosecutor in Durham County, North Carolina, persisted in his efforts to prosecute the players for raping a black woman at a party. In bringing charges against the three, Mr. Nifong discounted their alibis, the lack of forensic evidence, and the flawed lineup (in which the woman was unable to identify any of the accused young men) (Dewan, 2007).

After the accuser changed her story in December, Mr. Nifong dropped the rape charges but said he would pursue charges of kidnapping and sexual offense. In light of evidence that continued to emerge that questioned the charges, Nifong pressed on with the case. He did this despite the absence of physical evidence implicating the young men. In 2007, the North Carolina attorney general investigated the case, after which all charges were dismissed when it was found that the players were innocent. However, the three students had been dropped from the lacrosse team, suspended from Duke University, and had spent a year defending themselves against the spurious charges. Nifong was disbarred and was forced to resign his elected position as prosecutor (Dewan, 2007).

Of course, Nifong is not the first—nor will he be the last—prosecutor who has engaged in prosecutorial misconduct. In fact, the courts have decided some cases alleging prosecutorial misconduct. For example, in 2004, in the case of *Banks v. Dretke*, the U.S. Supreme Court overturned the death sentence of a Texas inmate because of misconduct by a prosecutor. In the case, prosecution witnesses lied and prosecutors failed to alert the court when they were aware witnesses were giving false testimony (*Banks v. Dretke*, 540 U.S. 668 [2004]).

In other cases, prosecutors have failed to share evidence with the defense or withheld exculpatory material or evidence from the defense or the court. Such tactics are in direct violation of the American Bar Association standards, which state that a prosecutor should not intentionally fail to make timely disclosure to the defense "... of the existence or information which tends to negate the guilt of the accused." It is a violation of the section of the standards which states that "A prosecutor should not knowingly offer false evidence, whether by documents, tangible evidence, or the testimony of witnesses, or fail to seek withdrawal thereof upon discovery of its falsity" (Dzienkowski, 2005, pp. 921 and 923).

There are no studies that give statistics about the extent of prosecutorial misconduct. However, a study published in the journal *Crime and Delinquency* in 1986 indicated that it is estimated by experts in the criminal justice field that about .05 percent of convictions are of innocent people (Huff, Rattner, & Sagarin, 1986). While this seems like a small percentage, it could translate into about 36,000 people wrongfully convicted each year (Bohm & Haley, 2002). And while the blame cannot solely be placed on prosecutors, they do share some of the responsibility.

FOR FURTHER CONSIDERATION

Historical Events Relevant to Chapter Eight

February 6, 1881: Plea bargaining gains favor in American courts as Albert McKenzie receives the first plea bargain.

April 28, 1965: The U.S. Supreme Court issues its opinion in *Griffin v. California*. The issue in this case was whether the guarantee of the Fifth Amendment privilege against self-incrimination is violated when prosecutors and judges comment adversely on a defendant's failure to testify in a criminal proceeding. In holding that it does violate the Fifth Amendment, the Court said that such a practice makes the defendant pay a price for refusing to speak. Even an innocent person, the Court said, may have many reasons for not taking the witness stand in his own defense.

December 12, 1984: Nineteen-year-old Jay Wesley Neill and 21-year-old Robert Johnson rob a bank in Geronimo, Oklahoma, of $17,000. During the robbery, three bank employees are stabbed to death and four customers are shot, one fatally. Three days later, Neill and Johnson are arrested in San Francisco with the money. They were tried together in 1985 and both were sentenced to death. In 1992, the Oklahoma Court of Criminal Appeals reversed their convictions finding that they should have been tried separately. On retrial, Johnson received life in prison, Neill got a death sentence. In closing arguments, the prosecutor told the jury: "I want you to think about the man you're sitting in judgment on and determining what the appropriate punishment should be ... [think] of what kind of person he is ... He's a homosexual ..." He went on to emphasize this several more times.

The 10th Circuit Court of Appeals considered the inappropriateness of the prosecutor's remarks on two separate occasions and both times narrowly (2–1) voted to uphold the death penalty. The dissenting judge (Judge Carlos Lucero) said, "The prosecutor's blatant homophobic hatemongering at sentencing has no place in the courtrooms of a civilized society."

Neill was executed by lethal injection on December 12, 2002.

Important Court Cases

- **United States v. Cowan, 524 F. 2d 504 (1975):** The U.S. Appeals Court for the Second District ruled that it must be conceded that the attorney general and his subordinates have the absolute power and discretion to institute prosecutions. Likewise, the Court said, the prosecuting attorney has a similar power to terminate prosecutions.
- **Santobello v. New York, 404 U.S. 257 (1971):** After negotiations with the prosecutor, a defendant withdrew his previous not-guilty plea to two felony counts and pleaded guilty to a lesser offense, with the prosecutor agreeing not to make a recommendation on the sentence. When the defendant returned for sentencing several months later, a new prosecutor recommended the maximum sentence, which the judge imposed. The defendant then wanted to withdraw his guilty plea but his conviction was affirmed on appeal. The case was appealed to the U.S. Supreme Court, and the High Court held that the promises made by the prosecution in plea bargaining must be kept. In this case, the Court required that the sentence be vacated or that the defendant be allowed to withdraw his plea under the original agreement.
- **Banks v. Dretke, 540 U.S. 668 (2004):** Delma Banks Jr., a Texas man, was convicted of capital murder and sentenced to death. Prior to trial, the prosecution advised Banks's attorney there would be no need to litigate discovery issues, as the prosecution would provide all discovery (evidence) to which they were entitled. Despite that assurance, prosecution withheld evidence that would have allowed Banks to discredit two essential prosecution witnesses. The state did not disclose that one of those witnesses was a paid police informant, nor did it disclose a pre-trial transcript revealing that the other witness's trial testimony had been intensively coached by prosecutors and law enforcement officers. And despite the prosecutor being aware that one of the state's witnesses was lying on the witness stand, the prosecutor told the jury that that witness had been truthful and honest in his testimony. The Court overturned the death sentence.

Websites to Check Out

- *What is a criminal prosecutor? Yale Law School.* Available at: *www.law.yale.edu/documents/pdf/.../PUB_Version-Crim_Pro2010.p...* This website, provided by Yale Law School, describes what a prosecutor is and the training needed to become a prosecutor.
- *The Federal Prosecutor. Speech given by Robert H. Jackson in 1940.* Available at: *http://www.roberthjackson.org/the-man/speeches-articles/speeches/speeches-by-robert-h-jackson/the-federal-prosecutor/.* A website that is centered around the remarkable legal career of Jackson, who became a Supreme Court justice, but in 1940 was the attorney general of the United States when he gave this speech on what a federal prosecutor is.
- *Plea Bargaining Pros and Cons. LawInfo.* Available at: *http://resources.lawinfo.com/en/articles/plea-negotiations-criminal-lawyer/federal/the-pros-and-cons-of-plea-bargaining.html.* This site features a discussion of the pros and cons of plea bargaining, plus links to other legal information.

Books

- Delsohn, G. (2003). *The Prosecutors*. New York: Dutton.
- Flynn, S. (2000). *Boston D.A.* New York: T.V. Books.
- Merola, M. (1988). *Big City D.A.* New York: Random House.
- Stewart, J. B. (1987). *The Prosecutors*. New York: Simon & Schuster.

Movies

- *Presumed Innocent* (1990): Taken from lawyer and novelist Scott Turow's best-selling book features Harrison Ford as a prosecutor who finds himself accused of murdering a colleague with whom he's had an affair. Through his lawyer, this prosecutor discovers a great deal about himself and the seamy side of criminal law.
- *Beyond a Reasonable Doubt* (2009): An ambitious reporter takes an extraordinary risk to bring down a corrupt district attorney. He plans to frame himself for an unsolved murder in order to expose a district attorney as a fraud.
- *Mr. District Attorney* (1947): The Hollywood version of a story about an incorruptible district attorney.

TV Movies and Series

- *New York Justice: The Prosecutors:* This A&E TV video follows prosecutors as they investigate and prosecute cases in Brooklyn, New York.
- *Conviction:* Created by Dick Wolf, who also created *Law & Order,* this series was on for one season (2006). However, it was a well-done series that followed prosecutors in New York City as they pursued convictions in various kinds of cases, including murder and drug cases.
- *Law & Order:* This Dick Wolf police procedural and legal drama was on for 20 years before it went off the air. The show was noteworthy because it devoted the first half of the show to catching the criminal and the second half to the prosecution of the accused. The prosecutors discuss deals, prepare the witnesses and evidence, and conduct the people's case in the trial. The prosecutors work together and with the medical examiner's office, the crime laboratory, and other expert witnesses—all of whom testify in court. Unlike many legal dramas, the court proceedings are shown from the prosecution's point of view, with the regular characters trying to prove the defendant's guilt, not innocence.

Review for Chapter Eight:

Research Paper or Term Paper Topics:

- The role of the prosecutor in the criminal justice system
- Plea bargaining

Important Terms to Know

Information: A charging document which contains the criminal charges brought against a suspect.

Nolle prosequi: This is a process used by the prosecution to terminate a case without pursuing charges.

Plea bargaining: This is the process by which a prosecutor negotiates a guilty plea from a defendant in exchange for certain considerations.

Prosecutor: The prosecutor, referred to as the district attorney or the state attorney in some jurisdictions, decides on criminal charges against defendants and is responsible for prosecuting criminal cases.

Prosecutorial misconduct:

A prosecutor's use of unethical methods to prosecute a case. Misconduct by a prosecutor may include failing to disclose evidence to the defense, allowing witnesses to perjure themselves, and hiding exculpatory evidence.

Study Guide Questions

True or False:

1. It is the prosecutor who decides what formal charges will be brought against a defendant.

2. It is the judge who requests a grand jury.

3. A *nolle prosequi* refers to a prosecutor dropping charges.

4.   Ninety-five percent of all criminal cases end in a plea bargain.

Multiple Choice Items:

5.   The most critical factor in determining the prosecutor's decision to bring charges against a defendant may be
     a. the race of the defendant
     b. the cost of the prosecution
     c. the cooperation of the victim
     d. the amount of evidence provided by the police

6.   This is **not** one type of plea bargain:
     a. a charge bargain
     b. a reasonable bargain
     c. a sentence bargain
     d. a count bargain

7.   In the Supreme Court case of *Santobello v. New York*, the Court ruled that
     a. prosecutors may lie to defendants
     b. prosecutors may fail to keep their promises
     c. prosecutors may not lie to defendants
     d. prosecutors may withdraw a plea bargain whenever they choose

8.   The American Bar Association's Standards Relating to the Administration of Criminal Justice states that the duty of the prosecutor is to
     a. win at any cost
     b. convict by any means possible
     c. hide evidence from the defense
     d. seek justice, not merely to convict

References

Bohm, R. M., and Haley, K. N. (2002). *Introduction to Criminal Justice.* 3rd ed. New York: Glencoe-McGraw Hill.

Boyes-Watson, C. (2003). *Crime and Justice: A Casebook Approach.* Boston: Pearson Education, Inc.

Cole, G. F., and Smith, C. E. (2008). *Criminal Justice in America.* 5th ed. Belmont, CA: Thomson/Wadsworth.

Covey, R. D. (2008). Fixed justice: Reforming plea bargaining with plea-based ceilings. *Tulane Law Review* 82, 1237–1290.

Dewan, S., (September 8, 2007), "Duke Prosecutor Jailed; Students Seek Settlement," *New York Times* [online], Available at: http://travel.nytimes.com/2007/09/08/us/08duke.html?ref=dukelacrossesexualassaultcase.

Dues, M. (2010). *The Art of Conflict Management: Achieving Solutions for Life, Work, and Beyond.* Chantilly, VA: The Great Courses.

Dzienkowski, J. S., ed. (2005). *Professional Responsibility Standards & Statutes.* 2005–2006 ed. Belmont, CA: Thomson/West.

Horwitz, S., (April 11, 2012), "George Zimmerman is charged with 2nd degree murder in Trayvon Martin shooting," *Washington Post,* Available at: http://www.washingtonpost.com/politics/george-zimmerman-to-be-charged-in-trayvon-martin-shooting-law-enforcement-official-says/2012/04/11/gIQAHJ5oAT_story.html.

Huff, C. R., Rattner, A., and Sagarin, E. (1986). Guilty until proven innocent: Wrongful conviction and public policy. *Crime & Delinquency* 32: 518–544.

Inciardi, J. A. (2005). *Criminal Justice.* 7th ed. New York: McGraw Hill.

Lee, T., (March 22, 2012), "Trayvon Martin Case: State Attorney Quits Investigation as State Studies 'Stand Your Ground' Law," *Huffington Post* [online], Available at: http://www.huffingtonpost.com/2012/03/22/trayvon-martin-state-attorney_n_1374206.html.

Liston, B., (July 29, 2011), "Price tag for Casey Anthony case near $700,000," *Reuters* [online], Available at: http://www.reuters.com/article/2011/07/29/us-crime-anthony-idUSTRE76S72320110729.

Owen, S. S., Fradella, H. F., Burke, T. W., and Joplin, J. W. (2012). *Foundations of Criminal Justice.* New York: Oxford Press.

Reid, S. T. (2008). *Crime and Criminology.* New York: Oxford University Press.

Reid, S. T. (2009). *Criminal Law.* New York: Oxford University Press.

Documents

Available online at: *http://www.nytimes.com/interactive/2012/04/12/us/13shooter-document.html*

OFFICE OF THE STATE ATTORNEY
JRTH JUDICIAL CIRCUIT OF FLORIDA
WWW.SAO4TH.COM

ANGELA B. COREY
STATE ATTORNEY

220 EAST BAY STREET
JACKSONVILLE, FLORIDA 32202-3429
TEL: (904) 630-4767
FAX: (904) 630-2938

STATE OF FLORIDA VS. GEORGE ZIMMERMAN

EIGHTEENTH JUDICIAL CIRCUIT, SEMINOLE COUNTY FLORIDA

AFFIDAVIT OF PROBABLE CAUSE – SECOND DEGREE MURDER

Before me, personally appeared T.C. O'Steen and K.D. Gilbreath, who after being duly sworn; deposes and says:

Your affiants, Investigators T.C. O'Steen, and Dale Gilbreath are members of the State Attorney Office – Fourth Judicial Circuit, appointed in this case by State Attorney Angela B. Corey, who was assigned this case under Executive Order of the Governor 12-72.

Investigator O'Steen was previously employed by the Jacksonville Sheriff's Office, and has 35 years of law enforcement experience, including 20 years handling homicide investigations. Investigator Gilbreath was previously employed by the Jacksonville Sheriff's Office, and has 36 years of law enforcement experience, including 24 years handling homicide investigations.

Your Affiants, along with other law enforcement officials have taken sworn statements from witnesses, spoken with law enforcement officers who have provided sworn testimony in reports, reviewed other reports, recorded statements, phone records, recorded calls to police, photographs, videos, and other documents in detailing the following:

On Sunday 2/26/12, Trayvon Martin was temporarily living at the Retreat at Twin Lakes, a gated community in Sanford, Seminole County, Florida. That evening Martin walked to a nearby 7-11 store where he purchased a can of iced tea and a bag of skittles. Martin then walked back to and entered the gated community and was on his way back to the townhouse where he was living when he was profiled by George Zimmerman. Martin was unarmed and was not committing a crime.

Zimmerman who also lived in the gated community, and was driving his vehicle observed Martin and assumed Martin was a criminal. Zimmerman felt Martin did not belong in the gated community and called the police. Zimmerman spoke to the dispatcher and asked for an officer to respond because Zimmerman perceived that Martin was acting suspicious. The police dispatcher informed Zimmerman that an officer was on the way and to wait for the officer.

During the recorded call Zimmerman made reference to people he felt had committed and gotten away with break-ins in his neighborhood. Later while talking about Martin, Zimmerman stated "these assholes, they always get away" and also said "these fucking punks".

During this time, Martin was on the phone with a friend and described to her what was happening. The witness advised that Martin was scared because he was being followed through the complex by an unknown male and didn't know why. Martin attempted to run home but was followed by Zimmerman who didn't want the person he falsely assumed was going to commit a crime to get away before the police arrived. Zimmerman got out of his vehicle and followed Martin. When the police dispatcher realized Zimmerman was pursuing Martin, he instructed Zimmerman not to do that and that the responding officer would meet him. Zimmerman disregarded the police dispatcher and continued to follow Martin who was trying to return to his home.

Zimmerman confronted Martin and a struggle ensued. Witnesses heard people arguing and what sounded like a struggle. During this time period witnesses heard numerous calls for help and some of these were recorded in 911 calls to police. Trayvon Martin's mother has reviewed the 911 calls and identified the voice crying for help as Trayvon Martin's voice.

████████████ Officers recovered a gun from a holster inside Zimmerman's waistband. A fired casing that was recovered at the scene was determined to have been fired from the firearm.

Assistant Medical Examiner Dr. Bao performed an autopsy and determined that Martin died from the gunshot wound.

The facts mentioned in this Affidavit are not a complete recitation of all the pertinent facts and evidence in this case but only are presented for a determination of Probable Cause for Second Degree Murder.

By: _____

Investigator T.C. O'Steen, Affiant

By: _____

Investigator Dale Gilbreath, Affiant

Chapter Nine

The Defense

Most of us take the Sixth Amendment literally when it declares that, "In all criminal prosecutions, the accused shall enjoy the right ... to have the Assistance of Counsel for his defense" (Gaines & Miller, 2007, p. A7). Furthermore, some scholars consider the right to counsel the most important of all the defendant's constitutional rights (Reid, 1999).

However, the right to appointed counsel, which means a lawyer is provided at government expense, has not always been recognized in the United States—despite the words in the Sixth Amendment.

In 1932 in *Powell v. Alabama*, the Supreme Court gave only limited recognition of this right. That is, in *Powell v. Alabama*—a state case rather than a federal case—nine African American young men were charged with the rape of two white women in the town of Scottsboro, Alabama (Reid, 1999). Eight of the defendants were convicted and sentenced to death. Several issues were raised on appeal, but two of those issues pertained to lack of counsel (Reid, 1999).

When the case—usually referred to as the Scottsboro Boys case—was heard by the Supreme Court, the Court focused on the issue of whether appointed counsel should have been provided for the defendants because they could not have afforded attorneys, even if they had been given the opportunity to do so. In the majority opinion handed down by the Court, the Court said that the right to be heard had little meaning unless accompanied by a right to counsel (Reid, 1999). The Court held that there was a right to appointed counsel, but that right was limited to capital cases—that is, cases that carried the potential for the death penalty.

Defense counsel need present nothing, even if he knows what the truth is.

—*Justice Byron R. White, United States v. Wade, 388 U.S. 218, 256 (1967) (Dissenting opinion)*

113

Later, in *Betts v. Brady*, the Supreme Court refused to apply the right to appointed counsel to state cases. Furthermore, in this 1942 case, the Court established a fundamental fairness test, holding that an indigent defendant in a state trial would be appointed counsel in a non-capital case only where it could be shown that circumstances necessitated appointed counsel to receive a fair trial. The *Betts v. Brady* rule remained the law until it was overruled in a new Supreme Court decision in 1963.

GIDEON V. WAINWRIGHT

In the 1963 *Gideon v. Wainwright* decision, the Supreme Court reversed its previous ruling in *Betts v. Brady*. The facts of this case were fairly simple.

Clarence Earl Gideon, a Florida resident, was charged with breaking and entering with intent to commit petit larceny. When his case came to trial, Gideon asked for legal representation. The judge refused to appoint counsel for him, stating that in Florida the right to counsel only applied to defendants charged with a capital crime.

Gideon, a poor, uneducated drifter, defended himself the best he could, but he was convicted and sentenced to prison. In prison, he began studying law books in the prison library and wrote his own appeal, which he sent to the U.S. Supreme Court. In his appeal, he argued that he should have been entitled to appointed counsel. The Supreme Court chose to hear the case and decided in Gideon's favor, in the process establishing a new rule: Indigent clients should be provided with an attorney if they face a serious charge in a state court. According to the Court, a serious charge meant one in which the accused faced possible jail or prison time (Siegel & Worrall, 2012). In addition, the Court defined an indigent defendant as one who was too poor to afford his or her own attorney. Since the Gideon decision, it can more accurately be said—as the Supreme Court articulated in the *Miranda v. Arizona* decision in 1966—that prior to interrogation, the person in custody "... has the right to remain silent, that anything he says can be used against him in a court of law, that he has the right to the presence of an attorney, and that, if he cannot afford an attorney one will be appointed for him prior to any questioning if he so desires. Opportunity to exercise these rights must be afforded to him throughout the interrogation. After such warnings have been given, and such opportunity afforded him, the individual may knowingly and intelligently waive these rights and agree to answer questions or make a statement. But unless and until such warnings and waiver are demonstrated by the prosecution at trial, no evidence obtained as a result of interrogation can be used against him" (*Miranda v. Arizona* (1966), p. 23).

THE DEFENSE ATTORNEY

In an adversarial system, the defense attorney is the lawyer who represents the accused in the criminal justice process. According to the Supreme Court, every suspect and every accused person is entitled to legal representation at every stage of the process, starting with interrogation (Bohm & Haley, 2002).

In our criminal justice system, the defense attorney performs the key function of making sure that the prosecution proves its case in court or has substantial evidence of guilt before a guilty plea deal is worked out (Cole & Smith, 2008).

Myth: *In our justice system everyone receives an outstanding defense.*

Reality: *The real situation is that most defendants use court-appointed attorneys and these attorneys are often overworked and have few resources available to them.*

The defense attorney has the primary responsibility of representing the defendant by preparing the case and selecting the defense strategy. In addition to preparing a defense and presenting a case in trial, a defense attorney also has the following duties:

- Represent the client throughout the criminal procedure.
- Represent the accused from the time of arrest to ensure constitutional safeguards, from interrogation through the pre-trial stages.
- Review police reports and conduct further investigation to understand the details of the offense.
- Interview the police, the accused, and the witnesses in seeking out additional evidence on behalf of the accused.
- Discuss the offense with the prosecutor to gain initial insight into the strength of the state's case.
- Represent the accused at bail hearings and during plea negotiations.
- Prepare various pre-trial motions, filing and arguing those motions.
- Prepare the case for trial.
- Participate in jury selection.
- Represent the accused at trial.
- Provide advice and assistance at sentencing.
- Determine if there is an appropriate basis for an appeal and pursuing an appeal.
- Present written or oral arguments for an appeal.

Although the primary goal of a defense attorney is to get the best possible result for a client, it is not possible for all defense attorneys (or all prosecutors, for that matter) to take every criminal case to trial. Consequently, there is pressure on the defense—as well as on the prosecution—to plea bargain many cases. It is also part of the defense attorney's duties to represent his or her client in a plea negotiation, attempting to obtain the best possible outcome for the defendant.

PREPARING THE DEFENSE

As indicated, the defense has a duty to investigate the case and prepare a defense in case the defendant must be represented in a trial. If the case is not terminated with a plea deal, then the case goes to trial, and the defense attorney must decide on a criminal defense which will present a justification or an excuse for the criminal behavior charged against the defendant. Essentially, there are six possible defenses that a defense attorney can use in a trial:

1. The defendant didn't do it. The defense can attempt to show that the accused was not responsible for the alleged offense because she had an alibi.

2. The defendant was not responsible at the time of the offense. A defendant might try to show that he or she was not mentally competent at the time of the offense because of mental, emotional, or psychological reasons. This generally means that the defense will use the insanity defense, which will be discussed in more detail later on in this chapter.

3. The defendant had a good excuse for his criminal behavior. The accused might, the defense could argue, have a very good excuse for having committed the offense. For example, he might be a child and the infancy defense might be used. Common law has long established that children under the age of seven are presumed incapable of having the necessary criminal intent for any unlawful acts to be considered crimes (Fuller, 2010).

    Or another excuse could be duress. That is, the defendant claims that he committed an offense out of fear for his life or fear of bodily harm. An individual might contend that he participated in a robbery because he was afraid he would be killed if he didn't participate. Other excuses could include the assertion that the offense was a mistake. For instance, if an individual bought a television set through a Craig's List ad and the TV turned out to be stolen property, that person could claim it was an honest mistake because he believed the seller owned the TV he was selling.

    Finally, the defendant could say she was impaired due to intoxication or drug use. Although, most states do not allow an intoxication defense, it is possible to use this excuse if the drug use or drunkenness was involuntary. The defendant might assert that she was given drugs at a party, causing an impairment that led to an offense.

4. The defendant had a good reason to commit the offense. A good reason might be self-defense. For example, if her home was invaded by an armed gunman, whom she shot, she could claim that she had to defend herself against harm or death. Another good reason could be consent. If a man hit his pregnant girlfriend in the stomach with a baseball bat causing the death of a fetus, his defense might be that she wanted to abort the fetus and asked him to hit her with a baseball bat. Or in the case of a rape charge, a man may state that the victim actually had consensual sex with him.

    Finally, another plausible reason might be necessity. Hikers on a mountain get trapped by an avalanche and are lost for several days. In order to save their lives, they break into a cabin to get warm and obtain food and water. They might claim that it was necessary to break in, and they will willingly pay for any damage or anything taken or used.

5. The defendant did the offense but still should be acquitted. The defendant might argue that the statute of limitations has expired. For instance, if a man is charged with a robbery that happened 25 years before, his defense might be that the statute of limitations has expired and he can no longer be held responsible for the crime.

   Also, the defendant might contend that under the Fifth Amendment, he could not be tried for a particular crime because he was already convicted of that crime and already served his punishment (or had been tried and acquitted). Therefore, it would be double jeopardy to try him again for the same crime.

   Entrapment is another excuse why the accused should not be convicted of an offense that she admits she did. For instance, a woman could argue that while she did sell drugs, she didn't consider selling drugs until law enforcement enticed her to do it.

   Another argument why a defendant might claim that he should be acquitted is if there is police misconduct or prosecutorial misconduct. If the accused was tortured and forced to sign a confession by the police, he could use this as a defense. Or if the prosecutor withheld exculpatory evidence (evidence that could show the defendant was innocent) from the defense, the defendant would argue that he should be set free.

6. The defendant is guilty of the offense but was influenced by outside forces. Some defendants might readily admit they committed the offense, but might contend that it was some medical or psychological condition that caused them to violate a criminal law. For example, a veteran of three tours of duty in Iraq might argue that they were suffering from post-traumatic stress disorder and this led them to commit an armed robbery. Or a woman might say that she has severe pre-menstrual syndrome, and this condition was responsible for a violent offense.

Myth: *The insanity plea allows many dangerous felons to go free or get very light sentences.*

Reality: *The insanity defense is used in only a few cases each year—less than one percent—and when it is used as a defense it is often unsuccessful. If is successful, the defendant may end up in an institution for a longer period of time than if convicted by using a standard defense.*

THE INSANITY DEFENSE

The insanity defense is popular in the entertainment industry, as it is frequently featured in movies, plays, and television shows. The reason for this is easy to understand: The insanity defense makes for exciting drama. In reality, however, the insanity defense is rarely used. According to an eight-state study funded by the National Institute of Mental Health, the insanity defense was used in less than one percent of the cases coming before a state court (Callahan et al., 1991). This same study indicated that only 26 percent of all insanity pleas were successful and that 90 percent of those using the defense had been previously diagnosed with a mental illness.

From the point of view of criminal law, insanity is a legal concept, not a medical one. The legal definition of insanity usually has little to do with psychological or psychiatric understandings of mental illness. Instead, it is a concept developed to enable the judicial system to assign guilt or innocence to particular defendants (Schmalleger, 2012).

The legal definition of insanity as a defense refers to an individual whose mind was disordered because of defective mental processes at the time of committing a crime (Masters et al., 2013). Medical, psychological, and psychiatric experts will often contribute their opinions about a defendant's mental status and behavior at the time of the crime, but it is a jury (although sometimes it is a judge who renders a verdict in a trial) who will ultimately determine whether the defendant was insane at the time the offense occurred (Masters et al., 2013).

If a defendant is found not guilty by reason of insanity (NGRI), the individual is acquitted of the criminal charges and discharged from the criminal justice system. An alternative finding is guilty but mentally ill (GBMI). This finding means that the defendant was recognized as being mentally ill but is still criminally responsible for the crime. Because of the recognition of mental illness in GBMI, the individual is entitled to psychiatric treatment during incarceration.

There is no simple legal standard for determining insanity. Instead, there are three primary rules used in the United States. Those three rules or standards are the M'Naghten rule, the Durham rule, and the American Law Institute rule (Masters et al., 2013).

The oldest standard is the M'Naghten rule, named after Daniel M'Naghten, who assassinated Edward Drummond, the private secretary of the British prime minister, Edward Peel, in 1843 (Barkan & Bryjak, 2004). M'Naghten actually meant to kill Peel, but apparently shot Drummond by mistake. During the trial, M'Naghten claimed he was delusional when he shot Drummond. He was found not guilty by reason of insanity (Barkan & Bryjak, 2004).

This case led to the development of the M'Naghten Rule, which says that the defendant cannot be held criminally responsible if her or she has a mental defect that prevents him or her from understanding that his or her act was wrong (Barkan & Bryjak, 2004).

The M'Naghten rule is also referred to as the "right and wrong test." The right and wrong test says that to be found insane, the defendant must have had, at the time of the crime, a defect of reason, from a disease of the mind that renders the individual incapable of knowing what he was doing, or if he did know what he was doing, he did not know that it was wrong (Masters et al., 2013).

Some states have broadened the M'Naghten rule by including an irresistible impulse test. In this test, the jury must ascertain whether the defendant's mental disorder made him incapable of controlling his urges to behave in particular ways.

A majority of states use the M'Naghten rule, and about half of those states include the irresistible impulse test as part of the standard (Masters et al., 2013). The other states use either the Durham rule or the American Law Institute rule or do not allow a court definition of insanity (this is the case in four states: Kansas, Montana, Utah, and Idaho; these states do not allow the use of the insanity plea) (Gaines & Miller, 2007).

The American Law Institute rule is used in 19 states and is sometimes referred to as the substantial capacity test. This rule was put forward by the American Law Institute in 1962 in the Model Penal Code. This rule requires that the defendant have a mental disease or defect that causes the person to lack "substantial capacity either to appreciate the criminality of his conduct or to conform his conduct to the requirements of the law" (Masters et al., 2013, p. 126).

The third rule is the Durham rule, which is only used in New Hampshire. This rule holds that an individual may not be found guilty if his criminal act resulted from a mental disease or defect. This standard is seen as weaker and vaguer than either the M'Naghten Rule or the American Law Institute Rule, and, as a result, has not gained much popularity in other states (Barkan & Bryjak, 2004).

The insanity defense remains controversial and despite the fact that it is rarely used, it appears that the public is opposed to its use, believing that defendants use the insanity defense to get away with crimes (Masters et al., 2013). Even though, as mentioned earlier, it is seldom used, still there is no indication that the insanity defense impedes the prosecution of criminal cases (Walker, 2001).

APPOINTED COUNSEL

More than 90 percent of all persons accused of a crime cannot afford to retain their own attorney (Territo et al., 2004). For such defendants—those who cannot afford a private lawyer—the government must provide counsel at no cost to the defendant. However, if they choose, they can defend themselves.

Representing oneself is called *pro se* ("for one's own behalf"). Defendants have a constitutional right to act as their own attorney, although judges are usually very careful to make sure that a defendant who wishes to act as his or her own attorney thoroughly understands the risks of self-representation.

Defendants who wish to have appointed counsel are typically indigent, or poor, people. They are absolutely entitled to have the government appoint and pay for legal counsel. There are three methods by which indigent defense attorneys may be assigned. Some jurisdictions have public defenders. These attorneys work for the government, often in offices called public defenders' offices, to defend indigent clients.

A second method is the assigned counsel system. Here, individual lawyers in private law firms take indigent clients on a case-by-case basis and are paid based on a set fee schedule. The third method is a contract method in which law firms, non-profit agencies, or individual attorneys accept indigent cases for set fees for various duties in representing the defendants.

Myth:	*Court-appointed attorneys have many resources available to help defend clients.*
Reality:	*Being a court-appointed attorney means that an attorney may have as many as 200 to 300 clients and only the resources the court gives them. Many take whatever information the prosecution gives them and uses that information to offer a plea deal to the client.*

Most felony suspects in the United States are poor and most are represented by appointed counsel (Masters et al., 2013). Although it is sometimes thought that defendants represented by public defenders get a less competent defense, a study published in 2000 (National Legal Aid and Defender Association, 2000) found that defendants represented by public defenders were convicted at about the same rate as those represented by private counsel, but those with public defenders were more likely to be incarcerated.

Right to Effective Counsel

A defendant is not only entitled to legal counsel, but he is also entitled to effective counsel. In 1970, the Supreme Court ruled that defendants are entitled "to the effective assistance of competent counsel" (*McMann v. Richardson* [1970], p. 5). But some experts have contended that effective assistance of counsel is often lacking (Albanese, 2013). The reasons for this may be related to an inadequate number of experienced lawyers in some cities and jurisdictions, poor court supervision of the conduct of defense lawyers, and the lack of funds in some areas to pay good lawyers (Duncan, 2002). The fundamental question in many instances, though, is whether the legal advice given to a defendant is defective to such a degree that a defendant's case is hampered (Albanese, 2013).

In the case of *Strickland v. Washington*, the defendant, David Leroy Washington, on trial for various violent crimes including murder, was convicted and sentenced to death. On appeal, Washington contended that he had received ineffective assistance of counsel in violation of the Sixth Amendment (Albanese, 2013). In ruling on this appeal, the U.S. Supreme Court said that when ineffective assistance of counsel is claimed, "the defendant must show that counsel's representation fell below an objective standard of reasonableness" (*Strickland v. Washington*, p. 2). In order to win such appeals, defendants must identify specific errors made by their attorneys and show that these errors affected the results of the case and made the case unfair. This makes it very difficult for defendants (Cole & Smith, 2008).

FOR FURTHER CONSIDERATION

Historical Events Relevant to Chapter Nine

March 18, 1963: The U.S. Supreme Court announces its decision in the landmark case of *Gideon v. Wainwright*, establishing that an indigent defendant facing a serious charge has the right to appointed counsel.

April 4, 1859: The Daniel Sickles murder trial begins. Sickles was charged with killing Philip Barton Key II (the son of Francis Scott Key), whom Sickles suspected of having an affair with his wife. The jury verdict was announced on April 26, 1859, and Sickles became the first defendant to successfully use the insanity plea to prove innocence in a murder.

April 18, 1857: Famed defense attorney Clarence Darrow is born in Kinsman, Ohio.

April 19, 1926: The second *People v. Sweet et al.* trial begins in Detroit, Michigan. Clarence Darrow is the lead defense attorney and he successfully defends Dr. Ossian Sweet and other African Americans against murder charges.

June 1, 1942: The U.S. Supreme Court announces its decision in the *Betts v. Brady* case. The justices rule that the right to counsel is fundamental to criminal due process.

June 12, 1972: The U.S. Supreme Court decides the *Argersinger v. Hamlin* case. This ruling extended the rights of indigent defendants to have assistance of counsel. The Court said that the right to counsel is a right as long as the offense is punishable by more than six months' imprisonment.

September 9, 1925: Dr. Ossian Sweet and other family and friends are arrested by Detroit police and charged with the murder of Leon Breiner on Garland Avenue outside of Dr. Sweet's new home. All of the defendants are successfully defended by Clarence Darrow. The judge in the trial was Frank Murphy, who would later become a justice of the U.S. Supreme Court.

October 18, 1943: The first radio broadcast of *The Perry Mason Show* is heard on this date. Written by Erle Stanley Gardner, *The Perry Mason Show*, featuring Perry Mason as a fictional Los Angeles defense attorney, became a popular television series beginning in 1957.

Important Court Cases

- **Betts v. Brady, 316 U.S. 455 (1942):** After indictment for robbery, Betts asked the court to appoint an attorney to assist in his defense. The trial judge refused, and Betts was forced to defend himself. He was convicted and sentenced to prison. The case was appealed to the U.S. Supreme Court, which rejected the claim by Betts. The Court refused to extend the right to counsel to non-capital cases and to cases where there were no special circumstances.
- **Gideon v. Wainwright, 372 U.S. 335 (1963):** A Florida trial court refused to appoint counsel for Clarence Earl Gideon, charged with breaking and entering a poolroom with intent to commit a misdemeanor (which was a felony under Florida law). Gideon could not afford an attorney and was forced to represent himself. He was unsuccessful in defending himself and was sentenced to a prison term. He appealed his own case to the U.S. Supreme Court and the Court heard his appeal. A unanimous Court overruled the 1942 case of *Betts v. Brady* and declared that counsel be appointed to represent indigent defendants charged with serious offenses in state criminal trials.
- **McMann v. Richardson, 397 U.S. 759 (1970):** A defendant pleaded guilty to a felony charge based on the advice of counsel. The defendant also believed he had been forced to confess, and his attorney thought he had a better chance to plead guilty than go before a jury. In his appeal after sentencing, the defendant claimed incompetent advice by counsel. The U.S. Supreme Court ruled that a defendant's plea of guilty, based on reasonably competent advice, is an intelligent plea not open to attack as being involuntary on the ground that his counsel may have misjudged the admissibility of the defendant's confession.
- **Powell v. Alabama, 287 U.S. 45 (1932):** Nine black youth were arrested near Scottsboro, Alabama, on charges of having raped two white women riding on a freight train in 1931. The youths were hastily indicted and tried for the crime of rape. An attorney was appointed, but only minutes before the trial. Eight of the nine youths were convicted and sentenced to death after the brief trial. The case was ultimately appealed up to the U.S. Supreme Court. The Court's opinion was that the convictions of the youths must be reversed under the due process clause of the Fourteenth Amendment. Under the due process clause, the Court asserted, the youths were denied a fair trial because the right to counsel was an integral part of due process.
- **Strickland v. Washington, 466 U.S. 668 (1984):** The U.S. Supreme Court's decision in this case established a two-part test for supporting a claim of ineffectiveness of counsel. Under this test, a criminal defendant may not obtain relief unless he can show that defense counsel's performance fell below an objective standard of reasonableness and that counsel's performance gives rise to a reasonable probability that, had counsel performed adequately, the result of the proceeding—whether the trial, the sentencing hearing, or the appeal—would have been different.

Websites to Check Out

- *What you can expect from the best criminal defense lawyer. Findlaw. Available at: http://criminal.findlaw.com/criminal-legal-help/what-you-can-expect-from-the-best-criminal-defense-lawyer.html.* This website, provided by *Findlaw.com,* describes what you can expect from a criminal defense attorney.
- *10 Famous Defense Attorneys. Criminal Justice Degrees Guide. Available at: http://www.criminaljusticedegrees-guide.com/features/10-famous-defense-attorneys.html.* This website assists students in finding a career in criminal justice, and as part of its services, provides information about various aspects of law and justice.

- *Court findings of ineffectiveness of counsel in post-conviction appeals. Innocence Project.* Available at: *www.innocenceproject.org/docs/Innocence_Project_IAC_Report.pdf.* An Innocence Project site, this website features a discussion of the problem of ineffectiveness of counsel.
- *The Insanity Defense: A Closer Look. Washington Post.* Available at: *http://www.washingtonpost.com/wp-srv/local/longterm/aron/qa227.htm.* A *Washington Post* website, this features several articles on the insanity defense.

Books

- Abramson, L., and Flaste, R. (1997). *The Defense Is Ready: Life in the Trenches of Criminal Law.* New York: Simon & Schuster.
- Bailey, F. L., and Greenya, J. (1975). *For the Defense.* New York: Atheneum.
- Carter, D. T. (2007). *Scottsboro: A Tragedy of the American South.* rev. ed. Baton Rouge: Louisiana State University Press.
- Dershowitz, A. M. (1982). *The Best Defense.* New York: Random House.
- Irons, P., and Guitton, S., eds. (1993). *May It Please the Court: The Most Significant Oral Arguments Made Before the Supreme Court Since 1955.* New York: New Press.
- Lewis, A. (1964). *Gideon's Trumpet.* New York: Random House.
- Maeder, T. (1985). *Crime and Madness: The Origins and Evolution of the Insanity Defense.* New York: Harpercollins.
- McRae, D. (2009). *The Last Trials of Clarence Darrow.* New York: William Morrow.
- Simon, R. J., and Aaronson, D. E. (1988). *The Insanity Defense: A Critical Assessment of Law and Policy in the Post-Hinckley Era.* New York: Praeger.
- Tierney, K. (1979). *Darrow: A Biography.* New York: Thomas Y. Crowell.

Movies

- *Heavens Fall* (2006): Based on the Scottsboro Boys' case in Alabama in the 1930s, this movie covers the trial and subsequent events which culminated in the important Supreme Court decision.
- *Gideon's Trumpet* (1979): Henry Fonda portrays Clarence Gideon in this movie about the case that resulted in the landmark Supreme Court decision in the case of *Gideon v. Wainwright.*
- *Anatomy of a Murder* (1959): Perhaps the best Hollywood treatment of the insanity defense, this movie is a riveting courtroom drama as a murderer uses the defense of irresistible impulse to defend his killing of the man who raped his wife.
- *Murder on a Sunday Morning* (2001): An award-winning documentary that follows the trial of a teenager falsely accused of a murder. A public defender presents the defense for a 15-year-old African American youth and demonstrates that a public defender can do an excellent job of putting on a defense in a murder case.

TV Shows and Series

- *Scottsboro: An American Tragedy:* A documentary film made for the American Experience on PBS, this film covers the history of the nine black youths accused of raping two white women.
- *Murder One:* A drama series that aired on ABC in 1995 and 1996, this show followed a murder case from arrest to jury verdict. In each of the two seasons it ran on TV, the audience could follow the defense preparation for a murder trial, as well as the trial with the defense battling the strategies of the prosecution.

Review for Chapter Nine:

Research Paper or Term Paper Topics:

- The insanity defense
- The ineffectiveness of counsel
- The role and duties of the public defender

Important Terms to Know

Indigent defendant: A defendant who lacks the funds to hire a private attorney and is therefore entitled to free counsel.

Entrapment: A defense asserting that a crime was instigated by a government agent who offered inducements to commit a crime or makes false representations.

Exculpatory evidence: All information that is material and favorable to the accused defendant because it casts doubt on the defendant's guilt or on the evidence the government intends to use at trial.

Insanity defense: A criminal defense that enables the defendant to be found not guilty because he or she does not have the mental capacity required to be legally responsible for the criminal behavior.

M'Naghten rule: This rule defines a person as insane if at the time of the crime the defendant was laboring under such a defect of reason that he or she could not tell or know the nature and quality of the act, or if they did know it, that they did not know what they were doing was wrong.

***Pro se*:** Acting as one's own attorney.

Study Guide Questions

True or False:

1. The importance of the Scottsboro Boys' case (*Powell v. Alabama* [1932]) was that the Supreme Court declared that defendants had the right to counsel in capital cases.

2. The book *Gideon's Trumpet* was based on the Supreme Court case of Clarence Earl Gideon.

3. In our legal system, the defense attorney's primary responsibility is to make sure the prosecution proves its case against the defendant.

4. A defense attorney does not need to represent a defendant if he or she is convicted and wants to appeal his or her case.

Multiple Choice Items:

5. In the case *Betts v. Brady* (1942), the U.S. Supreme Court established a fundamental fairness test regarding a right to appointed counsel. This meant that
   a. a defendant may not only be indigent but also must have other special circumstances
   b. a defendant only had to ask for counsel
   c. a defendant had to be mentally retarded
   d. a defendant had to be a poor murderer

6. *Gideon v. Wainwright* (1963) brought about a change in the requirements for appointed counsel. In the decision, the U.S. Supreme Court ruled that
   a. an indigent defendant may ask for an attorney if he or she can read or write
   b. an indigent defendant may ask for an attorney if he or she faces a serious charge that could result in jail or prison time
   c. an indigent defendant may ask for counsel if he or she can demonstrate that he or she is incapable of defending him- or herself.
   d. an indigent defendant may ask for counsel if he or she has never studied law

7. The insanity defense is used in this percentage of all criminal cases:
   a. one percent or less
   b. five percent
   c. twenty-five percent
   d. fifty-five percent

8. If a defendant is found not guilty by reason of insanity (NGRI), then the individual is
   a. placed in a mental hospital
   b. sent to prison and prescribed medication
   c. placed on probation
   d. acquitted of the criminal charge and released from the criminal justice system

9. The M'Naghten rule is also referred to as
   a. the right and wrong test
   b. the guilty but insane test
   c. the wild beast test
   d. the irresistible impulse test

10. A convicted criminal could appeal his or her case on the basis of ineffectiveness of counsel. However, he or she would have to show
    a. that his or her counsel failed to show up for court hearings
    b. that his or her counsel never called any witnesses
    c. that his or her counsel's representation fell below an objective standard of reasonableness
    d. that his or her counsel used an unusual defense strategy

References

Albanese, J. S. (2013). *Criminal Justice.* 5th ed. Upper Saddle River, NJ: Pearson.

Barkan, S. E., and Bryjak, G. J. (2004). *Fundamentals of Criminal Justice* . Boston: Pearson.

Bohm, R. M., and Haley, K. N. (2002). *Introduction to Criminal Justice.* 3rd ed. New York: Glencoe-McGraw Hill.

Callahan, L. A., Steadman, H. J., McGreevy, M. A., and Robbins, P. C. (1991). The volume and characteristics of insanity defense pleas: An eight-state study. *Bulletin of the American Academy of Psychiatry and the Law* 19 (4), 331–338.

Cole, G. F., and Smith, C. E. (2008). *Criminal Justice in America.* 5th ed. Belmont, CA: Thomson/Wadsworth.

Duncan, M. J.. (2002), "The (so-called) liability of criminal defense attorneys: A system in need of reform," *Brigham Young University Law Review* [online], Available at: www.law2.byu.edu/lawreview/archives/2002/1/Dun1.pdf.

Fuller, J. R. (2010). *Criminal Justice: Mainstreams and Crosscurrents.* 2nd ed. Upper Saddle River, NJ: Prentice Hall.

Gaines, L. K., and Miller, R. L. (2007). *Criminal Justice in Action.* 4th ed. Belmont, CA: Thomson/Wadsworth.

Masters, R. E., Way, L. B., Gerstenfeld, P. B., Muscat, B. T., Hooper, M., Dussich, J. P. J., Pincu, L., and Skrapec, C. A. (2013). *CJ: Realities and Challenges.* 2nd ed. New York: McGraw-Hill.

McMann v. Richardson, 397 U.S. 759 (1970).

Miranda v. Arizona, 384 U.S. 436 (1966), Legal Information Institute [online], Available at: http://www.law.cornell.edu/supct/html/historics/USSC_CR_0384_0436_ZO.html.

National Legal Aid and Defender Association, (2000), "Compendium of Standards for Indigent Defense Systems: A Resource Guide for Practitioners and Policymakers," US Department of Justice, Office of Justice Programs [online], Available at: https://www.ncjrs.gov/App/Publications/abstract.aspx?ID=187860.

Reid, S. T. (1999). *Criminal Justice: Blueprints.* 5th ed. St. Paul, MN: Coursewise Publishing Co.

Siegel, L. J., and Worrall, J. L. (2012). *Introduction to Criminal Justice.* 13th ed. Belmont, CA: Wadsworth.

Schmalleger, F. (2012). *Criminal Justice: A Brief Introduction.* 9th ed. Upper Saddle River, NJ: Prentice Hall.

Strickland v. Washington (1984), Justia.com: U.S. Supreme Court Center [online], Available at: http://supreme.justia.com/cases/federal/us/466/668/case.html.

Territo, L., Halsted, J. B., and Bromley, M. L. (2004). *Crime and Justice in America: A Human Perspective*. 6th ed. Upper Saddle River, NJ: Pearson.

Walker, S. (2001). *Sense and Nonsense about Crime and Drugs: A Policy Guide*. 5th ed. Belmont, CA: Wadsworth.

Part Four

Going to Court

Chapter Ten

The Court System in America

The majority of criminal cases are heard in state courts. The reason for this is because most felonies are violations of state laws. State courts only deal with state laws. And all states have similar court systems, with three levels of jurisdiction: limited, general, and appellate. However, each state determines how its system is organized so the names of the state courts and their precise jurisdictions vary.

At the lowest level in each state are the courts of limited jurisdiction, such as municipal courts. These courts include all city, town, village, and district courts. Their legal authority is restricted to certain specific kinds of cases. For example, in most states these municipal or district courts handle trials for minor criminal and civil cases, deal with traffic and motor vehicle violations, and conduct probable cause hearings for felonies (Albanese, 2005).

At the next level are courts of general jurisdiction, which are often referred to as trial courts. It is in these courts, which are called by various names such as circuit courts or superior courts, where civil suits involving amounts that are too large to be handled in small claims courts and where felonies trials are held. Each county usually has one felony court, and nationwide there are about 3,200 trial courts (Albanese, 2005).

At the next highest level of state courts are appellate courts. These courts hear appeals from courts of general jurisdiction. There are two types of appellate courts: intermediate courts (often called the state court of appeals) and supreme courts. Some states have only one of these courts, while a few have both an appeals court and a state supreme court. Each appellate court is made up of a panel of three to 10 justices who hear arguments in cases that are referred from lower courts. Appellate courts hear arguments on

I love judges, and I love courts. They are my ideals, that typify on earth what we shall meet hereafter in heaven under a just God.

—William Howard Taft,
Quoted by Max Lerner in
Yale Law Review, 1290, 1311
n. 58 (1937)

specific legal issues that arise in trial courts, and if a significant error was made in law or procedure, the trial court finding could be set aside, and the case could be remanded back to the trial court for reconsideration.

The Federal Court System

In this country, we have a dual court system with both state courts and federal courts. Federal courts hear only cases involving allegations of violations of federal law. In most instances, federal laws, such as those related to kidnapping and bank robbery, are designed to deal with criminal behaviors that occur in more than one state.

There are three levels of federal courts. At the lowest level are the U.S. district courts. These courts hear both civil and criminal matters, but these are the courts in which federal trials are held. There are 94 U.S. district courts, with at least one (sometimes several in populous states) in every state. Above the district courts are the appellate courts. The intermediate appellate court are the U.S. courts of appeals. There are 13 such courts, and U.S. courts of appeals hear appeals from state courts.

Myth: *The U.S. Supreme Court only agrees to hear cases which are important.*

Reality: *It is true that the Supreme Court may base its decision on which cases to hear in part on whether a case is important. However, the Court also looks at whether an appeals court decision in a case conflicts with opinions of other courts and whether a lower court's decision may be wrong in terms of previous Supreme Court opinions.*

The nation's court of last resort is the U.S. Supreme Court. The U.S. Supreme Court, made up of nine justices nominated by the president and approved by the Senate, hears appeals on any case involving federal law, suits between states, and cases involving interpretations of the U.S. Constitution. The Supreme Court is referred to as the court of last resort because decisions of the Supreme Court cannot be appealed further. The Supreme Court can refuse to hear an appeal sent to it (in which case the previous court's ruling stands as the final decision) or it can choose to hear oral arguments by both sides in an appeal. The decision, which is contained in a written majority opinion, has the force of law and cannot be overruled by Congress. U.S. Supreme Court cases that determine how the Constitution is to be interpreted, as in *Miranda v. Arizona* or *Mapp v. Ohio*, are called landmark cases. Landmark cases are important in determining the constitutional rights of the defendant (Fagin, 2007).

CRIMINAL CASES IN STATE COURTS

In the American system of justice, the trial is regarded as the best method of determining a defendant's guilt or innocence. However, because of the high stakes and uncertainty that surround criminal trials, most defendants plead guilty as they get closer to the prospect of being judged by a random group of citizens drawn from the community (Cole & Smith, 2008).

A guilty plea, too, carries with it uncertainty and unpredictability about what the punishment will be. Prosecutors, though, create incentives for guilty pleas by offering reductions in charges and sentences in exchange for admissions of guilt. While a great majority of defendants plead guilty and accept a plea-bargained deal, there are some defendants who choose to go to trial. In this chapter, we examine the steps in the criminal justice process from arrest to conviction or acquittal and—sometimes—to appeal.

FROM ARREST TO TRIAL

Criminal offenses are broadly placed into two categories: felonies, which are the more serious crimes and can be punished by a sentence of a year or more in prison and frequently other punishments, and misdemeanors, which are less serious crimes and are punishable by a term of less than a year in jail and with, perhaps, other penalties, such as a fine. It is how a felony is processed in the criminal courts that we will follow in this chapter.

After an indictment is handed down by a grand jury or after an information is submitted by a prosecutor, the accused is arrested. The accused could be arrested based on probable cause or he or she could be arrested based on an arrest warrant signed by a judge. An arrest means that the accused is taken into custody and transported to a police station where the individual is booked. The booking process includes taking photographs and fingerprints; these form the basis of the case record.

If the accused is arrested without an arrest warrant, an initial hearing or initial appearance must be conducted within 48 hours. At the initial hearing, the charges are read, the individual is advised of his or her rights, and there is an opportunity to post bail. If the accused is arrested with an arrest warrant, it means evidence had already been presented to a judge who believed that evidence was strong enough to support a finding of probable cause (Cole & Smith, 2008).

BAIL DECISIONS

When an individual has been taken into custody and probable cause demonstrated to the satisfaction of the court, that person is presumed innocent because he or she has not been convicted of any wrongdoing. However, he or she may have been in pre-trial detention, although at the initial hearing, the issue of bail is addressed.

Often, a defense attorney may request the defendant's release on recognizance. Release on recognizance (or ROR) means that the person's word and his or her good standing in the community are accepted by the judge as assurance that the person will return for any or all court hearings. However, the judge may decide that releasing a defendant on his or her own recognizance is too risky and order that release will be dependent on the individual posting bail.

Bail is a sum of money or property in an amount specified by the judge. The accused would forfeit that money or property if he or she fails to appear in court as scheduled. The Eighth Amendment forbids excessive bail, but the U.S. Constitution does not spell out appropriate bail amounts. There are state bail laws, though, that are aimed at preventing discrimination in setting bail (Cole & Smith, 2008). In almost all instances, the amount of bail is determined by the judge based on the seriousness of the crime and the defendant's past record. However, prior to setting bail, the judge typically listens to arguments from both the prosecution and the defense as to the appropriate amount of bail. A judge can detain an individual without setting bail. A study of felony defendants in several counties across the country found that 62 percent of defendants were released on bail, 32 percent were unable to post bail, and six percent were detained without bail (Cohen & Reaves, 2006).

In order to make bail, defendants have to come up with 100 percent of the total amount of bail set by the court. That would mean, for instance, if bail was set at $10,000, the defendant would have to come up with $10,000 in cash. However, almost one in five defendants secures his or her release through the services of a bail bondsman (Barkan & Bryjak, 2004). Bondsmen are agents who guarantee the courts that the defendant will show up for court hearings or he or she will be responsible for the full amount of bail. The defendant must pay the bondsman 10 percent of the bail, which is non-refundable. Research shows that an overwhelming majority of people who post bail, either on their own or through a bondsman, do show up in court as scheduled (Barkan & Bryjak, 2004).

Myth: *It doesn't matter how you come up with the money for your bail.*

Reality: *It does matter. If the state thinks you have posted illegally obtained cash for your bail, a bail source hearing can be scheduled. This hearing is in front of a judge and defendants are asked to prove that the money was legally obtained.*

A preliminary hearing, sometimes referred to as a probable cause hearing and often heard in a municipal court, is another proceeding designed to determine if the accused must stand trial on felony charges. Probable cause hearings are used as checks on prosecutorial authority in jurisdictions that do not use grand juries (Owen et al., 2012). Both the prosecution and the defense may present evidence and arguments, but it is the judge who decides if there is probable cause. If the judge decides there is probable cause, then the judge binds the accused over for trial (Owen et al., 2012). If the judge, however, determines that probable cause is lacking, the judge may reduce felony charges to misdemeanor charges or may dismiss the charges completely.

After a defendant has been indicted by a grand jury or is bound over for trial by a judge, the next step is to hold an arraignment. An arraignment is a formal proceeding in which the charging document is read to the defendant and the defendant is asked to enter a formal plea on each charge (Owen et al., 2012). The defendant has options in terms of entering a plea. He or she can plead not guilty, guilty, no contest (*nolo contendere*), or stand mute. If the accused stands mute (or makes no plea), the judge enters a not guilty plea for him or her. If the judge enters a not guilty plea or if the individual pleads not guilty, the case is scheduled for trial. If the defendant enters a guilty plea or a no contest plea, the case proceeds to a sentencing hearing.

It is often after a plea of not guilty has been entered that plea bargaining takes place between the prosecution and the defense. As indicated previously, upward of 95 percent of all state and federal felony convictions are obtained by guilty pleas prior to trial (Covey, 2008). Plea bargaining can actually continue all through the court process—even up until the jury returns with a verdict. But it is up to the judge to accept a plea deal and enter a judgment based on that deal. If the judge refuses to accept the terms of the plea agreement, the defendant may withdraw from the plea deal and seek a trial (Owen et al., 2012).

After the arraignment and a trial date has been set, the process of discovery takes place. This is the process by which the prosecution and the defense exchange relevant information about a case. Although there is no constitutional right to discovery in criminal cases, a series of statutes, judicial decisions, and court rules have established that each side has an obligation to disclose certain information as part of a defendant's due process rights to a fair trial (Owen et al., 2012).

According to the Federal Rules of Evidence for United States Courts (Dzienkowski, 2005), both the prosecution and the defense, under provisions regarding discovery, must provide to the other parties:

- The names, addresses, and telephone numbers of each individual likely to have discoverable information.
- A copy of or a description of all documents, data compilations, and tangible things that they possess and which may be used in the trial.
- The identity of any person who may be used at trial to present evidence as an expert witness.
- The names of expert witnesses must also be accompanied by a written report prepared and signed by the witness.
- The names, addresses, and telephone numbers of each witness.

These disclosures must be done in a timely manner—if not, the opposing party may file a motion compelling disclosure or discovery and may request expenses and sanctions against the attorney not providing timely disclosure.

Myth:	*The prosecution must turn over all information it has obtained that might be favorable to the defendant.*
Reality:	*True. The prosecution must turn over such evidence. However, the prosecution can get around this by turning over thousands of pages of documents and forcing the defense to try to find useful information among all the pages.*

Additionally, the prosecution must disclose all exculpatory evidence to the defense. Exculpatory evidence is any evidence that may be favorable to the defendant at trial either by casting doubt on the defendant's guilt or by tending to mitigate the defendant's culpability. This was specifically stated by the U.S. Supreme Court in *Brady v. Maryland* in 1963 (*Brady v. Maryland*, 373 U.S. 83). The Court said that withholding of evidence violates due process "where the evidence is material either to guilt or to punishment" (*Brady v. Maryland*, 373 U.S. 83 [1963], p. 1).

All in all, the rules regarding discovery are designed to prevent unfair surprises at trial.

PRE-TRIAL MOTIONS

Both the prosecution and defense use pre-trial motions to challenge evidence or raise concerns about any other substantive and procedural issues. A motion is a formal request asking the court to make a specific ruling (Owen et al., 2012). In the criminal justice process, perhaps the most important motions may be related to changing the venue or suppressing evidence.

The Sixth Amendment guarantees the right to an impartial trial by jury. However, if the defense believes there has been too much pre-trial publicity negative to his or her client, then the defense can request a change of venue. This would mean, if granted, that the trial would be moved to another court in another jurisdiction (Samaha, 2006). Fair trials require an atmosphere that do not prejudice the jury against the defendant. Not only can judges grant a change of venue, but they can also sequester the jury during a trial. What this means is that the jury is put up in hotel rooms under guard where they cannot read newspapers, watch TV, or talk on the telephone (Samaha, 2006). Although judges are usually very concerned about conducting a fair trial, they are also aware that with the ubiquitous nature of the Internet, smart phones, and cable TV it is very difficult to find a different venue that may be more impartial (Siegel & Worrall, 2012).

When it comes to suppression of evidence, a motion for suppression is made, often by the defense, to prevent certain evidence from being introduced in the trial. The motion is based on the claim that the evidence was gathered in a manner that violated due process or was unconstitutional (Fagin, 2007). Most motions for suppression are related to physical evidence or confessions covered by the exclusionary rule. Obviously, suppression of evidence, if granted by the judge, can influence the outcome of a trial. The case against the defendant may be seriously weakened if the prosecutor cannot use the defendant's confession or is denied permission to use physical evidence gathered by the police at the scene of the crime (Fagin, 2007).

Other pre-trial motions that could be made prior to the start of the trial are motions for continuance (or a request to delay the start of the trial) and motions for dismissal. In the latter motion, the defense attorney claims that the charges against the accused should be dismissed on the grounds of lack of evidence, violation of due process, lack of jurisdiction, or any other reason why the case should not proceed to trial. If a judge grants a motion for dismissal, it could be done with prejudice (meaning that the defendant could not be recharged with the same crime) or without prejudice—meaning that the prosecutor may correct any defects and arraign the client again (Fagin, 2007).

Jury Selection

The selection of the jury may be considered the first real step in the trial process. In the jury selection process, prosecutors and defense attorneys seek to identify potential jurors who may be sympathetic or hostile to their side. When they believe they have identified such individuals among the jury pool, they attempt to exclude those who are hostile toward their side and include those who are more inclined to be favorable to their side. Of course, neither side is going to be able to select a perfect jury for its side because jury selection involves the interaction of the prosecution, the defense, and the judge—each of whom has different objectives in the jury selection process (Cole & Smith, 2008).

The jury selection process actually begins when potential jurors are randomly selected, usually from lists of registered voters. A summons is sent to the home of selected people and they are required to appear at the courthouse at a specific time on a specific date. The group of people who appear on that date are known as the *venire*. When a judge needs a jury for a trial, a number of individuals are randomly selected from this *venire* to go to the courtroom to engage in a process called *voir dire*. *Voir dire* comes from the French term meaning "to speak the truth." During *voir dire*, the potential jurors are sworn to tell the truth and they are then asked a variety of questions designed to screen out those individuals who cannot make a fair and impartial decision in the case. Sometimes the defense and the prosecution conduct the *voir dire*; sometimes the judge may prefer to ask the questions (Owen et al., 2012).

Jurors will typically be asked whether or not they or their immediate family members have been crime victims or otherwise involved in a criminal case, and if so, whether this could prevent them from making open-minded decisions about the evidence and the defendant. If an individual in this pool of potential jurors indicates that he or she will not be able to make fair decisions, the juror may be challenged for cause (this is a *voir dire* challenge for which an attorney states to the judge the reason why a prospective juror should not be included on the jury) by either the prosecutor or the defense attorney. The judge must then rule on the challenge. If the judge agrees, then the person is excused from that specific case. There is usually no limit on the number of jurors that can be challenged for cause (Cole & Smith, 2008).

Although challenges for cause fall under the judge's control, the prosecution and defense can exert control over the *voir dire* process through the use of peremptory challenges. With peremptory challenges, either the prosecution or the defense can excuse any juror without giving specific reasons. Normally, the defense is allowed eight to ten peremptory challenges, and the prosecution six to eight (Cole & Smith, 2008).

The use of peremptory challenges has, however, raised concerns that attorneys can use them to excuse jurors based on such criteria as race. In a series of decisions in the 1980s and 1990s, the Supreme Court prohibited using peremptory challenges to systematically exclude potential jurors because of their race or gender. *Batson v. Kentucky* (1986) was one of these decisions. In this case, Batson, an African American man, had been convicted of second degree burglary and other offenses by an all-white jury. The prosecutor had used his peremptory challenges to remove all African Americans from the jury. The Supreme Court ruled the use of peremptory challenges for purposeful discrimination constituted a violation of a defendant's right to an impartial jury (Schmalleger, 2012).

In the 1992 case of *Georgia v. McCollum*, the Supreme Court barred defendants and their attorneys from using peremptory challenges to exclude potential jurors on the basis of race. In *McCollum*, Justice Harry Blackmun, writing for the majority, said, "Be it at the hands of the state or defense, if a court allows jurors to be excluded because of group bias, it is a willing participant in a scheme that could only undermine the very foundation of our system of justice—our citizens' confidence in it" (*Georgia v. McCollum*, 505 U.S. 42 [1992], p. 4).

Then, two years later, in *J. E. B. v. Alabama*, the Court restricted the use of peremptory challenges to eliminate jurors because of their gender (Schmalleger, 2012). However, despite earlier rulings banning the use of peremptory challenges to remove potential jurors based on race, those kinds of cases continued to come before the U.S. Supreme Court. For instance, in the 2003 case of *Miller-El v. Cockrell*, the Court found that a convicted capital defendant's constitutional rights had been violated by Dallas County (Texas) prosecutors who engaged in intentional efforts to remove eligible African Americans from the jury. That decision was reaffirmed in the 2005 case of *Miller-El v. Dretke*, and again in the 2008 case of *Snyder v. Louisiana* (Schmalleger, 2012).

The Jury in a Criminal Case

In our jury system, we usually think of a jury as 12 citizens who decide the outcome of the case. However, some states now allow as few as six people to serve on a jury. This reform was recommended to modernize court procedures and reduce expenses (Cole & Smith, 2008). The use of smaller juries was upheld by the Supreme Court in *Williams v. Florida* (*Williams v. Florida*, 399 U.S. 78 [1970]). Six states use juries with fewer than 12 members in non-capital felony cases, and a larger number of states use small juries for misdemeanors (Cole & Smith, 2008). Although the Supreme Court ruled that juries smaller than 12 were constitutional, the Court did decide that six-member juries must vote unanimously to convict a defendant (Cole & Smith, 2008). The Court has also stated that unanimity is not required when a jury of 12 members is used. Some states do permit juries to convict defendants by votes of 10 to 2 or 9 to 3 (Samaha, 2006). Despite the Court's ruling that juries can consist of fewer than 12 jurors, only two states also allow less-than-unanimous verdicts in non-capital cases (LaFave & Israel, 1984).

FOR FURTHER CONSIDERATION

Historical Events Relevant to Chapter Ten

February 1, 1790:   The U.S. Supreme Court convenes for the first time in New York City.

April 19, 1994:   The U.S. Supreme Court renders its decision in the *J. E. B. v. Alabama* case. The Court, in this decision, prohibits gender discrimination in jury selection.

April 30, 1986:   The holdings in the case of *Batson v. Kentucky* are announced by the Supreme Court. The Court bans discrimination based on race in jury selection.

May 14, 1984:   The U.S. Supreme Court decides *Strickland v. Washington*. The High Court states that the right to counsel is the right to the effective assistance of counsel.

May 28, 2002:   In the case of *Bell v. Cone*, the Supreme Court asserted that defense counsel's failure to present mitigating evidence against imposition of the death penalty and defense counsel's waiver of a final argument does not amount to ineffective assistance.

June 11, 1984:   The U.S. Supreme Court decides *Nix v. Williams*. Chief Justice Warren Burger delivered the opinion of the Court. This case established the "inevitable discovery" exception to the exclusionary rule. It allows evidence obtained illegally to be admitted in court if the police would have "inevitably" discovered the evidence using legal means.

Important Court Cases

- ***Batson v. Kentucky*, 476 U.S. 79 (1986):** Batson, a black man, was tried for second degree burglary and the receipt of stolen goods. During *voir dire*, the prosecution used its peremptory challenges to remove all four black people on the jury. Batson's attorney moved for a dismissal of the jury, asserting that the removal of all the black panelists violated his rights to a jury drawn from a cross-section of the community. The judge denied the motion and the trial proceeded. Batson was convicted on both counts. The case was appealed, and when it reached the U.S. Supreme Court, the Court ruled in favor of Batson. The Court applied the equal protection principle to the exercise of peremptory challenges.
- ***Brady v. Maryland*, 373 U.S. 83 (1963):** Brady and a companion, Boblit, were found guilty of murder in the first degree and were sentenced to death. Their trials were separate, with Brady being tried first. At his trial, Brady took the stand and admitted his participation in the crime, but he claimed that Boblit did the actual killing. In his summation to the jury, Brady's counsel conceded that Brady was guilty of murder in the first degree, asking only that the jury return that verdict "without capital punishment." Prior to the trial,

Brady's attorney requested the prosecution to allow him to examine Boblit's statements. Several of those statements had been shown to the defense, but one in which Boblit admitted the actual homicide was withheld by the prosecution. After conviction and sentencing, defense counsel learned about that statement. The sentencing was appealed, and the Court of Appeals held that suppression of the evidence by the prosecution denied the petitioner due process of law and remanded the case for a retrial of the question of punishment, not the question of guilt. When it was appealed by the prosecution to the U.S. Supreme Court, it was held that the suppression by the prosecution of evidence favorable to an accused upon request violates due process where the evidence is material either to guilt or to punishment, irrespective of the good faith or bad faith of the prosecution. The case was remanded back to the trial court for a new punishment hearing.

- *Georgia v. McCollum,* **505 U.S. 42 (1992):** In a trial, involving three white people accused of assaulting two black people, the state of Georgia requested that the defense not use peremptory challenges to exclude jurors on the basis of race. When the case reached the Supreme Court, the Court held that a criminal defendant cannot use peremptory challenges based solely on race. The court had previously held in *Batson v. Kentucky* (1986) that prosecutors cannot make peremptory challenges based on race, but did not address whether defendants could use them.

- *J. E. B. v. Alabama,* **511 U.S. 127 (1994):** This was a paternity suit case in which the prosecution used its peremptory challenges to remove men from the jury and retain women. Ultimately, the jury was composed of 12 women. When the defendant was convicted, the defense appealed on the basis that the defendant was denied equal protection because the *Batson* case had precluded the use of gender-based peremptory challenges. The Supreme Court agreed that peremptory challenges could not be used to exclude men or women.

- *Miller-El v. Cockrell,* **537 U.S. 322 (2003):** When Dallas County prosecutors used peremptory strikes to exclude 10 of the 11 African-Americans eligible to serve on the jury at Miller-El's capital murder trial, the defendant moved to strike the jury on the ground that the exclusions violated equal protection. Miller-El's attorney presented extensive evidence supporting his motion at a pre-trial hearing, but the trial judge denied the motion, finding no evidence indicating a systematic exclusion of blacks. The trial proceeded and Miller-El was found guilty and he was sentenced to death. Subsequently, there were appeals and state *habeas* petitions filed in Miller-El's behalf, but all were denied. The Federal District Court denied similar petitions in deference to the state courts' acceptance of the prosecutors' race-neutral justifications for striking the potential jurors. The case was appealed to the U.S. Supreme Court and the high court concluded that the District Court did not give full consideration to the substantial evidence Miller-El put forth in support of his petition. In addition, the Supreme Court ruled that the District Court was incorrect in not inquiring whether a "substantial showing of the denial of a constitutional right" had been proved. The Supreme Court reversed lower court decision and remanded Miller-El back to the original court for a new trial.

Websites to Check Out

- *Discovery in criminal cases. Findlaw.com.* Available at: *http://public.findlaw.com/abaflg/flg-15-3e-1.html.* The *Findlaw.com* website features information about discovery as well as various other terms related to criminal law.

- *Nolo contendere. Nolocontendere.org.* Available at: *http://www.nolocontendere.org/.* This is an informational website that relays data about no contest pleas and how they work in every state.
- *Improving the Jury System: Peremptory Challenges. Public Law Research Institute.* Available at: *http://www.uchastings.edu/public-law/plri/spr96tex/juryper.html.* This website features an article on peremptory challenges, and it includes the historical background to the use of peremptory challenges.

Books

- Baum, L. (1995). *The Supreme Court.* 5th ed. Washington, DC: CQ Press.
- Cretacci, M. A. (2008). *Supreme Court Case Briefs in Criminal Procedure.* Lanham, MD: Rowman & Littlefield Publishers, Inc.
- Powe, L. A. (2000). *The Warren Court and American Politics.* Cambridge, MA: Belknap Press.

Movies

- *Runaway Jury:* This 2003 courtroom thriller is based on a John Grisham novel by the same name. It has a rather implausible plot, but it is an entertaining look at how a jury might be sold to the highest bidder.

TV Series

- *Murder One:* This entertaining show, which aired on television over two seasons from 1995 to 1997, does feature an extensive look at how jury selection takes place. Both the defense and the prosecution use challenges for cause as well as peremptory challenges.
- *Law & Order:* In *Law & Order,* which ran for 20 seasons, there are many episodes in which bail hearings are depicted and subsequent trials are held.

Review for Chapter Ten:

Research Paper or Term Paper Topics:

- Jury selection
- Pre-trial publicity and its effect on juries

Important Terms to Know

Appellate courts:	Courts which hear appeals from lower courts.
Arraignment:	A hearing in which the charging document is read to the defendant and the defendant is asked to enter a formal plea on each charge.
Bail:	A sum of money or property securing a defendant's release from detention pending a future court hearing.
Change of venue:	The defense may request a transfer to another court in another jurisdiction when it is thought that negative pre-trial publicity threatens a fair trial for the defendant.
Court of last resort:	The term applied to the U.S. Supreme Court, indicating that the Supreme Court makes the final decision and there is no appeal of a Supreme Court decision.
Discovery:	A process by which the prosecution and the defense exchange relevant information about a case.
Felonies:	The more serious crimes which can result in a punishment of a year or more in prison.
Misdemeanors:	Less serious offenses which can carry a penalty of a year or less in jail.
Nolo contendere:	A no contest plea, which means that the defendant does not admit guilt but will accept the punishment.
Peremptory challenges:	Either the prosecution or the defense can use a peremptory challenge to excuse any potential juror without giving a specific reason.
Preliminary hearing:	A preliminary hearing or probable cause hearing is held to determine if there is sufficient evidence against the accused to bind him or her over for trial.
Pre-trial motion:	A formal request to the court prior to the beginning of a trial in which each side can raise issues or concerns.
Release on recognizance (ROR):	This occurs when a court releases a defendant based on his or her word and/or good standing in the community.
U.S. district courts:	Federal courts which are the trial courts for both federal civil and criminal trials.

Venire: The pool of people available for jury duty. From this pool, potential jurors are randomly selected to appear in a court when a jury is needed for a trial.

Voir dire: A process by which potential jurors are questioned in order for both the defense and the prosecution to decide which individuals may be suitable or unsuitable to serve on the jury.

Study Guide Questions

True or False:

1. Nationwide, there are about 3,200 state trial courts.

2. In America, we have a dual court system made up of state courts and federal courts.

3. Release on Recognizance means being released from jail based on posting profits made from drug sales.

4. There is no precise maximum on the bail a judge may impose on the accused.

Multiple Choice Items:

5. In the federal court system, federal criminal trials are heard in U.S. district courts. In this country there are
    a. 54 district courts
    b. 74 district courts
    c. 94 district courts
    d. 124 district courts

6. U.S. Supreme Court cases that determine how the Constitution is to be interpreted are called
    a. hallmark cases
    b. landmark cases
    c. huge cases
    d. unanimous cases

7. Negotiations on a plea bargain between the defendant and the prosecutor take place after the defendant pleads
    a. no contest
    b. insanity

      c. guilty
      d. not guilty

8. According to the Federal Rules of Evidence, both the prosecution and the defense must provide the other side with
    a. a copy of or a description of all documents, data, and evidence they possess that might be used in the trial
    b. some of the evidence they have collected
    c. the names of key expert witnesses
    d. a copy of their opening statement

9. The prosecution and the defense may not use their peremptory challenges to remove
    a. potential jurors because of their race or gender
    b. jurors who may not favor their side
    c. jurors who are biased
    d. jurors who are poor

References

Albanese, J. S. (2005). *Criminal Justice.* 5th ed. Upper Saddle River, NJ: Pearson.

Barkan, S. E., and Bryjak, G. J. (2004). *Fundamentals of Criminal Justice.* Boston: Pearson.

Brady v. Maryland, 373 U.S. 834 (1963), Justia: U.S. Supreme Court Center [online]. Available at: http://supreme.justia.com/cases/federal/us/373/83/case.html.

Cohen, T. H., and Reaves, B. A. (2006). *Felony Defendants in Large Urban Counties.* Washington, DC: U.S. Department of Justice, Bureau of Justice Statistics.

Cole, G. F., and Smith, C. E. (2008). *Criminal Justice in America.* 5th ed. Belmont, CA: Thomson/Wadsworth.

Covey, R. D. (2008). Fixed justice: Reforming plea bargaining with plea-based ceilings. *Tulane Law Review* 82, 1237–1290.

Dzienkowski, J. S., ed. (2005). *Professional Responsibility Standards & Statutes.* 2005–2006 ed. Belmont, CA: Thomson/West.

Fagin, J. A. (2007). *Criminal Justice: A Brief Introduction.* Boston: Allyn & Bacon.

Georgia v. McCollum, 505 U.S. 42 (1992), Legal Information Institute, Cornell University Law School [online], Available at: http://www.law.cornell.edu/supct/html/91-372.ZO.html.

LaFave, W. R., and Israel, J. H. (1984). *Criminal Procedure.* Eagan, MN: West.

Owen, S. S., Fradella, H. F., Burke, T. W., and Joplin, J. W. (2012). *Foundations of Criminal Justice.* New York: Oxford Press.

Samaha, J. (2006). *Criminal Justice.* 7th ed. Belmont, CA: Thomson/Wadsworth.

Schmalleger, F. (2012). *Criminal Justice.* 9th ed. Upper Saddle River, NJ: Prentice Hall.

Siegel, L. J., and Worrall, J. L. (2012). *Introduction to Criminal Justice.* 13th ed. Belmont, CA: Wadsworth.

Williams v. Florida, 399 U.S. 78 (1970), Legal Information Institute, Cornell University Law School [online],. Available at: http://www.law.cornell.edu/supct/html/historics/USSC_CR_0399_0078_ZS.html.

Chapter Eleven

The Trial

Almost half of the Bill of Rights guarantees deal with criminal procedure, specifically referring to the trial stage. To many Americans, the trial—as seen in our popular culture—is the ultimate stage for the drama surrounding good and evil. And to criminal justice authorities, the trial takes on the powerful role of the ultimate forum for deciding the guilt or innocence of the accused (Territo et al., 2004).

The elaborate rules for every procedure in the criminal trial—choosing jurors, presenting each side's opening statements, examining and cross-examining witnesses, introducing evidence, the closing arguments by the prosecution and the defense, the judges' charging jurors, and the jury deliberating followed by the reading of the jury verdict—are all aimed at deciding the fate of the defendant. Has the prosecution proved its case beyond a reasonable doubt? Did the defense cast doubt on the evidence? Is the accused guilty or innocent?

BEYOND A REASONABLE DOUBT

In our legal system, the defendant is presumed to be innocent. This presumption of innocence is an important principle in the criminal justice system. If the defendant is presumed innocent, then the

There are two great things that are essential to be a good witness—one is the desire to tell the truth, and the other is the ability to tell the truth ... there are fortunately very many people who have that desire; but there are far less who have the ability.

—*Louis D. Brandeis,*
The Brandeis Guide to the
Modern World, *May 1910*

state has the burden of proving otherwise. This means that the prosecution has the responsibility of proving every element of the crime required for conviction.

And what are the elements of a crime that must be proved during a trial?

All serious crimes consist of three elements:

- The criminal act.
- The criminal intent.
- The concurrence of the criminal act and the criminal intent.

THE CRIMINAL ACT

In our system, the law cannot punish people for what they wish or hope or even what they intend. There has to be more than that. There must be a criminal act. That is referred to in criminal law as *actus reus* (Latin for "guilty act"). This is the physical element. There must be a dead body (or sufficient evidence to show that a murder took place even if the body was never recovered) to show a murder took place; or there must be the recovered money to prove bank robbery occurred; or there must be physical damage to property to demonstrate that malicious destruction of property happened. In the trial, one of the first tasks of the prosecution is to show that the crime did, in fact, take place.

This aspect of the criminal law doesn't mean that the accused had to complete a crime to satisfy the act requirement. There can be attempted murder or a conspiracy among several people to commit a robbery of a casino. These kinds of situations do have one thing in common: They all include some action that would potentially lead to a crime. Our system does make crimes out of attempts and conspiracies—this is a way to prevent future crimes.

THE CRIMINAL INTENT

In all serious crime, a criminal intent has to trigger the criminal act. This is *mens rea*, which is the Latin term meaning "guilty mind." In order for an act to be criminal, there must be some aspect of a guilty mind or knowledge that committing the act would result in an illegal activity.

But this element is somewhat complicated because there are four levels of criminal intent:

- *Purposeful*: Purposeful intent means the individual did it on purpose. For example, pointing a loaded gun at another person and pulling the trigger generally means you were aware what the end result would be.
- *Knowing*: Knowing intent means the person knew that committing the act would result in a criminal behavior but was not doing it for that reason. For instance, when a homeowner shoots an intruder in her

house, she knows the person might be harmed but is firing a weapon to protect her children—knowing her actions may well harm or kill the intruder.
- *Reckless*: Reckless intent means consciously creating a risk of causing criminal harm—for example, driving a car well over the speed limit while having several children in the car and failing to require them to use their seatbelts.
- *Negligent*: Negligent intent is much like reckless intent, except that there is an unconscious intent to create a risk—for instance, pointing a gun which is assumed to be unloaded at a friend and pulling the trigger. The individual is negligent when his friend is shot and dies because a reasonable person would not assume a gun was unloaded and a reasonable person would not point a gun at a friend and pull the trigger.

> **Myth:** *In presenting its case, the prosecution must show that the accused had a motive.*
>
> **Reality:** *There is no such burden on the prosecution. Courts have ruled that while juries may like to have a motive, a defendant can be convicted for a crime even though there is no known motive.*

THE CONCURRENCE OF THE CRIMINAL ACT AND THE CRIMINAL INTENT

The element of concurrence means that the *mens rea*—or criminal mind—must trigger the *actus reus*—or criminal act. In the case of Bob Bashara, whom we have met in several earlier chapters, if Bashara desired his wife to die and if he hired another person to bring about her death, and if she was, in fact, murdered, then there is concurrence of the *mens rea* (the intent to have her killed) and the *actus reus* (her murder). Bashara continues to deny any involvement with his wife's death (Castellano, 2012).

THE CRIMINAL PROSECUTION

In criminal cases, the prosecutor must prove beyond a reasonable doubt that the defendant is guilty of the charges. That is, the prosecutor must prove his or her case to the degree that it is completely consistent with the guilt of the defendant and inconsistent with any other plausible conclusion (Territo et al., 2004). All evidence that the state presents serves this purpose.

While there are various definitions of "proof beyond a reasonable doubt," the phrase is rather difficult to precisely define, but it is generally agreed that this standard of proof means that there is no reasonable doubt about the guilt of the defendant.

OPENING STATEMENTS

After the jury has been selected, both the prosecution and the defense can make an opening statement. In this opening statement, each side gives an overview of his or her side of the case. Prosecutors, for instance, give the jury a sort of road map as to what they are going to prove. But beyond that, they want to acquaint both the judge and the jury with the charges, to outline the facts, and to describe how the government will prove the defendant guilty beyond a reasonable doubt (Siegel & Worrall, 2012). The defense, on the other hand, will use the opening statement to take advantage of weaknesses in the state's case against the defendant.

Neither the defense attorney nor the prosecution is allowed to make prejudicial remarks or inflammatory statements or to bring up irrelevant facts. Both can, however, indicate what they will prove based on evidence they will submit. The prosecutor cannot refer to evidence that he or she knows to be inadmissible. Nor can the prosecutor comment on the defendant's prior criminal record, if one exists. Should the prosecutor do either of these things, it could result in a mistrial or a reversal of a conviction later in an appeal (Territo et al., 2004).

Myth: *Both the prosecution and the defense must make an opening statement.*

Reality: *The rules of court do not require either side to make an opening statement. Either side may opt for not giving an opening statement.*

THE PROSECUTION'S CASE

Following the opening statements, the government—as represented by the prosecutor—begins its case. The case will be presented through the introduction of evidence to the court through the witnesses. There are four main types of evidence the prosecution can present:

- *Testimonial evidence*: This is evidence given by police officers, citizens, and experts about what they heard, saw, or experienced (Siegel & Worrall, 2012).
- *Real evidence*: Real evidence consists of exhibits that can be entered as part of the court record and could include objects (such as a gun), photographs, maps, journals, or crime scene displays.
- *Documentary evidence*: This type of evidence includes forensic reports, public records, hospital records, or fingerprint identification.
- *Circumstantial evidence*: This is indirect evidence often inferred or indirectly used to prove a fact in question. Circumstantial evidence might include evidence that the victim's blood type was found in the trunk of the defendant's car or evidence that the defendant was seen in the area of the crime about the same time that the crime occurred.

The prosecutor will call several witnesses to provide testimony via direct examination. During direct examination, the prosecutor questions the witness to reveal facts believed relevant to the state's case. Prosecution witnesses are required to respond directly to the questions asked, and any attempts by the witness to avoid the question or to volunteer additional information beyond the scope of the prosecutor's questions are not allowed. The reason for this is to make sure that the jury does not hear material that is objectionable or inadmissible (Territo et al., 2004).

Furthermore, in direct examination, attorneys cannot ask leading questions—questions steering witnesses to the answers the lawyers want. When the prosecutor finishes with the presentation of each witness, the defense attorney has the option to conduct a cross-examination of the witness. The right to cross-examination of a witness is an essential part of a trial. During cross-examination, the defense attorney may challenge elements of the testimony, such as the witness's memory or accuracy.

ADMISSIBLE EVIDENCE

The law of evidence recognizes two types of evidence: physical evidence and testimonial evidence. The evidence that prosecutors use should help prove the elements of the crime. That is, it must be relevant evidence. But even relevant evidence is not admissible if it is:

- *Prejudicial evidence:* That means that its power to damage the defendant is greater than its power to prove the government's case.
- *Illegally obtained evidence*: Evidence gathered illegally, for instance without a search warrant, cannot be presented.
- *Hearsay evidence*: This is evidence not directly heard or seen by the witness.

THE CASE FOR THE DEFENSE

Once the prosecutor has provided all the evidence the state has against the defendant, he or she informs the court that the people rest its case. It is now the defense's turn.

> **Myth:** *In a jury trial, only the jury can decide guilt or innocence of the defendant.*
>
> **Reality:** *Not so. The defense, after the prosecution has put on its case, can ask for a directed verdict of acquittal. A judge can grant such a request. In effect, this means that the judge concludes that the prosecution did not present sufficient evidence for a reasonable jury to find the defendant guilty.*

The defense attorney at this point may ask for a directed verdict. This is a procedural device in which the defense asks the judge to order the jury to return a verdict of not guilty. Essentially, when requesting a directed verdict, the defense is arguing that the prosecution failed to present sufficient evidence to support the legal elements needed to prove the defendant guilty beyond a reasonable doubt. If the judge agrees, the case is terminated. If the court disagrees, the case continues and the defense must put on its case.

However, the defense attorney does not have to put on a defense. That is, the burden of proving guilt is on the prosecution, and if the defense believes that the burden has not been met, it may feel there is no need to present witnesses or evidence of its own (Siegel & Worrall, 2012).

If the defense chooses to put on a defense, the presentation of the case is similar to that put on by the prosecution. The defense counsel calls witnesses and directly examines them. Once direct examination is concluded, the prosecution can cross-examine each defense witness. Also, like the prosecution, the defense can submit relevant evidence in the form of real or documentary evidence, photographic, scientific, or opinion evidence. But the defense does not have to present any evidence or call any witnesses. The defense can be based entirely on the evidence and testimony presented by the prosecution (Territo et al., 2004). And the defendant is not required to give personal testimony.

A defendant's refusal to take the stand as a witness cannot be called to the attention of the jury by the prosecution or the judge. However, if the defendant does testify, then the defendant faces the same hazards of cross-examination as any other witness (Territo et al., 2004).

The defense lawyer is not obligated to prove the innocence of the defendant. The defense merely has to show that the prosecutor has failed to prove guilt beyond a reasonable doubt.

After the testimony of the last defense witness is completed and all of the defense's evidence has been introduced, the defense rests its case.

Rebuttal and Surrebuttal

When the defense has rested, the prosecutor has a chance for rebuttal. This means that the prosecution can call additional witnesses to reinforce its position, which may have been weakened by the defense's witnesses or evidence. The only testimony allowed in rebuttal is that which relates to matters covered in the defense's presentation of its case. But if the state introduces rebuttal witnesses, then the defense has an opportunity to place surrebuttal witnesses on the stand to try to make its case stronger. Again, there are limits on surrebuttal witnesses: They can only testify to matters covered by the state's rebuttal witnesses.

Closing Arguments

After both sides have presented all of their evidence and all rebuttal or surrebuttal witnesses have testified, both the prosecution and the defense make their closing arguments. Here is where each side gets to summarize its case and review the facts and evidence that were brought about during the trial. Often, both sides have a free hand in arguing about the facts, issues, and evidence, including applicable law. Neither side can comment on matters not previously presented as evidence. Normally, the prosecution goes first in presenting closing arguments, and then the defense can finish up. However, either the prosecution or defense can elect not to make a final summation to the jury.

Charging the Jury

There is one final step before the jury begins deliberations The jury must be given instructions. In a criminal trial, the judge will instruct, or charge, the jury on the principles of law that ought to guide and control their decision on the defendant's guilt or innocence.

Included in the charge will be information about the elements of the alleged offense, the type of evidence needed to prove each element, and the burden of proof that must be met to obtain a guilty verdict (Siegel & Worrall, 2012). The instructions to the jury are very important because they could serve as the basis for a subsequent appeal.

After the instructions are given to the jury, the jury retires to a room to decide whether the prosecution proved its case beyond a reasonable doubt. In the next chapter, we will discuss more about the jury and jury deliberations leading up to a verdict.

FOR FURTHER CONSIDERATION

Historical Events Relevant to Chapter Eleven

January 2, 1935: Bruno Hauptmann, charged with the kidnapping and murder of the infant son of famed aviator Charles Lindbergh, goes on trial. The trial ends on February 11, 1935. On February 13, 1935, Hauptmann is found guilty of murder in the first degree.

January 6, 2005: A Texas Court of Appeals overturns Andrea Yates's conviction in the drowning deaths of her five children in 2002. The conviction is overturned on the basis of a prosecution witness who told an untruth in the trial and a new trial was ordered.

February 2, 1935: The first lie detector was used in a court of law for consideration by a jury. This was the Keeler polygraph, invented by Leonarde Keeler of the Scientific Crime Detection Laboratory, Northwestern University School of Law, in Evanston, Illinois. Keeler conducted a lie detector test in Portage, Wisconsin, on two defendants and produced a graph of his test results in the case of *Wisconsin State v. Cecil Loniello & Tony Grignano*. Both defendants were found guilty of assault and sentenced by Judge Clayton F. Van Pelt of the Circuit Court of Columbia County, Wisconsin.

February 4, 1976: Heiress to the Hearst fortune and apolitical college student, Patty Hearst was kidnapped by the radical Symbionese Liberation Army (SLA) in February 1974. During her 18 months as a kidnap victim, she participated in illegal activities with the SLA. After she was rescued by the FBI, she was charged with bank robbery and other crimes. Her trial begins on this date and ends on March 20, 1976.

March 20, 1976: Newspaper heiress Patricia Hearst is convicted of armed robbery for her part in a San Francisco bank holdup while kidnapped by the SLA.

June 16, 1987: Subway gunman Bernhard Goetz is acquitted on all but gun possession charges after shooting four black youths who tried to rob him on the New York City subway.

July 8, 1994: After a preliminary hearing, the judge rules there is enough evidence to try former football star O. J. Simpson. He is ordered to stand trial on two counts of first degree murder in the slayings of his ex-wife, Nicole Brown Simpson, and her friend, Ronald Goldman.

July 17, 1922:   The James Frye murder trial begins in Washington, D.C. Frye, an African American, was charged with the murder of Dr. Brown. Frye had initially confessed, then later withdrew his confession. The defense was based on Frye's alibi plus William Marston's use of his crude lie detector test on Frye. Marston was convinced of Frye's innocence. However, Judge William McCoy refused to allow Marston to testify or to conduct a demonstration of his lie detector in the court. McCoy ruled that lie detection was not yet "a matter of common knowledge." The jury, however, heard the arguments and knew Marston believed Frye was innocent. The jury found him guilty not of first degree murder, but second degree murder. The court of appeals of the District of Columbia upheld McCoy's rejection of the test. In doing so, it laid down a rule that would ban the lie detector from criminal courts for the rest of the century and set criteria for the admission of all scientific evidence for the next 60 years. What mattered, the court of appeals declared in 1923, was whether the science was widely deemed acceptable by the relevant scientific experts. In its ruling, the court of appeals noted that the lie detector had yet to gain "general acceptance in the particular field to which it belongs."

July 22, 1994:   O. J. Simpson pleads "Absolutely 100% Not Guilty" to two charges of murder.

October 3, 1995:   The O. J. Simpson verdict is announced on national television. The jury acquits him of both counts of murder.

October 20, 1987:   Subway gunman Bernhard Goetz is sentenced to six months in jail.

Important Court Cases

- *Richmond Newspapers, Inc. v. Virginia*, **448 U.S. 555 (1980):** The U.S. Supreme Court in this case announced that the public and the press have a First Amendment right to attend criminal trials.
- *Daubert v. Merrill Dow*, **509 U.S. 579 (1993):** In the previous case (related to lie detector tests and results reported by expert witnesses in court) of *Frye v. United States* (1923), the Court held that in order for scientific testimony to be admissible as evidence it had to be generally accepted by scientists. This rule meant that most scientific testimony had to be based on data published in journals and subjected to peer review, and was designed to protect jurors from so-called junk science that could mislead them. In this 1993 case, the Court revised the rule previously given in Frye and held that pertinent evidence based on scientifically valid principles could be used as long as it was relevant and reliable. The Daubert ruling opened the door to more and different kinds of scientific testimony.

Websites to Check Out

- *Criminal Evidence. Findlaw.com.* Available at: *http://criminal.findlaw.com/criminal-procedure/criminal-evidence/.* The *Findlaw.com* website features information about evidence in criminal trials and has links to many articles about evidence.
- *Criminal Trial Procedures: An Overview. Nolo Law for All.com.* Available at: *http://www.nolo.com/legal-encyclo-pedia/criminal-trial-procedures-overview-29509.html.* This is an informational website that gives facts about various aspects of criminal trials.

Books

- Goldberg, J. (2010). *Preparation and Trial for a Federal Criminal case.* Bloomington, IN: Xlibris.
- Koski, D. (2003). *The Jury Trial in Criminal Justice.* Durham, NC: Carolina Academic Press.
- Spohn, C. C., and Hemmens, C. (2008). *Courts: A Text/Reader.* Thousand Oaks, CA: Sage.

Movies

- *Compulsion:* This 1959 movie is based on the trial of Nathan Leopold and Richard Loeb. Leopold and Loeb's murder of a young boy has been called the "crime of the century."
- *The Lindbergh Kidnapping* Case: Anthony Hopkins plays Bruno Hauptmann in this 1976 movie about the trial of the man accused of kidnapping and murdering the infant son of Charles Lindbergh.
- *Crime of the Century:* An HBO movie from 1996 about the trial and conviction of Bruno Hauptmann.

Plays

- *Never the Sinner:* An award-winning 1985 play about the Leopold and Loeb trial and their defense, which was handled by Clarence Darrow.

TV Shows

- *The O. J. Simpson Trial: Beyond Black and White:* A 1997 television show analyzing the African American perspective on the O. J. Simpson murder trial.
- *Why O. J. Won:* An A&E TV American Justice program that tries to answer the questions about how Simpson was acquitted of murder.
- *ABC News Nighttime: Closing Arguments in the O. J. Simpson Case:* ABC News analyzes the three days of closing arguments in the O. J. Simpson murder trial.

Review for Chapter Eleven:

Research Paper or Term Paper Topics:

- How a criminal trial is conducted
- What the defense and prosecution can and cannot do in closing arguments

Important Terms to Know

Actus reus:
In the criminal justice system, there must be a criminal act—something external to the mind of the accused—that shows that the defendant performed a physical action that was criminal in nature.

Beyond a reasonable doubt:
Defendants are presumed to be innocent, and it is the state's burden to prove them guilty. The standard for proof in the criminal justice system is "beyond a reasonable doubt." This means that jurors must be convinced beyond a reasonable doubt—or to a moral certainty—that the defendant is guilty.

Charging the jury:
The judge charges the jury after the closing arguments have been given and before the jury starts deliberating. The charge, or the judge's instructions to the jury, concerns the law that applies to the facts of the case in the trial.

Circumstantial evidence: Circumstantial evidence is indirect evidence which infers, rather than shows with certainty, that the defendant is guilty. The jury must make a connection between the indirect evidence and the crime.

Hearsay evidence:
Hearsay is a statement made in court by a witness about another statement uttered by a person not present in court. Generally, hearsay evidence is not acceptable in court.

Mens rea:
Mens rea is the mental act of a crime. Not only must a physical act have occurred, but the individual must have had a guilty mind or criminal intent.

Opening statement:
In a criminal trial, both the prosecution and the defense get to make an opening statement in a trial. The opening statement often serves as a road map as the attorney (either the prosecution or the defense) outlines what he or she plans to prove with evidence during the trial.

Rebuttal:
A rebuttal is evidence introduced in a trial to counter, disprove, or contradict the opposition's evidence. It is the prosecution that may call a rebuttal witness to bolster its position in proving the defendant guilty.

Study Guide Questions

True or False:

1. The "presumption of innocence" means that every defendant who has a criminal trial is presumed—or assumed—to be innocent.

2. *Mens rea* is a Latin term meaning "the guilty mind."

3. Testimonial evidence refers to real evidence.

4. At the end of the prosecution's case, the defense can ask the judge for a directed verdict of not guilty.

Multiple Choice Items:

5. The burden of proof in a criminal trial is
    a. a preponderance of the evidence
    b. proof through forensic evidence
    c. an accumulation of circumstantial evidence
    d. beyond a reasonable doubt

6. Neither attorney in his or her opening statement is allowed to
    a. accuse the defendant of a brutal crime
    b. talk about the defendant's life
    c. make prejudicial statements
    d. talk about the defendant's mental state

7. The prosecutor's evidence against the defendant must be relevant. However, the evidence presented by the prosecution will be inadmissible if it
    a. implies the guilt of the defendant
    b. is illegally obtained
    c. upsets the defense counsel
    d. came about through the prosecutor's investigation of the case

8. If the defense fails to put on a defense, then
    a. the jury can imply nothing from this
    b. the jury must find the defendant guilty
    c. the judge can force the defense to present a case
    d. the defendant should ask for new counsel

References

Castellano, A., (June 26, 2012), "Grosse Pointe killing: Bob Bashara accused of trying to kill alleged hit man," *ABC News* [online], Available at: http://abcnews.go.com/blogs/headlines/2012/06/grosse-pointe-murder-bob-bashara-accused-of-trying-to-kill-alleged-hit-man/.

Siegel, L. J., and Worrall, J. L. (2012). *Introduction to Criminal Justice*. 13th ed. Belmont, CA: Wadsworth.

Territo, L., Halsted, J. B., and Bromley, M. L. (2004). *Crime and Justice in America*. 6th ed. Upper Saddle River, NJ: Pearson.

Chapter Twelve

The Jury Decides

The Jury in Criminal Trials

Before we discuss what happens in jury deliberations leading up to a description of the final verdict, it may be good to backtrack and talk more about criminal trials and juries.

One of the most distinctive features of the criminal justice system in the United States is a trial by a jury of one's peers. As we indicated previously, that is a right given to every citizen by the Sixth Amendment. However, as we saw in Chapter Ten, prosecutors and defense attorneys have found ways around guaranteeing a defendant a trial by a jury of his or her peers. The *voir dire* process gives opportunities for prosecutors, particularly, to eliminate jurors that might—at least in some instances—provide for a more fair trial by a jury.

But there is another problem that is perhaps even more serious than the use of challenges to eliminate jurors the prosecutor doesn't want on the jury. That other problem is plea bargaining. When we discussed plea bargaining in a previous chapter, it was stated that upward of 95 percent of all defendants never go to trial where it is up to a jury to decide the guilt or innocence of that defendant. That means that somewhat less than five percent of all cases actually go to trial—all the rest plead guilty and accept a plea deal.

When a case does go to trial, the jury itself is often composed of people who could not find an excuse not to serve (Kappeler & Potter, 2005). That may mean that more juries have people serving who are senior citizens, have a job that pays them to serve on a jury,

Because we believe that trial by jury in criminal cases is fundamental to the American scheme of justice, we hold that the Fourteenth Amendment guarantees a right of jury trial in all criminal cases which—were they to be tried in a federal court—would come within the Sixth Amendment guarantee.

—*Justice Byron R. White,* Duncan v. Louisiana, *391 U.S. 145 149 (1968)*

or who are not working or are not gainfully employed. Some critics of our jury system go so far as to contend that the end result of the jury selection process is that juries are often composed of people who are uneducated, uninformed, and generally inexperienced at making any type of well-considered decision (Schmalleger, 2012).

And that raises the question: What is a jury of one's peers?

In many jurisdictions, jury pools are selected from voter registration lists. About 30 percent of eligible voters do not register; in some areas that rate can be as high as 60 percent (Bohm & Haley, 2012). People who are not registered voters are, therefore, excluded from jury service. Some studies show that the people least likely to register to vote are the poor, the poorly educated, the young, and people of color (Bohm & Haley, 2012). Again, this indicates that these categories of citizens are least likely to serve on juries.

To deal with the problem of an unrepresentative jury pool, some parts of the country now use multiple-source lists for obtaining jurors. In addition to voter registration lists, their sources include lists of licensed drivers, lists of utility users, and names listed in telephone directories. Appellate courts have ruled that master jury lists must reflect an impartial and representative cross-section of the population (Bohm & Haley, 2012). The courts have also ruled that people cannot be excluded systematically from juries because of race, ethnicity, or gender. This does not mean that women or people of color must be included on all juries—just that they cannot be denied the opportunity to serve as jurors.

The lack of diversity on juries has been addressed in some jurisdictions such as Wayne County, Michigan, which includes the city of Detroit. While Wayne County has a 20 percent minority rate in the population, it has been found that only about 11 percent of the people seated on juries in the Detroit area are minorities. To counteract this problem and increase the diversity of juries, a group of circuit court judges and an ad hoc committee have made several recommendations. Among those recommendations are:

- Improve the accuracy of address records.
- Use stronger language on the second notice, if there was no response to the first jury summons.
- Use state tax lists to randomly select potential jurors (Pardo, 2012).

What about jury tampering? Kappeler and Potter (2005) suggest that skillful defense attorneys as well as prosecutors find ways to tamper with juries within the bounds of what is legal. For instance, as Kappeler and Potter point out, the law only prevents direct contact with jurors during or before the trial. The law does not prohibit using the media to plant seeds in the public's—and potential jurors'—minds. Another legal resource, if the defendant can afford it, is the jury consultant. A jury consultant investigates each juror or potential juror to try to predict how he or she will respond to almost every aspect of the trial. Depending on what the consultant figures out about each juror, he or she can advise the defense attorney about how to frame his or her opening argument, how to cross-examine certain witnesses, and how to give his or her closing argument.

JURY DELIBERATIONS

After the instructions are given to the jury, the jury retires to a room to decide whether the prosecution proved its case beyond a reasonable doubt. The conduct of jurors and the procedures governing jury deliberations are established by local statutes and court rules. In general, however, the rules usually restrict jurors from communicating with anyone except the bailiff or the judge during their deliberations.

Most jurisdictions do not allow the jury to separate once deliberations have begun (Territo et al., 2004), although in most unsensational cases in a trial, court jurors may be allowed to go home to sleep and then return the next day to continue deliberation. A review of the case by the jury may take hours or even days.

Myth:	*A jury is always 12 people.*
Reality:	*A jury can be any size as long as it is made up of at least six individuals.*

WHAT HAPPENS IN THE JURY ROOM?

In cases in which the evidence is either very clear or very weak, jury deliberation may be brief, lasting only a matter of hours, or even just minutes. Some juries, on the other hand, deliberate days or sometimes weeks, carefully weighing all the nuances of the evidence they have seen and heard (Schmalleger, 2012).

When there are prolonged deliberations, it is often the case that one or two jurors are holding out for a different verdict than the majority of other jurors. Some jurors are not able to separate their emotions from the facts and thus they perceive things markedly different from the other jurors. And because jurors are drawn from all walks of life and with many diverse personality traits and cognitive abilities, many are unable to understand modern legal complexities and to appreciate all the nuances of trial court practice (Schmalleger, 2012). It is also likely that for some jurors, even the instructions given them by the judge are too detailed and complex (Elwork, Sales and Alfini, 1982).

JURY NULLIFICATION

The right to a jury trial is based on the belief that the defendant is entitled to have his or her case decided by those who represent community values (Reid, 2009). Because of this, a jury may ignore the facts and the law and acquit a defendant even when the facts clearly point to guilt. This is called jury nullification.

> **Myth:** *Jurors are always instructed in the law by the judge; therefore, during deliberations, they will put aside their own feelings in order to decide guilt or innocence based strictly on the law.*
>
> **Reality:** *Once they are in the jury room, jurors can decide a case based on their own emotions or on their interpretation of the law.*

At times, jury nullification has played a noble role in upholding the conscience of the community against unjust laws (for instance, by acquitting a family member who has performed a mercy killing of another family member who was dying and in constant pain), but at other times it has played a more ignoble role by maintaining inequality within the society (such as when all-white juries convict African American defendants when there is scanty evidence of guilt) (Boyes-Watson, 2003).

The courts have upheld the ultimate power of the jury to acquit defendants by going against the facts by recognizing that it is a power that cannot be taken away from juries (Boyes-Watson, 2003). In the 1920 case of *Horning v. District of Columbia*, the U.S. Supreme Court recognized the undisputed power of the jury to "decide against the law and the facts" if that is what they choose (*Horning v. District of Columbia*, 254 U.S. 135, 138 [1920], p. 135).

Yet, the courts have decided that juries should not be fully informed of this power, either in the judge's instructions or by statements in front of the jury by defense counsel (Boyes-Watson, 2003). The courts have said that to inform juries of this power is to invite anarchy. Consequently, the defense is not allowed to tell juries that they may disregard the law in making their decision (*Horning v. District of Columbia*, 254 U.S. 135 [1920]).

> **Myth:** *A hung jury will result in the prosecutor retrying the defendant in a new trial.*
>
> **Reality:** *Many times prosecutors decide that it is too costly in terms of time and money to retry a case.*

The number of juries failing to reach a consensus in criminal trials—resulting in a hung jury and a mistrial—has generally remained constant at about five percent (Barkan & Bryjak, 2004). However, in some jurisdictions, that number has dramatically increased, and this has been attributed to race-based decisions (Biskupic, 1999). Race also seems to be related to an increasing number of acquittals. For instance, in the New York City borough the Bronx, where more than 80 percent of juries are comprised of African Americans and Hispanics, African American defendants are acquitted in 47.6 percent of felony cases (Barkan & Bryjak, 2004).

Because juries need not discuss their deliberations with others after the verdict is rendered, no one knows how often their decisions are affected by factors that are not supposed to be considered in criminal cases—such as the defendant's race, gender, social class, or physical attractiveness (Masters et al., 2013).

Reaching a Consensus

If a verdict cannot be reached, the trial might result in a hung jury. However, most judges will generally send the jury back for further deliberation before declaring a mistrial. If a mistrial is declared by the judge, it is up to the prosecution as to whether the defendant will have a completely new trial. Recent data shows that in the small number of jury trials, hung juries occur infrequently (in about three to six percent of the trials) (Bohm & Haley, 2012). Defense attorneys routinely ask judges to acquit the defendant when a mistrial has been declared because of a hung jury. Should this request be denied, the prosecutor must decide if the case warrants a second trial. A new trial is most likely when the case is a high-profile case and the prosecutor believes that the reputation of the department is at stake, or when the prosecutor believes that the public wants the case retried (Barkan & Bryjak, 2004).

When the jury has reached a verdict, they return to the courtroom and the decision is read. Although it is uncommon, either attorney may request that the court poll the jury, with the judge asking each juror if the verdict reflects his or her opinion (Barkan & Bryjak, 2004). Approximately two thirds of all criminal trial juries find for the state and convict the defendant (Barkan & Bryjak, 2004). If the verdict is not guilty, the defendant is released from the criminal justice system. If the verdict is guilty, the individual is taken into custody to await sentencing. Although in misdemeanor cases the judge may announce an immediate sentence, in felony cases typically the judge sets a date for sentencing.

In the next chapter, we explore what happens after a guilty verdict is delivered by the jury.

FOR FURTHER CONSIDERATION

Historical Events Relevant to Chapter Twelve

March 23, 1987:   Jury selection begins in the trial for Bernhard Goetz, who, while riding on a New York City subway train in December 1984, shot four black youths who had approached him and demanded money. Goetz was brought to trial on 13 charges, ranging from attempted murder to criminal possession of a gun. The jury deliberated over three days before reaching verdicts on the 13 counts. The jury found him not guilty on all counts except for one: criminal possession of a firearm in the third degree.

June 10, 1868:   Jury selection begins in the murder trial of Hester Vaughan, a young, unmarried woman, accused of killing her newborn baby. The ultimate jury was all men; the prosecutor was a man, her defense attorney was male, and the judge who sentenced her to die after she was found guilty of murder was a man. The case got the attention of many prominent women, including Elizabeth Cady Stanton, Susan B. Anthony, and other members of the Working Women's National Association. They called on Pennsylvania's governor (John W. Geary) to pardon Ms. Vaughan. Cady, Stanton, and other women across the country protested the trial and the sentence, claiming that Ms. Vaughan had been denied a fundamental right: a trial by a jury of her peers. They contended that women should be tried by a jury of their peers, and in addition, should have a voice in making the laws and electing judges. Finally, in the summer of 1869, Governor Geary pardoned Vaughan.

July 15, 1968:   The trial for Huey P. Newton, an African American man and cofounder and "minister of defense" for the Black Panther Party, begins on this date. He was charged with murdering a police officer. During the *voir dire*, Newton's defense attorney, Charles Garry, probed the jurors' attitudes about race, the Black Panther Party, the Vietnam War, and the police. Garry implied that Newton could not get a fair trial because of the public's (and the jurors') attitudes about blacks and the Black Panther Party. The jury returned after the trial concluded with a verdict of not guilty of murder but guilty of voluntary manslaughter.

November 3, 1919:   After a trial lasting 45 minutes, an all-white jury in Arkansas deliberated for five minutes before returning a verdict of guilty against Frank Moore and 11 other African Americans, who were all charged with the murder of a white man. The sentence of death for Moore and the others was given by the judge. The case was appealed to the U.S. Supreme Court by the NAACP, and the Supreme Court overturned the verdict and the sentence. Led by Justice Oliver Wendell Holmes, the Court said that a threatening mob inflamed racial prejudice, making the trial "absolutely void."

Important Court Cases

- ***Williams v. Florida,* 399 U.S. 78 (1970):** Williams was tried for a felony and convicted by a jury of six persons in Florida. Florida had passed a law in 1967 permitting a six-person jury for all but capital cases. Williams had argued in a pre-trial motion that he should have a jury of 12, because a smaller jury would deprive him of his Sixth Amendment right to trial by jury. Justice Byron White, in writing the majority opinion, stated that a six-person jury was the "functional equivalent" of a 12-person jury.
- ***Maxwell v. Dow,* 1767 U.SD. 581 (1900):** Charles Maxwell challenged his conviction for robbery on the basis that he was denied due process rights under the Fourteenth Amendment because the jury was composed of eight people, not twelve. The Supreme Court rejected his argument, although Justice John Marshall Harlan dissented and said that states could not avoid the Sixth Amendment's guarantee of a trial by a jury of twelve persons.
- ***Apodaca v. Oregon,* 406 U.S. 404 (1972):** The U.S. Supreme Court in this case held that the Sixth Amendment jury trial guarantee does not require a unanimous jury verdict in non-capital criminal cases. The Court was split 5 to 4 in this decision, with the dissenters arguing that a non-unanimous verdict was inconsistent with the constitutional requirement that a criminal jury's decision be "beyond a reasonable doubt." However, since this decision in 1972, few states have adopted the non-unanimous rule.
- ***Ballew v. Georgia,* 435 U.S. 223 (1978):** Ballew was tried and convicted of a misdemeanor by a jury of five persons. He appealed, arguing that his Sixth and Fourteenth Amendment rights to a trial by jury were violated. By a 9 to 0 decision, the U.S. Supreme Court ruled in favor of Ballew. Justice Harry Blackmun, writing for the Court, stated that a criminal jury of five was unable to fulfill the constitutional purposes and functions of a jury. Blackmun cited studies which raised significant questions about both the wisdom and constitutionality of juries below six in number.

Websites to Check Out

- *American Bar Association. Jury trials and juries.* Available at: *http://search.americanbar.org/search?q=jury+trials&client=default_frontend&proxystylesheet=default_frontend&site=default_collection&output=xml_no_dtd&oe=UTF-8&ie=UTF-8&ud=1.* The American Bar Association's website features considerable information about juries and jury trials in criminal cases.
- *Jury Instructions. American College of Trial Lawyers.* Available at: *http://www.actl.com/Content/NavigationMenu/Publications/AllPublications/default.htm.* The American College of Trial Lawyers' website, this site has many articles available to read relating to trials and juries.

Books

- Abramson, J. (2000). *We, the Jury: The Jury System and the Ideal of Democracy.* Cambridge, MA: Harvard University Press.
- Conrad, C., and Conrad, C. S. (1999). *Jury Nullification: The Evolution of a Doctrine.* Durham, NC: Carolina Academic Press.

- Kassin, S. M., and Wrightsman, L. S. (1988). *The American Jury on Trial: Psychological Perspectives.* New York: Taylor and Francis.

Movies

- *Twelve Angry Men:* This classic 1957 movie depicts what goes on in the jury room during negotiations following a homicide trial. It was remade in 1997 for television, with much of the action and dialogue similar to the original.
- *Inside the Jury Room*: This is a documentary film produced in 1986 and seen on television that takes viewers inside a jury room in a real criminal court trial.

TV Shows

- *Law & Order: Trial by Jury:* This *Law & Order* spinoff was on for one season in 2005–2006. In its 13 episodes, it provides a view of both the prosecution and the defense preparations for trial. In addition, the show gave a glimpse of jury selection and action among the jurors during deliberations.

Review for Chapter Eleven:

Research Paper or Term Paper Topics:

- Jury nullification
- What is a jury of one's peers?

Important Terms to Know

Hung jury:	A hung jury is one that cannot reach a verdict. It means that the jury will be dismissed and the defendant may be retried in a second trial.
Jury deliberations:	Discussion among jury members to weigh the evidence that was presented during the trial and arrive at a verdict.
Jury nullification:	The power of jurors to ignore the law and decide cases according to extralegal considerations, such as emotions or community values.

Jury tampering: Attempts to influence a jury through any means other than presenting evidence and argument in court, including conversations about the case outside the court, offering bribes, making threats, or asking acquaintances to intercede with a juror.

Study Guide Questions

True or False:

1. The Sixth Amendment guarantees defendants the right to a trial by an impartial jury.

2. In many jurisdictions, jurors are selected randomly from lists of registered voters.

3. A jury consultant tries to influence jurors to support one side.

4. A sequestered jury is one that has to sleep in the jury room.

Multiple Choice Items:

5. The problem with selecting jurors from voter registration lists is that
   a. voters are typically unintelligent
   b. up to 30 percent of adults don't register to vote
   c. people who register to vote may make poor decisions
   d. voters never update their addresses

6. During deliberations, jurors can only communicate with
   a. anyone on the Internet
   b. the defendant
   c. close friends and relatives
   d. the bailiff or the judge

7. An example of jury nullification is when
   a. the judge in a murder case says the jury's verdict is null and void
   b. the jury convicts an innocent man because they believe the evidence is conclusive
   c. the jury refuses to convict a defendant because they believe his crime was justified
   d. the prosecutor talks persuasively to the jury during deliberations

8. A hung jury means that
    a. the jury cannot reach a decision
    b. the jury members have all been sentenced to hang
    c. the judge disagrees with the jury's verdict
    d. the defendant will be allowed to go home

References

Barkan, S. E., and Bryjak, G. J. (2004). *Fundamentals of Criminal Justice.* Boston: Pearson.

Biskupic, J. (February 8, 1999). In jury rooms, form of civil protest grows. *Washington Post* p. A1.

Bohm, R. H., and Haley, K. N. (2012). *Introduction to Criminal Justice.* 7th ed. New York: McGraw-Hill.

Boyes-Watson, C. (2003). *Crime and Justice: A Casebook Approach.* Boston: Pearson.

Elwork, A. , Alfini, J. J., and Sales, B. D. (1982). Toward understandable jury instructions. *Judicature* 65:8/ 9:432–443.

Horning v. District of Columbia, 254 U.S. 135 (1920).

Kappeler, V. E., and Potter, G. W. (2005). *The Mythology of Crime and Criminal Justice.* 4th ed. Long Grove, IL: Waveland Press, Inc.

Masters, R. E., Way, L. B., Gerstenfeld, P. B., Muscat, B. T., Hooper, M., Dussich, J. P. J., Pincu, L., and Skrapec, C. A. (2013). *CJ: Realities and Challenges.* 2nd ed. New York: McGraw-Hill.

Pardo, S., (June 25, 2012), "Lack of jury diversity studied," *Detroit News* [online], Available at: http://www.detroitnews.com/article/20120625/METRO01/206250346.

Reid, S. T. (2009). *Crime and Criminology.* 12th ed. New York: Oxford University Press.

Schmalleger, F. (2012). *Criminal Justice: A Brief Introduction.* 9th ed. Upper Saddle River, NJ: Prentice Hall.

Territo, L., Halsted, J. B., and Bromley, M. L. (2004). *Crime and Justice in America.* 6th ed. Upper Saddle River, NJ: Pearson.

BEHIND CLOSED DOORS

A Guide for Jury Deliberation

Introduction

You will be instructed on the law in this case. Please read this information for tips on how you may consider evidence and how you may reach a verdict. You are free to deliberate in any way you wish. These are suggestions to help you proceed with the deliberations in a smooth and timely way.

Before you get started, it would be useful to think about the following guidelines for jurors:

- Follow judge's instructions about the law.
- Respect each other's opinions and value the different viewpoints you each bring to the case.
- It is okay to change your mind.
- Listen to one another, do not let yourself be bullied into changing your opinion, and do not bully anyone else.
- Do not rush into a verdict to save time. The people in this case deserve your complete attention and thoughtful consideration.

Getting Started

Q. How do we start?
A. At first, you might want to:
- Take some time to get to know one another.
- Talk about your feelings and what you think about the case.
- Talk about how you want to go ahead with the deliberations and lay out some rules to guide you.
- Talk about how to handle voting.

Selecting the Presiding Juror

Q. What qualities should we consider when choosing the presiding juror?
A. Suggestions include someone who:
- Is a good discussion leader.
- Is fair.
- Is a good listener.
- Is a good speaker.
- Is organized.

From *Behind Closed Doors A Guide for Jury Deliberation*, pp. 3-10. Copyright © 1999 by American Judicature Society. Reprinted with permission of the American Judicature Society. Content prepared by the American Judicature Society in cooperation with the Superior Court of Arizona in Maricopa County, under a grant from the Bureau of Justice Assistance, U.S. Department of Justice #97-DD-BX-0054.

Q. What are the responsibilities of the presiding juror?
A. The presiding juror should:
- Encourage discussions that include all jurors.
- Keep the deliberations focused on the evidence and the law.
- Let the court know when there are any questions or problems.
- Tell the court when a verdict has been reached.

Q. Are there any set rules to tell us how to deliberate?
A. No. You could:
- Go around the table, one by one, to talk about the case.
- Have jurors speak up anytime, when they have something to say.
- Try to get everyone to talk by saying something like, "Does anyone else have anything to add?"
- Show respect to the other jurors by looking at the person speaking.
- Do not be afraid to speak up and express your views.
- Have someone take notes during your deliberations so that you do not forget the important points.
- Write down key points so that everyone can see them.

Discussing the Evidence and the Law

Q. What do we do now?
A. First, review the judge's instructions on the law because the instructions tell you what to do.

Q. Is there a set way to examine and weigh the evidence and to apply the law?
A. The judge's instructions will tell you if there are special rules or a set process you should follow. Otherwise you are free to conduct your deliberations in whatever way is helpful. Here are several suggestions:
- Look at the judge's instructions that define each charge or claim and list each separate element that make up that charge or claim.
- For each of these elements, review the evidence, both the exhibits and witness testimony, to see if each element has been established by the evidence.
- If there is a lot of evidence, try listing each piece of it next to the elements it applies to.
- Discuss each charge or claim, one at a time.
- Vote on each charge or claim.
- Fill out the verdict form(s) given to you by the judge.

Q. What if someone is not following the instructions, refuses to deliberate, or relies on other information outside of the evidence?
A. This is a violation of a juror's oath and the court should be told.

Voting

Q. When should we take the first vote?
A. There is no best time. But, if you spend a reasonable amount of time considering the evidence and the law and listening to each other's opinions, you will probably feel more confident and satisfied with your eventual verdict than if you rush things.

Q. Is there any correct way to take the vote?
A. No, any way is okay. You might vote by raising your hands, by a written ballot, or by a voice ballot. Eventually, a final vote in the jury room will have to be taken with each of you expressing your verdict openly to the other jurors.

Q. What if we cannot reach a verdict after trying many times to do so?
A. Ask the judge for advice on how to proceed.

Getting Assistance from the Court

Q. What if we don't understand or are confused by something in the judge's instructions, such as a legal principle or definition?
A. Ask the judge because you must understand the instructions in order to do a good job.
- There may be some information you ask for that the judge is unable to give you.

Q. How do we get more information?
A. Write the question on a piece of paper and have the presiding juror give it to the jury bailiff.

Q. Is there any type of information we cannot ask for?
A. Yes, some examples of information you cannot ask for include:
- Police reports, doctors' reports, etc., that were referred to during the trial, but were not received in evidence as an exhibit.
- Reports and other information that were not referred to during the trial, but which you assume might or should be available.

The Verdict

Q. After we have reached a verdict and signed the verdict form(s), how do we turn our verdict over to the court?
A. The following steps are usually followed:
- The presiding juror tells the attending jury bailiff that a verdict has been reached.
- The judge calls everyone, including you, back into the courtroom.
- The clerk in the courtroom asks the presiding juror for the verdict.
- The verdict is read into the record in open court.

Q. Who reads the verdict?

A. The verdict will be read into the record by the clerk, the judge or some other court official. The judge may ask for an individual poll of each of you to see if you agree with the verdict. You need only answer "yes" or "no" OR "not guilty" or "guilty" to the question asked by the judge.

Once Jury Duty is Over

Q. Now that the case is over, may we speak with others about the case and the deliberations?

A. Yes, if you choose to do so.

Q. How do we know we have done the right thing?

A. If you have tried your best, you have done the right thing. Making decisions as jurors about the lives, events and facts in a trial is always difficult. Regardless of the outcome of this case, you have performed an invaluable service for the people in this case and for the system of justice in our community.

We thank you for your time and thoughtful deliberations.

This guide is not intended to take the place of any instructions given you by the judge.

This guide was originally developed by the American Judicature Society. With their permission, the Wisconsin Chief Judges' Subcommittee on Juror Treatment and Selection tailored the guide for use in Wisconsin Courts.

Part Five

Sentencing, Corrections, and Alternatives

Chapter Thirteen

The Sentencing Hearing

There are over one million felony convictions each year in state courts and more than 75,000 felony convictions in federal courts (Fagin, 2007). For each conviction, there must be a sentence. That means that following each conviction—whether it comes about through a plea bargain or through the verdict of a jury—a judge must impose a sentence. But as will be discussed in this chapter, there is great variety in the sentencing of defendants. Before discussing sentences, though, it is important to discuss appeals of convictions.

APPEALS

The imposition of a sentence does not mean that the defendant must serve it immediately. He or she typically has the right to appeal. Furthermore, the right to counsel for indigent defendants continues through the first appeal (Priehs, 1999).

An appeal is a request to a higher court to review actions taken in a completed trial. An appeal is contained in a brief, which explains the alleged errors made during the trial. Usually such alleged errors have to do with claims of errors of law or procedure made during the investigation, arrest, or trial process (Cole & Smith, 2007). Appeals are related to questions of procedure, not on issues of the defendant's guilt or innocence. Appellate courts will not

For the past three decades, those arrested for crack offenses—mostly young, African American men—faced far harsher penalties than the white and Hispanic suspects most often caught with powder cocaine.

—*Editorial,* Washington Post, *August 3, 2010*

normally second-guess a jury, but instead will check to make sure that the trial followed proper procedures (Cole & Smith, 2007).

The appellate court, consisting of a panel of several judges, will review the brief and the trial transcript. If the court finds that there is no basis for the appeal, the appeal is dismissed. If the panel believes there may be merit to the appeal, the court holds a hearing in which the defense and the prosecution present arguments on the issue raised in the brief (Albanese, 2013). Sometime after the hearing and a review of the brief and the trial transcript, the judges on the appeals court will discuss the issue and vote either to affirm the conviction by leaving it undisturbed, or to reverse the conviction by overturning it on the grounds that a significant legal error was made either before or during the trial.

Most appeals are unsuccessful (Albanese, 2013). If the appeal is unsuccessful, the defendant has no alternative but to accept the trial court's verdict. If, however, there is an allegation of a violation of the defendant's constitutional rights, then the appeal could go to the federal courts. However, the U.S. Supreme Court is the court of last resort in an attempt to overturn a conviction. In the rare event that a conviction is reversed, the case usually is retried in the original court. The reversal of the conviction renders the initial trial a mistrial, and the retrial is treated as the first trial under the law (Albanese, 2013).

Myth:	*If a defendant is convicted in a trial, appealing the decision can result in the conviction being overturned.*
Reality:	*An appeal might result in the conviction being overturned, but in a majority of cases the original verdict is affirmed by a higher court.*

A five-state study found that appeals have increased in recent decades. Although this study found a majority of appeals occurred after trial convictions, about a quarter of the appeals related to non–trial proceedings, such as guilty pleas and probation revocations (Chapper & Hanson, 1989). Furthermore, the study found that homicides and other serious crimes against people account for more than 50 percent of appeals, and the issues raised at appeal most often tend to concern the introduction of evidence, the sufficiency of evidence, and jury instructions (Chapper & Hanson, 1989). Finally, in almost 80 percent of the cases Chapper and Hanson examined, the decision of the trial courts was affirmed.

DETERMINING THE SENTENCE

How do judges determine the sentence they hand down? Judges are guided by the law and by sentencing guidelines put out by the federal government. Sentencing guidelines are usually enacted when criminal laws are passed by municipalities and the state legislature, as the laws often include the type and range of punishments that accompany those criminal statutes. Because laws are passed by legislators, those laws—and the punishments prescribed for criminal offenses—are frequently based on public sentiment related to civic reaction to recent crimes. There is, however, a degree of latitude afforded judges, which allows judges to individualize sentences on the basis of the nature of the offender and the circumstances of the offense.

PUNISHMENT

The history of punishment in the United States is rooted in economic sanctions, corporal punishment, and death (Fagin, 2007). However, the concept of incarceration in jail or prison as punishment for crime is a fairly new philosophy in the criminal justice system. Historically, punishments in England, and later in the American colonies, consisted primarily of fines, ordeals, and torture. Criminals who could not afford to pay the fines imposed on them as punishment could be sold into economic servitude—a form of slavery—to pay the fines. Corporal punishment included whipping, branding, dunking, the stocks or pillory, and other pain-inflicting rituals (Fagin, 2007).

There are five basic philosophies regarding the purpose of punishment:

- Deterrence
- Incapacitation
- Retribution
- Rehabilitation
- Restorative justice

Deterrence aims to prevent crime through the example of an offender's punishment. General deterrence is directed at preventing crime among the general population, while specific deterrence is aimed at preventing future crimes by a particular offender (Albanese, 2013). A major problem with deterrence as a philosophy is that it is difficult to demonstrate its effectiveness. There is virtually no reliable evidence that suggests that punishment and sanctions deter crime (Albanese, 2013).

Incapacitation is a philosophy that seeks to prevent future criminal behavior by a specific offender by physically restraining the offender. The primary method of incapacitation in the United States is through incarceration. One criticism of incapacitation is that it is unclear how long an offender must be imprisoned before he or she no longer poses a threat to society. Also, it is economically unfeasible to lock up large numbers of offenders for long periods of time. Higher prison costs, the need to support families on welfare, and the inability to predict future criminal behaviors make incapacitation both expensive and uncertain over the long term (Albanese, 2013).

> **Myth:** *Putting more people in prison will reduce the crime rate because all the criminals will be locked up and incapacitated.*
>
> **Reality:** *Scientists have concluded that placing more people in prison has little to no effect on the crime rate.*

Retribution is a philosophy of deterrence based on the premise that criminals should be punished because they deserve it (Fagin, 2007). Retribution is associated with "get-tough" sentencing and the philosophy of an eye for an eye, which advocates that those who do wrong should pay for their crimes in equal measure (Fagin, 2007). Those who believe in retribution often want to see offenders receive harsh punishments and they frequently believe that prison conditions should be harsh and cruel.

Rehabilitation is a philosophy and an approach that tends to view criminal behavior as a consequence of social conditions or psychological problems. The purpose of a sentence using the rehabilitation philosophy is to correct or treat the underlying conditions or problems in order to prevent future crimes. It is assumed in this approach that we can identify and treat the social conditions or psychological shortcomings of offenders. However, the results of rehabilitation efforts to date have been discouraging (Albanese, 2013). When rehabilitation has proven successful, it is often because offenders are carefully screened and treatments are just as carefully chosen to respond to the needs of the offender.

Restorative justice is a philosophy that focuses as much on the victim as on the offender. The underlying restorative justice philosophy is that crime causes harm to the community and thus it is the responsibility of the offender to heal the community, as well as the direct victim of the criminal behavior (Fagin, 2007). Some of the strategies used in restorative justice include community service, restitution to the victim, and dialogues between victims and offenders.

Sentencing

Although the jury decides a defendant's guilt, it is the judge who is responsible for determining the sentence. Typically, the sentencing hearing takes place a number of weeks after the verdict. In sentencing, the judge evaluates the circumstances of the offense and the offender. In addition, the judge evaluates the possible sentences allowed by law and then selects the sentence that in his or her opinion best fits the case.

The traditional criminal sanctions imposed by American judges include fines, imprisonment, or probation—or some combination of some of these options. In some states and in the federal court system, the death penalty is an option as well. Judges, as indicated previously, are guided by the law as to the minimum and maximum sentence that a convicted defendant can receive. However, the difference between the minimum and maximum punishment may vary greatly. Thus, each sentence requires the judge to give careful consideration to the individual circumstances of the case (Fagin, 2007).

There has been considerable controversy over sentencing strategies in this country for many decades. At one time, judges had nearly complete discretion in sentencing offenders because most states and the federal courts used the indeterminate model of sentencing (Fagin, 2007). Indeterminate sentences involve prison terms that do not state a specific term to be served. For example, if an offender were convicted of armed robbery, in imposing an indeterminate sentence, the judge might order the individual to serve a five-to-15-year prison term. The exact numbers of years to be served would be determined by the prisoner's behavior and the decision of the parole board.

> **Myth:** *Racist cops and judges result in more African Americans and other minorities being incarcerated.*
>
> **Reality:** *More often it is the laws and the behaviors that we criminalize in this country that result in the incarceration of minorities.*

During the 1950s and 1960s, a progressive attitude in corrections led to a greater reliance on indeterminate sentences. By shifting the discretion for deciding the length of incarceration from the judge to the prison staff and the parole board, the length of stay in prison was seen to be based on the willingness of the inmate to take advantage of the rehabilitative services available (Fuller, 2010). However, by the 1970s and 1980s, the prevailing attitudes had changed, and indeterminate sentences had lost favor in the criminal justice system.

The main reasons for this were because released inmates continued to engage in crime, there were wide discrepancies in sentencing (and it was found that length of incarceration was likely to be based on race or social class), inmates were not being rehabilitated, and rehabilitation services did not appear to be effective (Fuller, 2010). Consequently, the length of sentences shifted away from the discretion of the prison staff and parole boards to a greater role played by state legislatures, prosecutors, and established sentencing guidelines. This represented a shift to determinate sentencing.

In determinate sentencing, judges impose a fixed term of incarceration. Determinate sentencing is also known as flat sentences or fixed sentences (Fagin, 2007). In its strictest form, determinate sentencing would require a judge to impose a particular sentence for a particular crime. These are referred to as mandatory sentences. For example, in Michigan and some other states, a conviction of first degree murder results in mandatory life imprisonment without the possibility of parole. In its more common form, however, there are sentencing guides that specify a minimum and a maximum term for each crime. One form of determinate sentencing is the presumptive sentence, which allows judges limited discretion to consider aggravating or mitigating circumstances and thus depart from the guidelines (Fuller, 2010).

The supposed advantage of determinate sentencing was uniformity. That is, similar cases would be treated in similar ways; therefore, such factors as social class, race, and gender would not affect sentencing decisions (Fuller, 2010). But the shift to determinate sentencing has, according to some criminal justice experts, caused unintended consequences. For instance, determinate sentencing has removed the power to make decisions from those closest to the case, such as judges (Fuller, 2010). Also, legislators who helped bring about determinate sentencing were not always aware of the long-term consequences—such as prison overcrowding, strained corrections budgets, and the lack of resources within the criminal justice system to handle longer sentences.

MANDATORY MINIMUM SENTENCES

Mandatory minimum sentences are a form of determinate sentencing that has become widely used to address certain types of offenses (Fuller, 2010). Typically, mandatory-minimum laws do not allow for probation and stipulate incarceration for a term of not less than a specified number of years (Fuller, 2010). Mandatory minimum sentences were adopted because of the public perception that offenders were "getting off too easy" (Fagin, 2007). Concerned that judges were too lenient in sentencing, many states adopted legislation mandating that offenders convicted of crimes serve the full sentence for those crimes as specified by law. Some of the types of offenses that are likely to carry mandatory minimum sentences are:

- *Weapons violations*: Mandatory sentencing has been applied to individuals who use (or simply possess) a gun during the commission of a felony. The intent of these laws is to tack on additional years to the sentence, and in many states, reduce the possibility of a probationary sentence while making sure that a felon using a gun (in some states other weapons) will serve longer prison terms. The idea of this approach is to get tough on people using guns and other weapons in crimes, thus bringing about a reduction in weapons-use crimes.
- *Repeated drunk driving*: In some states, those people who continue to drink while intoxicated are sentenced to mandatory prison or jail time. Groups such as Mothers Against Drunk Driving (MADD) have been effective in changing laws that they viewed as too lenient on repeat offenders (Fuller, 2010).
- *Drug-sales and drug-kingpin laws*: As a result of the nation's war on drugs, mandatory sentencing has been employed to put people who sell illicit drugs in prison for long periods of time. Both states as well as the federal government passed laws specifying mandatory prison time for the sale of drugs and for those individuals identified as drug kingpins.
- *Three-Strikes-and-You're-Out Laws*: Mandatory sentencing has been applied to repeat offenders through habitual offender laws. These laws, such as California's three strikes law, take the approach that getting tough on repeat offenders and removing them from the street will reduce crime. Critics of this approach argue that these laws create situations in which offenders are receiving disproportionately long prison terms for minor crimes. As a result of these "get tough" laws, the number of convicted felons serving life sentences has increased 83 percent since 1992 (Fagin, 2007).
- *Truth in sentencing laws*: These laws specify that the offender must serve a substantial portion of his or her sentence before being released. These laws limit the flexibility of parole boards by ensuring that inmates spend most of the original sentence (often 85 percent) behind bars (Fuller, 2010).

Mandatory sentences have been adopted not only by the federal government but also by every state. The assumption for these laws is that they deter crime and have an incapacitating effect. But such laws disregard the fact that not all offenders are alike, even though they may commit the same crime. While it sounds good to many to have mandatory prison terms for offenders who callously sell drugs to young people, a study of drug offenders sentenced to mandatory prison terms in Massachusetts found that nearly half of those people sentenced had no prior record of violent crimes (Weinstein, 2003).

Some states such as New York have reduced mandatory drug sentences because first offenders and non-violent offenders were getting caught up in the sweep of mandatory sentencing laws. A study of California's three-strikes law found that it did not reduce crime rates (Albanese, 2013). Two U.S. Supreme Court justices, Stephen Breyer and Anthony Kennedy, criticized mandatory minimum sentences in separate speeches before the American Bar Association in 2003. Breyer stated that such sentences have set back "the cause of fairness in sentencing" (Finucane, 2003), and Kennedy argued that "our resources are misspent, our punishments too severe, our sentences are too long" (*Washington Post*, 2003, p. A8). With budgetary concerns, more states are likely to rethink long prison terms because they place tremendous strain on state budgets—especially those budgets related to corrections.

FEDERAL SENTENCING GUIDELINES

Both the states and the federal government have established sentencing guidelines. The reasons for such guidelines has been to ensure equal treatment, lessen racial disparity in sentencing, and reduce a perceived leniency in sentencing by federal judges (Masters et al., 2013).

Congress established the U.S. Sentencing Commission in 1984 to create sentencing guidelines for federal offenses. These guidelines took effect in January 1989, and as of 2011, more than one million defendants had been sentenced under the guidelines (Masters et al., 2013). Federal judges are expected to sentence offenders within the guidelines for specific crimes. Furthermore, each state has its own classification for the seriousness of a crime and the corresponding length of sentence that can be imposed for that crime.

Sentencing guidelines are supposed to have the advantage of reducing disparities in sentencing while allowing greater flexibility in sentencing by judges. But the results of their use call these missions into question. Research into racial disparity and sentencing has found that sentencing differentials have not been eliminated. In general, white offenders still receive lighter sentences than black and Latino offenders (Brennan & Spohn, 2008). But under the guidelines, some federal judges have considered the sentences required for federal drug offenses so high that those judges have refused to impose them (Albanese, 2013).

Perhaps the greatest disparity in sentencing has been in respect to the sentences of crack cocaine users versus powder cocaine users. First-time offenders caught with five grams of crack cocaine receive a mandatory minimum sentence of five years in prison, whereas a first-time powder cocaine offender must possess 500 grams of the drug to receive the same sentence. This 100 to one ratio has been called excessive and discriminatory in light of the fact that the cheaper crack cocaine is used more often by blacks and the more expensive powdered cocaine is used more often by whites (Albanese, 2013). President Barack Obama signed into law the Fair Sentencing Act of 2010, which aims to cut down on the inequality between crack and powder cocaine offenses (White House, 2010).

FOR FURTHER CONSIDERATION

Historical Events Relevant to Chapter Thirteen

January 6, 2005: A Texas Court of Appeals overturns Andrea Yates's conviction in the drowning deaths of her five children; a new trial is ordered. The conviction is overturned on the basis of a witness who told an untruth in the trial.

February 23, 1976: The first Ted Bundy trial begins. Bundy, a serial killer, was charged with aggravated kidnapping and went on trial in Salt Lake City, Utah. He had attempted to abduct Carol DaRonch, who escaped. He asked for a trial in front of a judge, rather than a jury. He was found guilty and sentenced to one to 15 years in prison.

March 13, 1980: John Wayne Gacy is sentenced to death. Gacy sexually assaulted and murdered at least 33 teenage boys and young men between 1972 and 1978. He buried 26 of his victims in the crawl space of his home, buried three others elsewhere on his property, and discarded the remains of his last four known victims in a nearby river. He was convicted of 33 murders and sentenced to death for 12 of these killings. He was executed in May 1994.

March 26, 1999: Dr. Jack Kevorkian was convicted of second degree murder and delivery of a controlled substance for giving a lethal injection to a man whose death was shown on the television show *60 Minutes*. He was given a sentence of 10 to 25 years in prison. He was released from Coldwater Prison in Michigan after serving eight years and was placed on parole for the next two years. One of the conditions of his parole was that he could not assist in any suicides.

April 5, 1790: The first American law is passed which establishes imprisonment at hard labor as the normal method of punishing convicted criminals.

April 19, 1995: The Oklahoma City bombing takes place. The Oklahoma City bombing was a terrorist bomb attack on the Alfred P. Murrah Federal Building in downtown Oklahoma City—it would be the most destructive act of terrorism on American soil until the September 11, 2001, attacks. The Oklahoma blast claimed 168 lives, including 19 children under the age of six, and injured more than 680 people. Timothy McVeigh, responsible for detonating the truck bomb that caused the explosion, was found guilty and sentenced to death. He was put to death by lethal injection on June 11, 2001.

May 22, 1924: The body of 13-year-old Bobby Franks is found in Chicago. This quickly leads to the arrests of Nathan Leopold and Richard Loeb. They pleaded guilty to the murder.

May 23, 2005:   The U.S. Supreme Court announces its decision in *Deck v. Missouri*. This case deals with the constitutionality of shackling a prisoner during the sentencing phase of a trial. In a 7–2 opinion delivered by Justice Breyer, the Court held that it is a violation of due process rights to shackle a defendant in the sentencing portion of a trial, unless the shackling relates to a specific defendant interest or a certain state interest.

September 10, 1924:   Nathan Leopold and Richard Loeb are defended by famed defense attorney Clarence Darrow, whose main goal is to prevent them from being executed. They are found guilty on this date and subsequently sentenced to 99-year prison terms for the so-called "thrill killing."

October 2, 1996:   Mark Fuhrman, the Los Angeles police department detective who testified as an expert witness in the O. J. Simpson murder trial, pleads no contest to perjury for lying under oath at the Simpson trial. He was sentenced to three years of probation and a $200 fine.

Important Court Cases

- *Apprendi v. New Jersey*, **530 U.S. 466 (2000):** The Supreme Court ruled that the Sixth Amendment prohibited judges from increasing criminal sentences beyond statutory maximums based on facts other than those presented to the jury.
- *Blakely v. Washington*, **542 U.S. 296 (2004):** The U.S. Supreme Court applied the same prohibition as in *Apprendi v. New Jersey* (2000) to state mandatory sentencing guidelines. That is, trial judges are not allowed to enhance sentences beyond statutory maximums based on facts other than those decided by the jury or admitted to by the defendant.
- *Mistretta v. United States*, **488 U.S. 361 (1989):** This case represented a challenge to the Sentencing Reform Act of 1984, which created a U.S. Sentencing Commission located within the judicial branch of government. The Supreme Court upheld the sentencing law in all respects. The Court stated that locating the commission within the judicial branch did not violate the separation of powers doctrine.
- *Stone v. Powell*, **428 U.S. 465 (1976):** Prior to this court case, an act of Congress allowed state prisoners to petition a federal court for a writ of *habeas corpus*, challenging the constitutionality of their state conviction. *Stone v. Powell* was a reevaluation of a court ruling entitling a state prisoner to a federal court hearing on all federal constitutional issues. In this ruling, the Supreme Court said that Fourth Amendment claims once raised and decided in state courts could not be heard again in a federal *habeas corpus* proceeding when the state had provided an opportunity for a full and fair hearing.
- *United States v. Booker*; *United States v. Fanfan*, **543 U.S. 220 (2005):** Booker and Fanfan were two convicted drug dealers who were given sentences that were lower than those required by federal guidelines. The government appealed and the Supreme Court ruled that federal sentencing guidelines are discretionary and that judges may follow them but they cannot be required to do so.

Websites to Check Out

- *The United States Sentencing Commission.* Available at: *http://www.ussc.gov/.* The U.S. Sentencing Commission has a website that provides information about federal sentencing guidelines, along with facts, research, and the legal aspects of sentencing guidelines.
- *Families Against Mandatory Minimum Sentences.* Available at: *http://www.famm.org/.* Families Against Mandatory Minimums (FAMM) is a non-profit, non-partisan organization fighting for fair and proportionate sentencing laws that allow judicial discretion while maintaining public safety. This group and their website call for state and federal sentencing reform.

Books

- Petersilia, J., and Reitz, K. R. (2000). *The Oxford Handbook of Sentencing and Corrections.* New York: Oxford University Press.
- U.S. Congress House of Representatives (2010). *Federal Rules of Criminal Procedure.* Washington, DC: BiblioGov.
- U.S. Sentencing Commission. (2011). *Federal Sentencing Guidelines Manual, 2011.* Charleston, SC: CreateSpace Publishing.

Movies

- *The Thin Blue Line: The Thin Blue Line* is a 1988 documentary film by Errol Morris. The film tells the story of Randall Dale Adams, who was convicted and sentenced to life in prison for the murder of a police officer. But it was a crime he did not commit. Adams's case was reviewed, and he was released from prison approximately a year after the film's release.

Review for Chapter Thirteen:

Research Paper or Term Paper Topics:

- Three-Strikes-and-You're-Out-Laws
- Mandatory minimum sentences

Important Terms to Know

Appeal: A proceeding to have a court decision reviewed by a higher court.

Determinate sentence: Offenders are given a sentence of incarceration for a fixed period of time.

Deterrence: The act or process of discouraging criminal behavior or the prevention of future criminal behavior by fear of punishment.

Incapacitation: The process of disabling an individual from committing a criminal action. Incapacitation is often brought about through imprisonment.

Indeterminate sentence: In this approach, convicted offenders are given a sentence that could range from an earliest date to a latest date for release.

Mandatory minimum sentence:
A sentence requiring—often by legislation—a minimum prison term.

Presumptive sentencing:
A statutory sentencing method that specifies normal sentences of particular lengths, with limited judicial leeway to shorten or lengthen the term of the sentence.

Restorative justice: An approach to corrections which attempts to have offenders heal the community. It is the community that is seen as the victim in this approach. Offenders are often involved in offender-victim mediation, restitution, and community service.

Retribution: A philosophy of punishment that believes offenders should be punished for purposes of revenge.

Sentencing Reform Act of 1984:
Convinced of a need for more uniformity in fixing the sentences for convicted offenders, Congress passed the Sentencing Reform Act of 1984. This act created the United States Sentencing Commission.

Three-Strikes-and-You're-Out Law:
Preventive detention laws that mandate, as demonstrated in California's such law in 1994, a 25-years-to-life sentence for felons with two previous violent felony convictions who get convicted of a third offense—even if the third crime is not violent.

Truth-in-sentencing laws:
These laws specify that the offender must serve a substantial portion of the sentence before being released. These laws limit the flexibility of the parole

board by ensuring that inmates serve most of the original sentence (often 85 percent) behind bars.

United States Sentencing Commission:

Created in 1984, the sentencing commission's authority was to establish ranges of sentences for all categories of federal offenses. The commission was established as an independent body within the judicial branch of the government and was to consist of seven members appointed by the president. At least three members of the commission were required to be federal judges.

Study Guide Questions

True or False:

1. After a conviction and/or a sentence, a defendant has the right to appeal.

2. Most appeals are successful.

3. Restorative justice is an approach to corrections that sees crime as harm to the community.

4. Weapons violations are one kind of offense very likely to carry mandatory minimum sentences.

Multiple Choice Items:

5. Incapacitation is a philosophy of corrections that attempts to prevent future criminal behavior by
     a. psychotherapy
     b. the death penalty
     c. making it impossible for the offender to commit crimes
     d. rehabilitation

6. Three-Strikes-and-You're-Out Laws take the approach that
     a. you have to get tough on offenders
     b. offenders need sympathetic and caring handling
     c. you must give offenders a second chance
     d. offenders need to be on house arrest

7. The greatest concern about mandatory sentences is that they
     a. are too lenient toward violent offenders

b. require short prison terms

c. imprison too many drug kingpins

d. sweep up too many non-violent offenders and first offenders

8. The U.S. Sentencing Commission was created to

a. reduce all sentences for violent offenders

b. find out which sentences deterred crime most effectively

c. determine sentencing guidelines for federal crimes

d. help judges figure out how to sentence drug dealers

References

Albanese, J. S. (2005). *Criminal Justice.* 5th ed. Upper Saddle River, NJ: Pearson.

Brennan, P., and Spohn, C. (2008). Empirical research on the impact of sentencing reforms: Recent studies of state and federal sentencing innovations. *Journal of Contemporary Criminal Justice* 24: 340–344.

Chapper, J. A., and Hanson, R. A. (1989). *Understanding Reversible Error in Criminal Appeals.* Williamsburg, VA: National Center for State Courts.

Cole, G. F., and Smith, C. E. (2007). *The American System of Criminal Justice.* 11th ed. Belmont, CA: Thomson/Wadsworth.

Fagin, J. A. (2007). *Criminal Justice: A Brief Introduction.* Boston: Allyn & Bacon.

Fuller, J. R. (2010). *Criminal Justice: Mainstream and Crosscurrents.* 2nd ed. Upper Saddle River, NJ: Pearson.

"Justice criticizes sentencing guidelines," (August 120, 2003), *Washington Post* [online], Available at: http://www.prisontalk.com/forums/archive/index.php/t-23870.html.

Masters, R. E., Way, L. B., Gerstenfeld, P. B., Muscat, B. T., Hooper, M., Dussich, J. P. J., Pincu, L., and Skrapec, C. A. (2013). *CJ: Realities and Challenges.* 2nd ed. New York: McGraw-Hill.

Priehs, R. (1999). Appointed counsel for indigent criminal appellants: Does compensation influence effort? *Justice System Journal* 21, 57–79.

Weinstein, I. (2003). Fifteen years after the federal sentencing revolution: How mandatory minimums have undermined effective and just narcotics sentencing. *American Criminal Law Review* 40, 87–132.

White House, "President signs Fair Sentencing Act of 2010" [online], Available at: http://www.whitehouse.gov/blog/2010/08/03/president-obama-signs-fair-sentencing-act.

Chapter Fourteen

Corrections, Punishment, and Rehabilitation

In Chapter Thirteen, we learned that there are over one million felony convictions each year in state courts and more than 75,000 felony convictions in federal courts. In this chapter, you will learn that there are about seven million men and women who are under the supervision of the criminal justice system at any one point in time. These seven million individuals are either in prison, in jail, on probation, or on parole. This means that while two million or more people are in jail or prison, more than five million other offenders are living and working within the community. That may come as surprise to you that so many people—well over five million—are people you may have contact with in your daily life.

But before we describe who these people are and what they are doing in the community, we should start with an overview of the correctional system.

THE CORRECTIONAL SYSTEM

The third part of the criminal justice system, along with law enforcement and the courts, is the correctional system. The correctional system incapacitates convicted offenders and attempts to aid in their treatment and rehabilitation. In the broadest sense, the correctional system is made up of jails, prisons, community supervision, and parole programs. Corrections ordinarily represents

The gallows has long been the penalty of murder, and yet we can scarcely open a newspaper, that does not relate a new case of that crime.

–Abraham Lincoln, Speech, December 26, 1839

the post-adjudicatory care given to offenders when a sentence is imposed by the court and the offender is placed in the hands of the correctional system (Siegel & Senna, 2008).

The correctional system, as a whole, costs the U.S. taxpayers about $60 billion a year (Siegel & Senna, 2008). It is made up of about 6,000 correctional institutions and more than 3,500 probation and parole departments. As a result of the enormous number of people processed through law enforcement agencies and courts each year, the correctional system population has been at all-time highs in the past several years (Siegel & Senna, 2008).

We can break down the functions of the correctional system into three broad areas:

- *Correctional treatment*: Upon sentencing, an offender is transferred to the correctional system for secure confinement or to serve a probationary term. In addition to either confinement or probation, the individual may be asked to participate in rehabilitation or other programs designed to ultimately lead to readjustment to society.
- *Release:* After completing his sentence and his period of correction, the offender is released back into society. However, most inmates do not serve the full term of their sentence but are released from jail or prison to finish their term under community supervision.
- *Post-release:* Following release from a correctional facility, offenders may be placed in a community correctional center or a reentry program. Since reentry into society poses difficulties, there are various reentry programs to help bring about adjustment to society.

CORRECTIONAL TREATMENT

Although many offenders are sentenced to jail or prison, we are going to postpone our discussion of incarceration until Chapter Fifteen. In the rest of this chapter, our focus will be on community corrections.

The principle of community-based correction rests on the fundamental fact that offenders are either incarcerated or remain at home in their community. Therefore, many types of sentences are viewed as community-based correction. Essentially, as we use the term today, community-based correction includes activities and programs within the community that are generally of a rehabilitative rather than a punitive nature. Such community-based programs can include those services that are employment-related, educational, social, or clinical. In addition, community-based corrections will involve supervision by a community or governmental agency.

Community-based corrections covers a vast array of services, including pre-trial diversion programs, probation, parole, educational projects and services, work-release programs, restitution, and halfway house facilities. Some, such as diversion programs and probation, are called intermediate sanctions because they fall between the extremes of fines and incarceration.

> **Myth:** *The best way to handle criminal offenders is to lock them up.*
>
> **Reality:** *The reality is that prison may be the worst thing to do to many offenders. Taking offenders away from their homes, families, and communities may be very disruptive and lead to greater maladjustment after release.*

Why not just incarcerate every offender? While some people might believe that every criminal offender should be locked up, community-based correctional strategies exist for a number of reasons:

1. There are many criminal offenders who represent a low risk to society.

2. For a number of offenders, imprisonment has unfavorable consequences, such as detrimental effects on self-esteem, the risk of physical harm, adverse labeling, and exposure to criminal thinking and attitudes.

3. It costs far less to provide community supervision than it does to incarcerate an offender.

4. Community-based correctional strategies can help some offenders to play a positive and productive role in their families, neighborhoods, and communities.

5. Because of prison overcrowding, community corrections offers an alternative—especially for first-time and non-violent offenders.

6. There is no research that establishes that incarceration reduces recidivism. New, innovative approaches must be tried (Inciardi, 2005).

PROBATION

The term probation comes from the Latin word *probare*, which means "to test or to prove." Probationers are given a second chance to prove they are able to conform to the rules of society.

The first person to conceive of a formal function of court supervision was a wealthy philanthropist in Boston named John Augustus (Boyes-Watson, 2003). A bootmaker by trade, Augustus saw the evils of alcohol on society and made his first plea to a Boston court in 1841 to allow a petty criminal to serve a "season of probation" under his supervision. After his request was granted, Augustus had found his life's work—as a volunteer probation officer. From 1841 to 1858, John Augustus supervised almost 2,000 men and women to help them lead more sober and more responsible lives (Boyes-Watson, 2003).

The first paid probation officer was hired in Boston in 1878, and by 1891, Massachusetts had brought into existence a statewide probation system under the authority of the courts (Boyes-Watson, 2003). By 1900, four other states had enacted similar legislation, and probation became an established alternative to incarceration (Inciardi, 2005).

But what exactly is probation? The term can be confusing because it has been used in various ways. However, probation is a sentence of conditional release to the community. More specifically, as defined by Dean Champion (2001), probation is an alternative to incarceration, in which the offender stays under the state's authority. Probation involves conditions and retains authority in the sentencing court to modify the conditions of sentence or to resentence the offender if he or she violates the conditions.

As stated in the Champion definition, probation involves certain conditions imposed by the court. Those conditions imposed must be agreed to by the offender and usually include supervision by a probation officer, and may also involve counseling or other forms of psychological treatment, employment, restitution, community service, or regular attendance at such programs as Alcoholics Anonymous or Narcotics Anonymous. Typically, courts have broad discretion in imposing conditions of probation, but there are limits to probation conditions. For example, a Florida appellate court struck down a condition of probation that required that the defendant not father any children during the probation period (Schieb & Schieb, 1999).

Myth:	*The most common way of dealing with criminals is to put them in prison.*
Reality:	*The fact is that a majority of criminal offenders are placed on probation rather than incarcerated.*

Today, probation is the most common form of punishment in the United States (Gaines and Miller, 2007). Upon the granting of probation, and as part of their probation agreement, defendants are required to abide by a variety of regulations and conditions, which are fairly standard from state to state. Essentially, these regulations and conditions demand that the probationer live a law-abiding and productive life, work (or go to school), support his or her dependents, maintain contact with the probation officer, and remain within the jurisdiction of the court (Inciardi, 2005).

The probation officer, usually an employee of a court, has two basic roles. One is investigative and consists of conducting the presentence investigation. The second role is to supervise the probationer with the goal of helping that individual successfully complete probation. Although some probation officers establish close working relationships with probationers and may counsel them on a regular basis, they also have the responsibility of punishing them if they violate the conditions of probation or any laws (Gaines & Miller, 2007). Along this line, the U.S. Supreme Court has ruled that state regulations permit probation officers to conduct searches of probationers' homes without warrants, upon "reasonable grounds" to believe that contraband might be found (*Griffin v. Wisconsin*, 483 U.S. 868 [1987]). However, while warrantless searches of probationers, their automobiles, and premises are permissible if carried out by a probation officer with just cause, the courts have ruled that such searches cannot be extended to all law enforcement officers (Inciardi, 2005).

Although probation is often preferred over incarceration because it is more cost effective, there is usually no limit to the size of the caseloads of probation officers. Caseload size varies from state to state and court to court, and Petersilia found that the average probation officer in the United States has a caseload of 175 offenders (Petersilia, 2002). Another study found that 20 percent of adult felony probationers had no personal contact with their probation officers whatsoever (Langan & Cunniff, 1992). Still another study discovered that, on average, probation officers do not know the whereabouts of nine percent of the probationers on their caseload (Claxton, Sinclair, & Hanson, 2002).

Despite these alarming statistics which may suggest that dangerous felons are roaming the streets without supervision, the majority of probationers complete their terms of probation without being arrested (Gaines & Miller, 2007). A research project comparing the recidivism rates of probationers and offenders released from prison found that probation appears to be more effective than incarceration. In the study, only 38 percent of probationers were rearrested and only 31 percent were incarcerated, while 72 percent of former prisoners were rearrested, with 47 percent incarcerated yet again (Petersilia & Turner, 1986). However, as pointed out by the American Bar Association (*ABA urges states to increase the use of parole and probation*, 2012), probation not only reduces revocation (and incarceration) rates, but also saves money.

INTERMEDIATE SANCTIONS

Intermediate sanctions are more restrictive than probation and less restrictive than imprisonment. Intended to alleviate pressure on overcrowded correction facilities and understaffed probation departments, there are several intermediate sanction options:

- *Fines:* Fines, which are often ordered in misdemeanor cases, may be financial penalties based on court costs and other fees for services provided to the offender. A more recent popular idea is that of "day fines," with the judge setting the amount of the fine in relation to the daily earnings of the offender (Gottfredson, 1999).
- *Community service:* As part of a probation order or in lieu of incarceration, offenders are ordered to engage in community service. This generally means providing some kind of labor, often for a non-profit service agency. Offenders might be required to pick up litter on roadways, paint public buildings, landscape parks, build playgrounds, serve meals to the homeless, or do some other kind of work that benefits the community.
- *Restitution:* Restitution is required compensation to the victim for losses suffered because of the crime. Unlike victim compensation, which the state usually pays to the victim, restitution requires the offender to pay the victim.
- *Forfeiture:* This is a penalty in which the state seizes money or property. Forfeitures often are related to drug crimes, where the offender's house, car, boat, or other valuable property gained from or used in criminal activity is seized. In the case of *Bennis v. Michigan*, the U.S. Supreme Court ruled that a person's home or car could be forfeited, even if the owner was unaware that it was connected to illegal activity (*Bennis v. Michigan*, 516 U.S. 442 [1996]).
- *Pre-trial diversion programs:* Since not every criminal violation requires the courtroom process, some judges have the discretion to order an offender into a pre-trial diversion program. These programs represent an

"interruption" of the criminal proceedings and are generally reserved for young or first-time offenders who have been arrested on charges of illegal drug use, child or spousal abuse, or sexual misconduct (Gaines & Miller, 2007). Pre-trial diversion programs usually include counseling or treatment as well as educational programs.

- *House arrest:* House arrest may be used along with probation or intensive probation. The offender is confined to his or her house either all the time or during certain hours each day. House arrest may be used in conjunction with electronic monitoring with daily reports provided to the probation officer regarding the offender's compliance with the house arrest.
- *Electronic monitoring:* With advances in technology, electronic monitoring has become very sophisticated. There are a great many electronic monitoring systems, but all of them provide some kind of tracking—through a telephone, tether, or modem—that alerts the probation or parole officer as to the offender's whereabouts and compliance with the court's orders.

Myth: *Harsh and punitive punishments such as boot camps and* Scared Straight! *programs are very effective in helping people avoid further criminal offenses.*

Reality: *In truth, these kinds of approaches to criminal offenders seem to have the opposite effect. They may result in more offending—rather than less offending.*

- *Boot camps:* Boot camps are programs that emphasize military-like discipline and a regimented lifestyle. These programs not only rely on the military model of boot camp, but they also impose a routine of mandatory physical exercise, drill, and hard labor on the offender. Used initially for young offenders, federal and state boot camp programs have been designed for adult offenders as well. At their peak of popularity in the mid-1990s, state and federal boot camps housed more than 7,000 inmates. In 2005, however, the Federal Bureau of Prisons announced plans to close down its three boot camps, following the lead of numerous states that had been unwilling to continue to fund these programs that had no measureable effect on recidivism rates (Gaines & Miller, 2007).
- *Intensive probation:* Intensive probation is a form of probation in which the probation officer provides close and intense supervision. Not only might the probation officer have visits several times a week with the probationer, but there are often other requirements—such as counseling, drug abuse treatment, and community service—that are monitored closely by the probation officer. Caseloads for probation officers offering intensive probation are usually reduced to facilitate providing the very close supervision.

Drug Courts

Over the past two decades, various specialty courts have developed. The first was drug courts in 1989, followed by gun courts, and more recently, mental health courts. However, it is drug courts that have caught on and become a highly successful approach to sentencing and rehabilitation.

Research projects over several years have shown that drug courts are effective. For instance, a recent study over two and a half years in Minnesota demonstrates that an intensive, treatment-centered drug court program is more likely than a traditional correctional approach to improve the lives of drug-using offenders and at the same time save taxpayers money. This study compared the experiences of 535 drug court offenders with 644 offenders with similar profiles who did not opt for the drug court's regimen of treatment, intensive supervision, incentives for good behavior, and sanctions for reoffending. Among the findings:

- Two and a half years after entering the program, 26 percent of the drug court cohort had been charged with a new offense, compared with 41 percent in the comparison group.
- Drug court participants spent fewer days incarcerated (jail plus prison) than did the comparison group, on average saving the state $3,200 per participant over two and a half years.
- More than half—54 percent—of drug court participants finished the program, which typically involves about 18 months of frequent court appearances, random drug tests, and completion of treatment. Sanctions including incarceration are quickly imposed if a participant is found to be using drugs.
- Drug court participants show gains in employment, educational achievement, home rental or ownership, and payment of child support over the run of the program. That in turn leads to reduced taxpayer costs, as formerly homeless and unemployed people become taxpayers (Minnesota Statewide Drug Court Evaluation, 2012).

Myth: *Drug courts are just an easy way out of jail, don't hold people accountable, and are too costly.*

Reality: *The reality is that drug courts create accountability for drug offenders, have been shown to change behavior, and reduce costs.*

Numerous studies attest to the success of drug courts, at least in terms of recidivism rates. Two studies, one by the National Institute of Justice, found that the recidivism rate of the drug court participants was 29 percent lower than that of the non-participating counterparts (Rempel, Fox-Kralstein, & Cissner, 2004; Roman, Townsend, & Bhati, 2003).

PUNISHMENT

The history of corrections can be traced back to ancient Greece, Israel, Rome, and Egypt. Punishment in ancient times included confiscation of property, fines, imprisonment, and death in Greece (Ortmeier, 2006). But in other countries such as Israel and Egypt, mutilation was sometimes used. Ancient Romans punished by exacting compensation from the offender, but they also used exile as well as execution. Although the ancient countries used non-lethal forms of punishment, the most common punishments involved some form of death (Ortmeier, 2006).

By the 1500s, incarceration as punishment began to replace hanging and other forms of executions. By the 1600s, there was more criticism, especially in Europe, of capital punishment, and at the same time there were advocates for more humane conditions for prisoners, as well as for punishments that fit the crime. Nonetheless, hanging was a frequent punishment for various serious and not-so-serious crimes in England up to the end of the 18th century.

Approaches to American colonial corrections were patterned after English approaches. Although England continued to use hanging for various crimes, American colonists preferred corporal punishment, fines, and confinement (Ortmeier, 2006). After the Revolutionary War and into the 19th century, large-scale penitentiaries—as places where offenders could do penance and reflect on their evil ways—replaced many other forms of punishment.

During the period from about 1825 to 1865, punishment began to take new directions. For one thing, crime was more often viewed as a critical social problem (Oliver & Hilgenberg, 2006). For another, crime was beginning to be seen as a problem that should be addressed by the government. The penitentiary system in America was growing, and the view that prisons could help solve the problems of crime was taking root. With the building of Eastern State Penitentiary in the 1820s, this ultramodern (for its time) facility in Pennsylvania reflected some of the new ideas of the reformers (Oliver & Hilgenberg, 2006). Both solitary confinement and productive work for inmates was emphasized in Eastern State Penitentiary. Eastern State Penitentiary was viewed as a prison that allowed for control of inmates, but at the same time it was seen as a more humane facility to house offenders.

After Eastern State Penitentiary was opened, other new prisons were built around the United States—Auburn Prison and Sing Sing in New York and Jackson Prison in Michigan, for instance. These prisons generated a great deal of publicity and notoriety in the 19th century, both in America and in Europe. But Americans viewed prison as the best way of dealing with criminals; consequently, there was a prison-building boom well into the 20th century.

THE DEATH PENALTY

The death penalty as the ultimate form of punishment came with the American colonists from England and other European countries. However, during the 19th century, several developments occurred that triggered a debate that has continued into the 21st century. Just as the concept of prison was changing in the so-called Jacksonian era (from about 1825 to 1865), so did ideas about the death penalty. For instance, Tennessee, Alabama, and Mississippi made hanging an option rather than mandatory—even if an individual was convicted of first degree murder (Oliver and Hilgenberg, 2006).

During this period of time, Michigan became the first state to outlaw the death penalty in 1846. Wisconsin and Rhode Island would follow suit by banning executions in 1847 and 1852, respectively (Oliver & Hilgenberg, 2006). A number of other states debated in their legislatures doing away with capital punishment, but the death penalty narrowly survived votes in the legislatures of Pennsylvania, New Hampshire, and New York.

Also, with the building of state penitentiaries, executions were moved from public areas to taking place inside state prisons. No longer would hangings be public spectacles. Pennsylvania, in 1834, was the first state to order that executions be moved inside of prisons, and other states made the same move very quickly, which eventually was the norm for all states (Oliver & Hilgenberg, 2006).

Capital punishment today has been abolished in 17 states, with 33 still having the death penalty as an option. The latest state to do away with the death penalty was Connecticut in April 2012 (Death Penalty Information Center, 2012). But capital punishment remains a lively topic of debate in this country, even though very few first-degree murder convictions result in the death penalty (Ortmeier, 2006).

Critics of the death penalty point out that two dozen countries have abolished the death penalty since 1986 (Gaines & Miller, 2007) and that the United States is the only Western democracy that continues to execute inmates. It is also argued by opponents of the death penalty that capital punishment cannot serve the interests of justice when the people who are placed on death row and are actually executed are mostly those without money and likely to be minorities (Gaines & Miller, 2007).

Death penalty advocates believe that the death penalty is a deterrent and that executing criminals is an effective way of preventing other crimes, especially murder. Others believe that it is less expensive than incarcerating inmates for long sentences (Kappeler and Potter, 2005). The fact is that research that has studied this belief finds that the costs associated with capital punishment are at least twice that of incarceration (Potter, 2000).

For more than 150 years, the U.S. Supreme Court has made decisions regulating capital punishment in this country. During these years, the Supreme Court has upheld the constitutionality of various methods of execution, including electrocution (In re *Kemmler*, 1890). Currently, there are five methods of execution authorized by the Court: lethal injection, electrocution, lethal gas, hanging, and firing squad. However, lethal injection is now the primary method of execution used in all states with the death penalty (Bohm & Haley, 2012).

On June 29, 1972, the Supreme Court set aside death sentences for the first time in its history. In its decision in the case of *Furman v. Georgia* (1972), the Court ruled that capital punishment statutes in three different cases were unconstitutional because they gave the jury complete discretion to decide whether to impose the death penalty or a lesser punishment in capital cases (*Furman v. Georgia* [1972]). The majority of the Court pointed out that the death penalty had been imposed arbitrarily and often selectively against people of color. The majority of the Court also noted that the statutes allowing this in Georgia and Texas constituted cruel and unusual punishment under the Eighth and Fourteenth Amendments.

The practical effect of the *Furman* decision was that the Supreme Court voided the death penalty laws in the 35 states that then practiced capital punishment. Within two years, most of these states passed new laws that were designed to meet the Court's objections. The constitutionality of these new laws were challenged, and on July 2, 1976, the Supreme Court issued its ruling in five test cases (although they are generally all referred to as *Gregg v. Georgia*) (Bohm & Haley, 2012). Those new statutes, the Court decided, struck a balance between giving the jury some guidance and allowing it to consider the background and character of the defendant and the circumstances of the crime.

The most dramatic effect of the *Gregg v. Georgia* (1976) ruling by the Court was that executions could resume. On January 17, 1977, the first execution since 1972 took place when Gary Gilmore, a convicted murderer, was executed by firing squad in Utah. Since January 1977, there have been 1,300 executions in the United States (as of June 2012) (Death Penalty Information Center, 2012). Fifty-six percent of the inmates executed have been white, and more than 75 percent of the murder victims of those executed were white (Death Penalty Information Center, 2012). Race appears, however, to play an important role in who is sentenced to death and who is actually executed. For example:

- In Louisiana, the odds of a death sentence were 97 percent higher for those whose victim was white than for those whose victim was black (Pierce & Radelet, 2011).
- A study in California found that those who killed whites were more than three times more likely to be sentenced to death than those who killed blacks and over four times more likely than those who killed Latinos (Pierce & Radelet, 2005).
- A comprehensive study of the death penalty in North Carolina found that the odds of receiving a death sentence rose by three and a half times among those defendants whose victims where white (Boger & Unah, 2001).
- In 96 percent of states where there have been reviews of race and the death penalty, there was a pattern of either race-of-victim or race-of-defendant discrimination, or both (Baldus, et al., 1998)
- Ninety-eight percent of the chief district attorneys in death penalty states are white; only 1% are black (Pokorak, 1998).

Does the Death Penalty Deter Crime?

Numerous studies have failed to establish that the death penalty deters crime (Kappeler and Potter, 2005). Research has failed to find that the death penalty has any effect on homicide rates (Gaines & Miller, 2007). The latest major study on the issue found no evidence that the number of executions had any effect on the incidence of murder in the Houston, Texas, area over a five-year period (Stolzenberg & D'Alessio, 2004).

These kinds of facts perhaps will have little effect on proponents of the death penalty, who are likely to go on believing that murderers will "think twice" about committing a murder when they are aware they could be executed for their crime.

On the other hand, both the economic argument and the fallibility argument are more likely to sway public opinion in the death penalty debate.

Is It Cheaper to Execute Inmates?
Do the Wrong People Get Executed?

It is commonly assumed that execution offers a less expensive alternative to incarceration. However, the facts are that the costs associated with capital punishment are at least twice that of incarceration (Potter, 2000). Every aspect of a capital trial is more complex, more time consuming, and, as a result, more expensive. The costs associated with capital trials relate to prosecution costs, greater use of expert witnesses, greater use of equipment and displays, and costs of hiring defense attorneys for indigent clients. In a majority of capital cases, the defendant is indigent and the cost of trials and subsequent appeals must be borne by the government (Miller-Potter, 2005).

Furthermore, because executions are irreversible sentences, almost every state that has the death penalty requires an automatic review of all death sentences. Defendants often file multiple appeals. Not only are appeals expensive, but the average length of the entire review process is about nine years (Liebman, Fagan, & West, 2000).

However, a more persuasive argument against the death penalty relates to the fallibility of the criminal justice system. While many people believe capital punishment should be used to kill people who commit heinous crimes, very few people believe that the innocent should be executed. According to the Death Penalty Information Center, between 1976 and 2012, about 140 American men and women convicted of capital crimes and sentenced to death were later found to be innocent (Death Penalty Information Center, 2012). It is not known how many innocent people have been executed; however, projects such as the Innocence Project and other wrongful conviction programs continue to help exonerate the wrongfully convicted. The Innocence Project's website reports that as of July 2012, there have been 292 post-conviction DNA exonerations. As long as post-conviction exonerations continue to make the news, there will seemingly be a growing reluctance to rush to execution when the convicted person could very well be innocent.

FOR FURTHER CONSIDERATION

Historical Events Relevant to Chapter Fourteen

January 1, 1889:   The state of New York legalizes the use of the electric chair for executions.

January 13, 1947:   The case of *Francis v. Resweber* is decided by the U.S. Supreme Court. The question before the Court was whether returning Willie Francis to the electric chair a second time, after the current failed to kill him the first time, constituted cruel and unusual punishment. A majority of the Court rules that it is not a violation of the U.S. Constitution to send Willie Francis to the electric chair a second time.

January 17, 1977:   Gary Gilmore, a convicted murderer, becomes the first person in the United States to be executed after the U.S. Supreme Court reinstituted the death penalty in 1976 by virtue of its ruling in the *Gregg v. Georgia* case. Gilmore opts to die at the hands of a firing squad on this date in Utah.

January 31, 1843:   The state of Michigan's House votes in favor of Flavius J. Littlejohn's bill to abolish capital punishment in Michigan. This marks the first time that a legislative house of any state votes to outlaw capital punishment. However, on February 3, 1843, the Michigan Senate kills the bill by voting it down. Later, in another vote, both the House and the Senate approve such legislation, and Michigan does become the first state to ban capital punishment. It is on March 1, 1847, that Michigan officially becomes the first English-speaking territory in the world to abolish the death penalty.

February 21, 1862:   The first federal execution takes place at the Tombs Prison in New York City. Nathaniel Gordon, a native of Portland, Maine, is hanged for piracy under the law of May 15, 1820, which defines slave trading as piracy. Gordon was captain of the *Erie*, a ship transporting Africans to a slave market.

March 7, 1995:   New York becomes the 38th state to adopt the death penalty. In 2004, the state of New York's appeals court rules the law is unconstitutional. But a new version of the law passes, allowing New York to be a death penalty state.

March 20, 1899:   Martha M. Place of Brooklyn, New York, becomes the first woman to be executed in the electric chair. She was previously convicted of murdering her stepdaughter. The execution occurs in Sing Sing Prison in Ossining, New York.

March 30 and March 31, 1976:
    Oral arguments are heard by the United States Supreme Court in the case of *Gregg v. Georgia*. The Court announces its decision on July 2, 1976, and reinstates the death penalty in this country.

April 3, 1936:	Bruno Hauptmann is electrocuted in Trenton, New Jersey, for the kidnap-murder of Charles Lindbergh's baby.
June 20, 2002:	The U.S. Supreme Court rules in the case of *Atkins v. Virginia*. With Associate Justice John Paul Stevens writing the majority opinion, the Court declares that executions of the mentally retarded constitute cruel and unusual punishment.
June 29, 1972:	The U.S. Supreme Court rules by a 5 to 4 vote in the case of *Furman v. Georgia* that capital punishment in the way it is practiced on the state and federal level is unconstitutional. This, in effect, places a ban on capital punishment for the next four years.
August 6, 1890:	William Kemmler becomes the first person ever to be electrocuted in the electric chair after being convicted of murdering Matilda "Tillie" Ziegler, his common-law wife, with a hatchet on March 29, 1889. Prior to the electrocution, his lawyers appeal the sentence, arguing that electrocution is cruel and unusual punishment. George Westinghouse, one of the backers of alternating current as the standard for the distribution of main power, supported his appeal. The appeal failed, partly due to the support of Thomas Edison for the state's position. Thomas Edison was a backer of direct current power supplies, which powered the electric chair in Auburn Prison in Auburn, New York. Edison, whose own laboratories designed Auburn's electric chair, contended that alternating current was dangerous.
October 4, 1976:	In deciding *Gregg v. Georgia*, the U.S. Supreme Court lifts a ban against the death sentence in murder cases. Capital punishment had not been used in the United States since the Court's decision in *Furman v. Georgia* in June 1972. The first execution following *Gregg v. Georgia* takes place in January 1977, when Gary Gilmore, a career criminal who spent the last 18 of his last 21 years in jails and prisons and who had killed a gas station employee one night and a motel manager the next night during hold-ups, was executed by firing squad in Utah.

Important Court Cases

- *Atkins v. Virginia*, **536 U.S. 304 (2002):** The U.S. Supreme Court in this case directly overturned their own 1989 decision in *Penry v. Lynaugh*. In this case, the Court held that executing the mentally retarded is a violation of the Constitution's prohibition of the Eighth Amendment's cruel and unusual punishment provision. Taking into consideration the number of state statutes that prohibit the execution of the mentally retarded, the Court stated that the execution of such people violated contemporary standards of decency.
- *Bennis v. Michigan*, **516 U.S. 442 (1996):** Tina Bennis of Detroit was co-owner, along with her husband, John Bennis, of a 1977 Pontiac automobile, which John used to engage in oral sex with a prostitute. He was

convicted, and the trial court ordered his car seized. The facts in the case seemed clear that Tina Bennis did know of her husband's behavior with the prostitute and that she had provided most of the funds to buy the car. She claimed that her due process rights under the Fourteenth Amendment were violated. The U.S. Supreme Court found for the state of Michigan. Writing for the majority, Chief Justice William Rehnquist stated that the government acquired the car through a proper and legal set of proceedings and that property could be seized based on the use to which it was put.

- *Furman v. Georgia*, **408 U.S. 238 (1972):** By a five to four vote, the U.S. Supreme Court for the first time struck down the death penalty under the cruel and unusual punishment clause of the Eighth Amendment. A jury in Georgia had convicted William Furman for murder, and juries in Georgia and Texas had convicted two other men of rape. But all three juries imposed the death penalty. All three individuals were African American. Some justices among the majority found that jury discretion produced a random pattern among those receiving the death penalty and that this randomness was cruel and unusual. Justice William O. Douglas concluded that the death penalty was disproportionately applied to the poor and socially disadvantaged. The *Furman* decision had the effect of halting all executions in those states that had the death penalty. All 600 people on death row in America had their sentences changed to life in prison.

- *Gregg v. Georgia*, **428 U.S. 153 (1976):** A majority of the Supreme Court justices upheld statutes that guide judges and juries when imposing the death penalty. The Court rejected claims that capital punishment was unconstitutional *per se*, but it implied strongly that mandatory death penalty statutes would violate the Eighth Amendment's prohibition of cruel and unusual punishment. This decision had the effect of allowing states to begin executing prisoners again.

- *Griffin v. Wisconsin*, **483 U.S. 868 (1987):** Wisconsin law places probationers in the legal custody of the State Department of Health and Social Services and renders them subject to conditions set by the rules and regulations established by that department. One such regulation permits any probation officer to search a probationer's home without a warrant, as long as his supervisor approves and as long as there are reasonable grounds to believe in the presence of contraband. In determining whether reasonable grounds exist, an officer must consider a variety of factors, including information provided by an informant, the reliability and specificity of that information, the informant's reliability, the officer's experience with the probationer, and the need to verify compliance with the rules of probation and with the law. Another regulation forbids a probationer to possess a firearm without a probation officer's advance approval. When a probation officer received information from a police detective that there might be guns in Griffin's apartment, probation officers searched the apartment and found a handgun. Griffin was tried and convicted of the felony of possession of a firearm by a convicted felon. The Supreme Court, in accepting Griffin's appeal, ruled that no search warrant was necessary and that the search was reasonable.

- *Penry v. Lynaugh*, **492 U.S. 302 (1989):** In the *Penry v. Lynaugh* case, the Supreme Court held that the application of the death penalty to persons who are mentally retarded but not legally insane does not violate the Eighth Amendment's prohibition against cruel and unusual punishments. The Court also ruled that jurors in a capital case must be given the opportunity to consider mitigating evidence and to provide a "reasoned moral response" to that evidence in rendering its sentence decision.

- *Woodson v. North Carolina*, **428 U.S. 280 (1976):** Following the *Furman v. Georgia* decision in 1972, the state of North Carolina replaced its discretionary sentencing system with a mandatory death sentence for first-degree murder. Justice Potter Stewart, writing for the majority of the Court, said that evolving standards of decency have moved away from mandatory sentencing and that most death penalty laws reenacted after Furman did not provide for automatic death sentences. Therefore, North Carolina could use capital punishment, but it would be cruel and unusual to apply it as a mandatory sentence.

Websites to Check Out

- *American Probation and Parole Association.* Available at: *http://www.appa-net.org/eweb/.* The American Probation and Parole Association is an international organization. Its website provides considerable information about probation and parole as a career as well as resources about probation and parole services.
- *Death Penalty Information Center.* Available at: *http://www.deathpenaltyinfo.org/.* The Death Penalty Information Center is a storehouse of facts, resources, and up-to-date information related to capital punishment.
- *Eastern State Penitentiary.* Available: *http://www.easternstate.org/.* This website gives a history of Pennsylvania's Eastern State Penitentiary. It also allows people to book tours of the site on-line.

Books

- *Abadinsky, H. (2011). Probation and Parole: Theory and Practice.* 11th ed. Upper Saddle River, NJ: Prentice Hall.
- Banner, S. (2003). *The Death Penalty: An American History.* Cambridge, MA: Harvard University Press.
- Bedau, H. A., and Cassell, P. G. (2005). *Debating the Death Penalty: Should America Have Capital Punishment?* New York: Oxford University Press.
- Champion, D. J. (2007). *Probation, Parole, and Community Corrections.* 6th ed. Upper Saddle River, NJ: Prentice Hall.
- Lessenger, J. E., and Roper, G. F. (2010). *Drug Courts: A New Approach to Treatment and Rehabilitation.* New York: Springer Publishing Co.
- Turow, S. (2004). *Ultimate Punishment: A Lawyer's Reflection on Dealing with the Death Penalty.* New York: Picador.

Movies

- *Deadline*: This 2002 documentary film tells about Governor George Ryan's last few months in office as Illinois's governor. Ryan appoints a commission to review the conviction of all 167 prisoners on death row in Illinois. The film presents a look at capital punishment in America against the backdrop of an examination of many individual cases of men on death row in Illinois. Governor Ryan must decide what to do with the recommendations given him by the commission he has apppinted.
- *At the Death House Door*: A 2008 documentary film about Carroll Pickett, who served as the death house chaplain to the infamous "Walls" prison unit in Huntsville, Texas. Pickett presided over 95 executions in his 15-year career, including the very first by lethal injection. Initially pro-death penalty, he became an anti-death penalty activist.
- *The Green Mile:* Based on the Stephen King novel of the same name, this movie tells the story of an African American man found guilty of murdering two young girls and sentenced to death. While on death row, the viewer learns he is innocent but there will be no way to stop his inevitable execution.

- *Capote:* A 1959 murder of several members of a Kansas family becomes the basis for Truman Capote's book *In Cold Blood.* This movie gives the background of the book as Capote goes to Kansas to interview people and then develops a relationship with the murderers up until the time they are executed.
- *Dead Man Walking:* Sean Penn plays a man on death row in Louisiana. The man was convicted of killing a young couple, and while he is on death row, he turns to Sister Helen Prejean, played by Susan Sarandon, for help in his final days. It's a movie about forgiveness and redemption.

TV Movies

- *The Executioner's Song:* A 1982 made-for-TV movie starring Tommy Lee Jones as Gary Gilmore, it aired over two consecutive nights on NBC. The film was based on Norman Mailer's Pulitzer Prize-winning book of the same name. The book and the movie depict Gilmore's last nine months of his life before he is executed for murder by a firing squad in Utah.

Review for Chapter Fourteen:

Research Paper or Term Paper Topics:

- Community corrections
- Drug courts
- The death penalty

Important Terms to Know

Capital punishment: The imposition of the death penalty for the most serious crimes.

Community corrections: Locally operated services offering minimum security and the ability for offenders to live at home in their own community while serving a sentence.

Corrections: The system of programs, services, facilities, and organizations responsible for the management of people who have been accused of or convicted of criminal offenses.

Drug court: A specialty court that focuses on offenders who are drug users or addicts. Drug courts provide intensive probation, close supervision, incentives for good behavior, and sanctions for re-offending.

Intensive probation:	A form of probation in which the probation officer provides close and intensive supervision.
Intermediate sanction:	Sentences that are more restrictive than probation but less restrictive than imprisonment. Intermediate sanctions can include fines, community service, restitution, house arrest, and intensive probation.
Pre-trial diversion:	Removing a case from the criminal justice system while the defendant is required to comply with certain conditions such as counseling or treatment.
Probation:	The sentence of conditional release to the community; the most common form of punishment in the United States.
Restitution:	A sentence by the court requiring the offender to compensate the victim for their financial losses resulting from the crime.

Study Guide Questions

True or False:

1. The correctional system in the United States costs taxpayers about $60 billion a year.

2. Community corrections offers an alternative to incarcerating offenders.

3. Numerous studies attest to the effectiveness of boot camps.

4. New York was the first state in this country to ban the death penalty.

5. Capital punishment is now banned in 17 states in our nation.

Multiple Choice Items:

6. The most common form of punishment for criminal offenses in the United States is
    a. incarceration
    b. capital punishment
    c. community service
    d. probation

7. Intermediate sanctions do **not** include
    a. community service
    b. restitution
    c. maximum security
    d. house arrest

8. Death penalty proponents often believe that
    a. the death penalty is too expensive
    b. the death penalty deters crime
    c. the death penalty happens too quickly
    d. the death penalty is cruel and unusual punishment

9. The U.S. Supreme Court brought about a moratorium on capital punishment in 1972 with its decision in the case of
    a. *Gregg v. Georgia*
    b. *Furman v. Georgia*
    c. *Escobedo v. Illinois*
    d. *Miranda v. Arizona*

10. Opponents of the death penalty raise serious concerns regarding
    a. race and capital punishment
    b. the expense of lethal injection drugs
    c. the number of appeals death row inmates file
    d. the number of white people on death row

References

American Bar Association, (2012), "ABA urges states to increase the use of parole and probation" [online], Available at: http://www2.americanbar.org/sections/criminaljustice/CR203800/Pages/statepolicyproject.aspx.

Baldus, D. C., Woodworth, G., Zuckerman, D., Weiner, N. A., and Broffitt, B. (1998). Racial discrimination and the death penalty in the post-*Furman* era: An empirical and legal overview, with recent findings from Philadelphia. *Cornell Law Review*, 83, 1638–1770.

Bennis v. Michigan, 516 U.S. 442 (1996).

Boger, J. C., and Unah, I., (2001), "Race and the death penalty in North Carolina. The Common Sense Foundation," Available at: http://www.common-sense.org/pdfs/NCDeathPenaltyReport2001.pdf.

Bohm, R. M., and Haley, K. N. (2012). *Introduction to Criminal Justice*. 7th ed. New York: Glencoe/McGraw-Hill Co.

Boyes-Watson, C. (2003). *Crime and Justice: A Casebook Approach*. Boston: Pearson Education, Inc.

Claxton, M., Sinclair, N., and Hanson, R. (December 10, 2002). Felons on probation often go unwatched. *Detroit News* p. A1.

"Fact Sheet," (2012), Death Penalty Information Center, Available at: http://www.deathpenaltyinfo.org/documents/FactSheet.pdf.

Furman v. Georgia, 408 U.S. 238 (1972).

Gaines, L. K., and Miller, R. L. (2007). *Criminal Justice in Action*. 4th ed. Belmont, CA: Thomson/Wadsworth.

Gottfredson, D. M. (1999). *Exploring Criminal Justice: An Introduction*. Los Angeles: Roxbury Publishing Co.

Gregg v. Georgia, 428 U.S. 153 (1976).

Griffin v. Wisconsin, 483 U.S. 868 (1987).

Inciardi, J. A. (2005). *Criminal Justice*. 7th ed. New York: McGraw Hill.

In re *Kemmler*, 136 U.S. 436 (1890).

Liebman, J., Fagan, J., and West, V., (2000), "A Broken System: Error Rates in Capital Cases, 1973–1995," The Justice Project [online], Available at: http://www.justice.policy.net/cjedfund/jpreport/.

Miller-Potter, K. (2005). "Capital punishment: The myth of murder as effective crime control." In V. E. Kappeler, and Potter, G.W. *The Mythology of Crime and Criminal Justice*. 4th ed. (pp. 329–355). Long Grove, IL: Waveland Press.

Minnesota Statewide Drug Court Evaluation. (June 2012). State Court Administrator's Office. Minneapolis: Minnesota Judicial Branch.

Oliver, W. M., and Hilgenberg, J. F. (2006). *A History of Crime and Criminal Justice in America*. Boston: Allyn & Bacon.

Ortmeier, P. J. (2006). *Introduction to Law Enforcement and Criminal Justice*. 2nd ed. Upper Saddle River, NJ: Pearson.

Petersilia, J. (2002). "Community Corrections in Crime: Public Policies for Crime Control." In Wilson, J.Q. and J. Petersilia, eds. *Crime: Public Policies for Crime Control* (pp. 483–508). Ithaca, NY: ICS Press.

Petersilia, J., and Turner, S. (1986). *Prison versus Probation in California: Implications for Crime and Offender Recidivism*. Santa Monica, CA: Rand.

Pierce, G. L., and and Radelet, M. L. (2005). The impact of legally inappropriate factors on death sentencing for California homicides: 1990–1999. *Santa Clara Law Review* 46 (1), 1–41.

Pierce, G. L., and Radelet, M. L. (2011). Death sentencing in East Baton Rouge Parish: 1990–2008. *Louisiana Law Review* 71, 647–673.

Pokorak, J. J. (1998). Probing the capital prosecutor's perspective: Race of the discretionary actors. *Cornell Law Review* 83, 1811–1819.

Potter, G. (2000). Cost, deterrence, incapacitation, brutalization and the death penalty: The scientific evidence. *Advocate: A Journal of Criminal Justice Education and Research* 22 (1), 24–29.

Rempel, M., Fox-Kralstein, D., and Cissner, A. (2004). *Drug Courts: An Effective Treatment Alternative*. New York: Center for Court Innovation.

Roman, J., Townsend, W., and Bhati, A. S. (2003). *Recidivism Rates for Drug Court Graduates: Nationally Based Estimates, Final Report*. Fairfax, VA: Caliber Associates.

Siegel, L. J., and Senna, J. J. (2008). *Introduction to Criminal Justice*. 11th ed. Belmont, CA: Thomson/Wadsworth.

Stolzenberg, L., and D'Alessio, S. J. (2004). Capital punishment, execution publicity, and murder in Houston, Texas. *Journal of Criminal Law and Criminology* 94, 351–379.

Chapter Fifteen

Prison

THE PRISON SYSTEM IN AMERICA

One of the largest and most costly parts of the correctional system in America is the prison system. As we saw in Chapter Fourteen, prisons assumed a more prominent role in the criminal justice system in the 19th century as the courts placed a greater reliance on prisons to meet the needs of offenders. However, for most of the 20th century, the incarceration rate was fairly steady. But beginning in the early part of the 1970s, there was a continuing increase in incarceration rates, with each succeeding year showing a new high (Bohm, 2008).

According to the most recent statistics, there are about 749,000 offenders confined in jail facilities (Bureau of Justice Statistics, 2011). In addition, the latest figures show that there are about 1.6 million prison inmates (Reid, 2012). These numbers, however, are down slightly from the high of 2.4 million combined jail and prison inmates in 2008 (Bureau of Justice Statistics, 2011). With the number of inmates steadily increasing since the 1970s, and because that necessarily creates overcrowding, a jail building boom has been under way in this country. On the other hand, prisons have also been faced with the same set of problems, and that has been handled not only with the construction of new prisons but also contracting with private prisons and a more recent emphasis on paroling more prisoners (Siegel & Senna, 2008).

What all of this adds up to is a corrections system that is vast and very costly. The Federal Bureau of Prisons and every state government maintains prisons; most counties maintain jails and

But though his rights may be diminished by the needs and exigencies of the institutional environment, a prisoner is not wholly stripped of constitutional protections when he is imprisoned for a crime. There is no iron curtain drawn between the Constitution and the prisons of this country.

–*Justice Byron R. White,* Wolff v. McDonnell, *418 U.S. 539, 555–56 (1974)*

lockups. According to the Bureau of Justice Statistics, local governments, state governments, and the federal government spend more than $50 billion per year on corrections—an amount that rose 946 percent between 1977 and 2008 (Siegel & Senna, 2008).

PRISONS

Prisons house offenders who have been convicted of felonies and are sentenced to at least one year of incarceration. Those offenders sentenced to less than one year behind bars are housed in jails. Today, there are, according to the Bureau of Justice Statistics (2012), about 2,236 adult correctional facilities. This translates into 1,717 state prisons, 104 federal prisons, and 415 privately operated facilities.

Since 1990, the number of state facilities, both public and private, has risen by 351, or 29 percent (Barkan & Bryjak, 2004). However, all state facilities, again both public and private, are filled beyond capacity. In 2001, state prisons were 15 percent over capacity and federal facilities were 31 percent over the number of beds they were built to fill (Beck & Harrison, 2001). This is a fact, despite the existence of another fact, which was discussed in Chapter Three: The crime rate in America has been steadily declining since 1993.

JAILS

The 3,283 jails in this country (Bureau of Justice Statistics, 2011) are run by counties and sheriff departments, although in some areas they are operated by cities or towns. Typically, jails house inmates who have been convicted of misdemeanors or sentenced to a year or less, those individuals awaiting trial or awaiting transfer to a prison, individuals held for contempt of court or awaiting their preliminary hearing or arraignment, and mentally ill individuals awaiting transfer to a mental health facility (Barkan & Bryjak, 2004).

Because many of the people held in jails are not convicted and awaiting trials or hearings, those people are housed with convicted criminals, some of whom have committed serious offenses. Such confinement often subjects petty offenders or those not convicted (or indeed, the innocent) to the possibility of physical assaults and negative peer influences (Barkan & Bryjak, 2004).

STATE PRISON SYSTEMS

A wide range of state correctional institutions and programs exists for adult felons. These programs and facilities include prisons, reformatories, prison farms, forestry camps, and halfway houses. There are far more facilities and programs for men than there are for women, because, of course, there are fewer female felons.

State correctional facilities for men are usually classified by the level of security, with prisons classified as maximum, medium, and minimum (Cole & Smith, 2007). Thirty-eight states have prisons that exceed maximum security. These are usually referred to as "supermax" facilities. About 20,000 inmates live (Mears, 2006) in these supermax prisons, which are designed to house the most dangerous, violent, and incorrigible inmates. In these prisons, inmates spend up to 23 hours a day in their cells. They are shackled whenever they leave their cells, even during recreation, showers, and telephone calls (Cole & Smith, 2007). These supermax prisons are usually surrounded by stone walls with guard towers and with chain-link fences with rolls of razor wire along the tops of the fences—all of which are calculated to prevent escape. California's Pelican Bay institution and Connecticut's Northern Correctional Facility are examples of supermax prisons.

Myth: *Supermax prisons help violent prisoners achieve an adjustment.*

Reality: *With their absence of social interactions, lack of mental stimulation, and failure to provide exposure to what is normal, supermax prisons tax the ability of most prisoners to make any kind of reasonable adjustment.*

Maximum security prisons, which contain about 36 percent of state inmates, also, like supermax facilities, feature heavy security. However, inmates are given somewhat more freedom and flexibility, although discipline and custody are emphasized.

Medium security prisons resemble maximum security institutions in some ways, but they are organized differently—and the atmosphere is less rigid. Prisoners have more privileges and more contact with the outside world through visitors, mail, and access to radio and television (Cole & Smith, 2007). Although the inmates of medium security prisons have committed serious offenses, they are not perceived as hardened criminals.

Minimum security prisons house the least violent offenders. The inmates of these facilities are often long-term felons who have clean records in prison with few, if any, disciplinary problems, and frequently they include inmates who have nearly completed their sentence. In minimum security facilities, inmates often live in dormitories or in their own private room, rather than in barred cells (Cole & Smith, 2007). There is much more personal freedom, including being able to choose their own clothes. Furthermore, there are often more opportunities for rehabilitation programs, education, and work release programs.

WOMEN'S PRISONS

Only about 6.7 percent of the prison inmate population is female. Therefore, there are fewer correctional facilities for women. However, the growth rate in the number of incarcerated women has exceeded that of men since 1981 (Clear, Cole, & Reisig, 2006). Although the ratio of arrests is approximately six men to one woman, still, since 1996, the male population in state and federal correctional facilities increased 27 percent, whereas that of women has increased 38 percent (Clear, Cole, & Reisig, 2006). A higher proportion of female defendants receive probation and intermediate sanctions, and one reason may be that men are more likely to commit the more violent crimes (Cole & Smith, 2007). Currently, there are about 105,000 women incarcerated in prisons in this country (Women in Prisons, 2010). But since 1981, the rate of increase for women inmates has increased faster than for men (Cole & Smith, 2007). Despite their growing numbers, female inmates are convicted of different offenses than are males. Women are more likely to be incarcerated for drug offenses, whereas men are more likely to be imprisoned for violent offenses (Barkan & Bryjak, 2004).

The 105,000 female inmates are housed in 98 institutions for women and 93 facilities which are co-ed. Conditions in correctional institutions for women are generally much more pleasant than the conditions for men. There are no supermax prisons for women, and few institutions for women even appear to be maximum security. However, the institutions for women are often located in rural areas; thus, female inmates may be more isolated from their families and communities than are male inmates. Furthermore, women in correctional facilities often experience sexual abuse—most often from male correctional officers (Barkan & Bryjak, 2004).

Female inmates also differ from their male counterparts in that women who are in prison are much more likely to have been physically or sexually abused before their incarceration. Almost 60 percent of women inmates, against only 16 percent of male inmates, report such abuse (Barkan & Bryjak, 2004). Another important difference between men and women in prison is that 65 percent of females in prison have children under the age of 18, compared to only 55 percent for male inmates (Barkan & Bryjak, 2004). More importantly, 64 percent of these mothers were living with their minor children at the time they were sent to prison. Only 44 percent of men were living with their children at the time they began serving their prison sentence (Barkan & Bryjak, 2004).

PRIVATE PRISONS

Since the early 1970s, we witnessed the largest incarceration boom in our country's history (Bohm, 2008). However, even with the construction of new prisons, the new and existing institutions could not keep up with the number of beds needed for defendants sentenced to prison. Enter private correctional companies.

Private correctional companies offered an alternative to the lack of space in state and federal prisons. Private companies, such as the U.S. Corrections Corporation, began to contract with states, along with the federal government, to build and operate prisons. One of the earliest privately operated state prisons for adult offenders was Kentucky's minimum security Marion Adjustment Center, which opened in January, 1986 (Bohm, 2008).

> **Myth:** *Private prisons only have an interest in providing service to the prisoner population.*
>
> **Reality:** *Private prisons are businesses that make a profit from an ever increasing incarceration rate.*

Today, more than 415 privately operated facilities are under contract with state or federal authorities to house prisoners. And these facilities currently have over 140,000 inmates (State and Federal Prison Facility Characteristics, 2012).

The results of placing inmates in privately run prisons are mixed at this time. Some evaluations suggest that inmates released from private prisons have lower rates of recidivism than do inmates who leave public prisons (Siegel & Senna, 2008). However, there has been criticism of some of the research, which some critics contend has featured flawed comparisons (Masters et al., 2013). There have also been charges of lax oversight in the running of private prisons (Masters et al., 2013). There have been several escapes from private prisons in the last few years, which have been coincident with questions raised about security, efficiency, and training of personnel in privately operated prisons (Masters et al., 2013).

PRISON INMATE CHARACTERISTICS

Most male inmates are currently incarcerated for committing a violent crime, and the proportion of violent inmates has been rising at a much faster pace than inmates incarcerated for other types of crime (Siegel & Senna, 2008). That is not to say that there has not been an increase in offenders imprisoned for non-violent offenses, especially drug offenses. Inmates imprisoned for drug offenses still rank as one of the most significant reasons for incarceration. In 1980, only about six percent of prisoners were behind bars for drug offenses. More recently, that figure has jumped to more than 20 percent of state prisoners incarcerated for drug offenses, while about 55 percent of federal prisoners are imprisoned for drug violations (Cole & Smith, 2008).

For the most part, male inmates (who comprise more than 90 percent of prison inmates) tend to be young, single, poorly educated, and minority group members (Siegel & Senna, 2008). Many were either underemployed or unemployed prior to their arrest. Many had incomes of less than $10,000 a year, and many suffered drug abuse and other personal problems (Siegel & Senna, 2008). Almost 40 percent of all prison inmates are African American, and a significant proportion of the entire black male population is now behind bars (Siegel & Senna, 2007). Recent statistics reveal that about five percent of black males aged 25 to 29 are now in prison (Masters et al., 2013).

> **Myth:** *When prisoners are released from prison, they can make an adequate adjustment back into society if they try hard enough.*
>
> **Reality:** *The vast majority of prisoners were seriously disadvantaged before entering prison. Most have serious social and medical problems, are uneducated and unskilled, and very often have little family support.*

As indicated, many inmates have substance abuse problems. There is, in fact, a strong association between substance abuse and inmate status. One study of Texas inmates found that almost 75 percent suffered from substance abuse or dependence (Peters, Greenbaum, Edens, Carter, & Ortiz, 1998). About 80 percent of inmates report having used drugs at some time during their lives, and more than 60 percent are regular drug users (Siegel & Senna, 2008).

Prison inmates also report a long history of physical abuse and mental health problems. About 19 percent of male inmates report some form of physical abuse (Harlow, 1999). About 16 percent of state prison inmates report having some form of mental health problem (Ditton, 1999). Mentally ill inmates are more likely to be arrested for violent offenses and to have suffered a variety of personal and emotional problems than the general inmate population (Siegel & Senna, 2008).

ADJUSTING TO PRISON

There is a vast difference between living in a community with a great deal of individual and personal freedom and living in a prison. In prison, there is little freedom and inmates are deprived of both independence and material goods. There is much less privacy, and life in prison features constant insecurity, stress, and unpredictability (Bohm, 2008). Therefore, making the transition from an independent and free lifestyle into the new, more repressive lifestyle of a prison community requires an important—but difficult—adjustment.

Different inmates with very diverse backgrounds and personalities adapt to the prison environment in different ways. For instance, predatory, violent convicts who have had lengthy prior records of incarceration will seek power and status by dominating and victimizing others (Bohm, 2008). Criminologist John Irwin suggests that in coping and adjusting to prison, each inmate will develop a prison career or lifestyle (Irwin, 1970).

Three of the lifestyles described by Irwin (1970) are "doing time," "jailing," and "gleaning." Those inmates who are classified as "doing time," are those whose lifestyle centers around getting out of prison as soon as possible and avoiding hard time in the process. Avoiding hard time means maximizing comfort and minimizing discomfort in a way that does not get him in trouble or place himself in danger. The "jailing" inmate is one who embraces the lifestyle and position of those who know their way around prison and the "jailing" inmate is on the lookout to achieve a position of influence in the inmate society. The inmate who adopts the "gleaning" style is the prisoner who wants to take advantage of the resources available to him in the prison and make his life better, particularly after release. Such an inmate may spend time in the library, take classes, or attend therapy groups.

PROBLEMS AND CHALLENGES IN THE PRISON SYSTEM

Becoming a prisoner presents various challenges to the new inmate. Among the problems and challenges encountered by inmates are:

- Racial concerns
- Gangs and violence
- Sexual assault
- Drugs
- Solitary confinement
- Overcrowding

RACIAL CONCERNS

Much of the violence that occurs in men's prisons today has to do with tensions and hostilities between gangs of different racial affiliations (Masters et al., 2013). As a result, racial and ethnic tensions are a significant feature of prison life. But unlike the world outside of prisons, the environments of most prisons are dominated by people of color. This, according to some experts, makes the minority white inmate have more difficulty adjusting to the prison culture (West & Sabol, 2009). Whites also tend to be victimized more often in prisons and more severely. There is some evidence that whites are sexually assaulted more than any other racial group (Knowles, 1999).

GANGS AND VIOLENCE

Prison gangs are a major aspect of prison life. In fact, when a national survey of prison wardens and state corrections administrators was conducted, they identified three significant problems they face in prison: prison overcrowding, understaffed treatment programs, and gang-affiliated inmates (McEwen, 1995).

Gangs operate in prisons in at least 40 states, as well as in federal prisons (Masters et al., 2013). Many inmates, particularly in maximum security institutions, view prison life as dangerous; belonging to a gang in prison provides gang members with protection, as well as a sense of stability (Alarid & Cromwell, 2002). Most gangs are racially segregated, and many of the prison gangs come from the same city—often even from the same neighborhood (Masters et al., 2013).

Within the prison, gangs manage drug trafficking, and through an active black market they are able to control illegal goods and services to other inmates.

Sexual Assault

In 2008, according to the Department of Justice, there were 7,444 reports of sexual violence in jails and prisons, including allegations of sexual assault by correctional staff (Beck & Guerino, 2011). It is generally agreed that this number is much lower than the actual number of incidents because many men who are victims of sexual assault are reluctant to report these incidents due to embarrassment or fear of retaliation (Masters et al., 2013). One study in the federal prison system found that about half of inmates who were sexually assaulted had not told anyone what happened (Masters et al., 2013).

Often, correctional officers and prison officials ignore sexual assaults, sometimes believing that rape or assault is the price inmates should pay for their crime. At other times, corrections officers may contribute to the problem by placing certain inmates in cells with known rapists (Masters, et al., 2013).

Drugs

Even though illicit drugs are prohibited in prisons, still there is ready availability of drugs in most prisons. Despite careful security and searches of all visitors, drugs are smuggled in by visitors, as well as correctional staff (Marx, 1992). Once in the prison, they then become products available in the prison black market.

One of the problems associated with drug use in prison is that inmates under the influence of certain drugs may pose risks for violence against other inmates or staff.

Solitary Confinement

All prisons have the ability to place unruly inmates in solitary confinement when it is deemed necessary. Solitary confinement cells are bare and provide virtually no sensory stimulation. As a result, inmates become disoriented and may emerge from solitary confinement with mental disorders that did not exist before their isolation (Andersen, Sestoft, & Lillebaek, 2003; Gawande, 2009).

Studies have found that prolonged isolation from human contact produces brooding, retaliation fantasies, hallucinations, panic attacks, withdrawal, and in some cases an almost catatonic state, in which the individual's movements and expressions significantly decline (Masters et al., 2013).

Some groups favor abolishing solitary confinement altogether. The British have all but eliminated the use of solitary confinement in their prisons by finding alternatives that tend to prevent violence rather than using punishment and confinement to deal with violent behavior. Alternatives used in British prisons include giving prisoners more control and increasing opportunities for education, work, and mental health treatment (Gawande, 2009).

Overcrowding

The explosion in the prison population, especially since the 1970s, has led to overcrowding and new construction. Most state correctional facilities are operating at or over capacity (Albanese, 2013). As a result of prison overcrowding, states have turned to private prisons as one alternative, and they have also housed thousands of inmates in local jails because of the lack of available prison space (Albanese, 2013). Hundreds of state prisons are under court orders to reduce overcrowding or correct some of the associated conditions—such as health or safety hazards—that violate the law.

The national average cost to house a prisoner is more than $20,000, which includes facility construction and renovation, repair, wages of corrections employees, food service, medical care, transportation, and various programs (Albanese, 2013). These costs are simply not sustainable for a majority of states. Consequently, not only are courts ordering prisons to release inmates in overcrowded prisons, but states themselves have seen no alternative but to release inmates. As state legislatures have tried to deal with the country's severe recession during the first decade of the 21st century, they have had no alternative but to slash state department of corrections' budgets. The direct result has been that corrections departments in literally every state have had to release inmates who are non-violent or eligible for parole.

Prisoner Rights

Overcrowding in prisons has led to lawsuits being filed on behalf of prisoners because of a lack of adequate bed space, a lack of services, reduced medical care, and other problems that come about when prisoners are squeezed into too little space. The U.S. Supreme Court has ordered California, for instance, to reduce its state prison population by 30,000 inmates (Liptak, 2011). The Court ruled that the overcrowding in California's prisons was so bad that it constituted cruel and unusual punishment.

However, it was in a 1964 Supreme Court ruling in the case of *Cooper v. Pate* that the Supreme Court refused to stay uninvolved in what was going on in prisons. In this court case, the Court said that through the Civil Rights Act of 1871 prisoners are *persons* whose rights are protected by the Constitution (*Cooper v. Pate*, 1964). The act of 1871 imposes civil liability on any person who deprives another of his or her constitutional rights. It allows suits against state officials to be heard in federal courts. Because of *Cooper v. Pate*, the federal courts now recognize that prisoners may sue state officials over such things as brutality by guards, inadequate nutrition, poor medical care, the theft of personal property, and the denial of basic rights.

Because of prisoner lawsuits, there has been a series of court cases in the past half century establishing that prisoners have rights under the First, Eighth, and Fourteenth Amendments. Some of the most significant decisions by the courts include the following:

- Prisoners have freedom of speech and freedom of expression. The Supreme Court ruled in *Procunier v. Martinez* in 1974 that inmates' mail could be censored only when prison officials could demonstrate a compelling government interest in maintaining security.
- Prisons must give prisoners the opportunity to practice their religion (*Gittlemacker v. Prasse* [1970]).

- The Muslim faith must be recognized as a religion and prison officials may not restrict members from holding services (*Fulwood v. Clemmer* [1962]).
- Deliberate indifference to serious medical needs of prisoners constitutes the unnecessary and wanton infliction of pain, and thus violates the Eighth Amendment (*Estelle v. Gamble* [1976]).
- When courts have found brutality, unsanitary facilities, overcrowding, and inadequate food, judges have used the Eighth Amendment to order sweeping changes and even, in some cases, to take over administration of entire prisons or corrections systems (Cole & Smith, 2007).
- The basic elements of procedural due process must be present when decisions are made concerning the discipline of an inmate (*Wolff v. McDonnell* [1974]).
- The involuntary transfer of a prisoner to a mental hospital requires a hearing and other minimal elements of due process, such as notice and the availability of counsel (*Vitek v. Jones* [1980]).

Given the application of the Bill of Rights to prisoners, beginning in the 1960s, there have been significant improvements in the living conditions in prison for inmates. Law libraries and legal assistance are now generally available, communication with the outside is easier, religious practices are protected, inmate complaint procedures have been developed, and due process requirements are recognized. Although overcrowding remains a serious problem, many conditions are much improved and the most devastating and brutalizing aspects of prison life have been reduced or eliminated (Cole & Smith, 2007).

SPECIAL PROBLEMS AND NEEDS IN PRISONS

The inmates in state and federal prisons are diverse and as a result, many have special needs and problems. The most critical special needs and problems involve elderly inmates, inmates with HIV/AIDS, mentally ill prisoners, and sex offenders.

ELDERLY INMATES

Getting tough on crime by sentencing more defendants to longer sentences in prison has led to one unintended consequence that perhaps few legislators gave much thought to when enacting tough-on-crime laws. That is, the problem of elderly inmates.

The prison population is aging, with the number of older inmates—those aged 55 and over—increasing by 200 percent since the 1990s (Masters et al., 2013). Now, one out of every 23 prisoners is in the 55-years-and-older category. Between 1994 and 2004, the number of prisoners serving life sentences increased by 83 percent (Masters et al., 2013).

So, why is this a problem? Very simply, the cost of imprisoning older inmates is high—costing taxpayers $2.1 billion annually (Abner, 2006). Most of the added expense for elderly prisoners is related to health care costs.

Medical problems and expenses involve such inmate needs as hearing aids, bath rails, wheelchairs, and walkers. Furthermore, those inmates with age-related dementia and senility may need constant supervision. Also, older and more fragile prisoners may need to be protected—and separated—from the general prison population.

Finally, prisons were never built to provide long-term medical care or aging services. Older inmates with significant health issues may not only require expensive medical treatment such as transplants or other surgeries, but if they have a contagious disease they will have to be isolated from other inmates.

Inmates with HIV/AIDS

As indicated in the previous section, inmates with significant health issues—for instance, tuberculosis, cancer, or AIDS—require extensive health care in prison. Two groups of people at high risk of contracting HIV are intravenous drug users who share needles and males who engage in homosexual sex. Both are common in prison (Siegel & Senna, 2008).

Although constantly changing, the rate of HIV infection among state and federal prisoners is currently stabilized at around two percent (Siegel & Senna, 2008). All state and federal facilities do some AIDS testing, but only 18 states and the Federal Bureau of Prisons conduct mass screenings of all inmates (Siegel & Senna, 2008). About 40 percent of all state prison inmates have never been tested for AIDS (Siegel & Senna, 2008).

The rate of confirmed AIDS cases among prison inmates is about twice as high as that for the entire U.S. population (Barkan & Bryjak, 2004). A major reason for this difference is the high number of intravenous drug users among prison inmates. Also, unprotected homosexual sex and prison rape, along with sex with a partner with HIV, increase the rate of transmission within the prison population (Barkan & Bryjak, 2004).

Often prisons prohibit HIV or AIDS inmates from taking their required medication. However, one reason for this is because the medication is so expensive. The annual cost of such medication can be $12,000 or more per inmate (Barkan & Bryjak, 2004). Another reason for keeping medication away from inmates is related to the lack of doctors as well as other medical personnel to treat HIV and AIDS.

It is almost impossible to completely isolate inmates with HIV or AIDS. In fact, federal laws regarding inmates' rights of privacy often prohibit prison administrators from making it generally known which inmates are HIV-positive (Fagin, 2007). Therefore, prison staff and other inmates may not be aware of which inmates are affected. This lack of knowledge creates concern among both staff and inmates. Often correctional staff must treat all inmates as if they are potential infection risks.

Mentally Ill Inmates

A comprehensive Justice Department study of the rapidly growing number of prisoners with emotional and psychological disorders concluded that jails and prisons have become the nation's new mental health care facilities (Butterfield, 1999). Nearly one in five inmates in U.S. prisons report having a mental illness (Fagin, 2007).

In the 1960s, mental hospitals across the country began to release mentally ill patients who had often been held against their will. It was thought that the mentally ill would receive treatment and care at home or in the community. Despite these intentions, things did not work out as planned. There were too few community-based facilities, the mentally ill did not take their medications, and jails and prisons became the dumping ground for the mentally ill (Fagin, 2005).

Recent estimates have placed the number of inmates with mental disorders in jails and prisons at over 1.2 million (Masters et al., 2013). This total number breaks down into 56 percent of state prisoners, 45 percent of federal prisoners, and 64 percent of jail inmates with mental health problems (Glaze & James, 2006). These numbers strongly suggest the kinds of challenges the mentally ill inmate may present to the prison staff. Inmates who are suffering from hallucinations, delusions, paranoia, anxiety, and poor self-care are likely to be easy prey for institutional predators looking to take advantage of others. Some of these inmates will present discipline and management problems. Consequently, correctional staff must always be on the lookout for prisoners who are suicidal, may display erratic and violent behavior, or who require medication in order to bring about more tranquil behavior.

Sex Offender Inmates

As a group, sex offenders commit a wide range of offenses, and this range may include exhibitionism, child molestation, Internet child pornography, and rape. But of special concern to prison administrators are sex offenders who have victimized children. That is because they are often considered the lowest of the low in the status hierarchy of prison society (Masters et al., 2013). Given this lowly status, child sex offenders are very likely to receive threats, hostility, and beatings from other inmates (Masters et al., 2013).

A growing trend in this country—and a trend many consider troubling—is to incarcerate sex offenders beyond their prison term. This is carried out under civil commitment programs. In civil commitments, a judge decides that a person is mentally ill and a danger to himself or others. The judge then incarcerates that person indefinitely in a mental hospital rather than a prison. And he (most often sex offenders are male) might be held there until there is a ruling that he has been "cured" (Masters et al., 2013). Once a sex offender completes his sentence, though, he can then be subject to a state judicial hearing to determine whether he should still be held in a secure psychiatric facility. If the state finds that such an offender is eligible for a civil commitment, he could be confined in such a facility until he is no longer deemed dangerous (Masters et al., 2013).

Although civil commitment programs may be popular with the public who are frightened by sexual offenders returning to the community, they are very expensive. The cost of housing a sex offender for a year can be as much as $100,000 or more when treatment costs are figured in (Civil Commitment of Sex Offenders, 2011). Furthermore, many believe that extending a sex offender's sentence beyond the original term may be unconstitutional. And there is also concern that available treatments are not very effective with this population.

PAROLE

Sexual offenders who are subject to civil commitments aside, most inmates complete their sentence and return to society. For some inmates, their reentry into society comes by way of a parole. A parole is a release from prison before the expiration of the full prison sentence.

The decision to parole an inmate is determined by a parole board, which is an appointed body of men and women who review inmate cases and decide whether offenders have reached a rehabilitative level that allows them to return to their homes and the community (Siegel & Senna, 2008).

In some states, sentences can be reduced by more than half of the original sentence with corrections departments or parole boards paying attention (and releasing prisoners) based on eligible release dates (often determined by a state statute) and earned good time (Siegel & Senna, 2008). However, if after release the individual violates the rules and conditions of parole (which are also often determined by the parole board), he or she may be returned to prison to serve out the remainder of his or her sentence.

There is a great deal of opposition to parole by the general public in this country (Lawmakers Weigh Changes, 2012). This opposition is reflected in the abandonment of parole in the federal court system and in many states (Fagin, 2007). By the end of 2001, 15 states had abolished parole board authority for releasing all offenders, and another five states had abolished parole board authority for releasing certain violent offenders (Fagin, 2007). The public, it seems, wants criminals sentenced to prison to make sure they "get the amount of time they deserve." This fear seems to be based on the generalized apprehension that prisoners released early will return to a life of crime.

This fear may not be groundless. In 2004, only 46 percent of adults successfully completed the conditions of parole (Fagin, 2007). The failure rate for parolees is fairly high, despite the fact that they are under supervision, which requires them to report regularly to a parole officer.

At any given time, more than 750,000 former inmates are living in the community on parole (Gaines & Miller, 2007). When parolees do commit a new, serious crime, the public is justifiably outraged. However, their personal histories and personal problems—which often include drug and alcohol abuse, functional illiteracy, a lack of employable skills, and mental disorders—explain much of their high recidivism rates. In addition, many states have cut back on services for inmates which might be helpful in preparing them to reenter the community. By establishing and maintaining educational and treatment services in prisons, and by providing adequate supervision with appropriate and effective treatment in the community following release, many observers believe that more parolees could be successful after leaving prison (Barkan & Bryjak, 2004).

FOR FURTHER CONSIDERATION

Historical Events Relevant to Chapter Fifteen

January 28, 1936: Richard Loeb, who along with Nathan Leopold murdered a boy in Chicago, was stabbed to death in prison. Both Loeb and Leopold were sentenced to life in prison.

February 25, 1992: The Supreme Court rules that prison guards who use unnecessary force against inmates may be violating the Eighth Amendment's ban on cruel and unusual punishment (even if no serious injuries are inflicted). In the case of *Hudson v. McMillian* (503 U.S. 1 [1992]), the Supreme Court stated that a beating or other use of excessive force by a prison guard may violate the Constitution, even if it does not result in a serious injury to the prisoner. The decision overturned a ruling by a federal appeals court that the use of force against a prison inmate violates the Eighth Amendment only if it results in "significant injury." The case was appealed to the Supreme Court without legal assistance by a Louisiana prison inmate who had been beaten and punched by two prison guards while he was handcuffed and shackled. Because the inmate's injuries, which included bruises, swelling, and loosened teeth, did not require medical attention, the United States Court of Appeals for the Fifth Circuit in New Orleans overturned a decision by a federal magistrate, awarding him $800 in damages.

March 4, 2005: Martha Stewart is released from Alderson Federal Penitentiary in West Virginia today. "The experience of the last five months in Alderson, West Virginia has been life altering and life affirming," appears on her website today. "Someday, I hope to have the chance to talk more about all that has happened, the extraordinary people I have met here and all that I have learned." On June 9, 2003, Martha Stewart pleaded guilty to charges of obstruction of justice and giving false statements in relation to insider trading.

March 21, 1963: Alcatraz Prison in San Francisco Bay is emptied of its last prisoner on this date by order of U.S. Attorney General Robert F. Kennedy. "The Rock" opened in 1934 as a federal prison. During the years of its operation, it housed 1,545 men, including Al Capone for more than four years.

April 14, 2000: The Forgotten Victims of Attica call for support of their five-point plan and compensation for their loses, years of anguish, and lack of support as a result of the Attica Prison riot of September 1971. The riot started on September 9, 1971, when more than 1000 convicts took over the state prison at Attica, New York, and held 35 convicts as hostages. Four days later, 28 convicts and 11 corrections officers and civilian employees of the prison were killed. Only one died because of injuries inflicted by inmates. The other ten fatalities to the hostages were the result of New York state gunfire during the retaking of Attica on September 13, 1971.

September 14, 1966: State police use tear gas to end a strike attempt by 144 inmates at Cummins State Farm, a prison in Lincoln County, Arkansas. The movie *Brubaker* was based on the story of Thomas Murton, an Arkansas prison reform warden, who became the warden of Cummins in 1968.

September 21, 1862: Minnesota passes the first good-time law as an incentive for good behavior in prison. Prisoners could earn three days off their sentence for every month of good conduct.

October 4, 1873: The first women's prison run by women opens as the Indiana Reformatory Institution for Women and Girls receives 17 prisoners.

October 12, 1933: Alcatraz Island is made a federal maximum security prison. Situated on 12 acres in San Francisco Bay, it is one and a half miles from downtown San Francisco. In Spanish, the name Alcatraz means the Island of Pelicans. Alcatraz housed Al Capone and Machine Gun Kelly, among many other notorious prisoners before it closed in 1963.

November 16, 1676: The first colonial prison is established in Nantucket, Massachusetts. William Bunker was hired to organize the prison.

November 21, 1963: Robert Stroud, a violent prisoner housed in Leavenworth Prison and later in Alcatraz, dies on this date of natural causes. Stroud spent most of his prison life in a solitary cell because of his violence. He was first imprisoned in 1912 and never was released. On December 19, 1942, Stroud was transferred to Alcatraz, where he spent six years in segregation and another 11 years confined to the hospital wing. In 1959, Stroud was transferred to the Medical Center for Federal Prisoners in Springfield, Missouri, where he stayed until his death. However, at Leavenworth Prison he began to raise, study, and sell birds, and picked up the nickname later on of the Birdman of Alcatraz. A movie version of his life was made in 1962 called *The Birdman of Alcatraz.*

November 28, 1994: Convicted serial killer Jeffrey Dahmer is beaten to death by another inmate in prison as he was cleaning a toilet. Convicted of killing 17 men and boys between 1978 and 1991, Dahmer's murders involved rape, dismemberment, necrophilia, and cannibalism. At the time of his death, Dahmer was an inmate at the Columbia Correctional Institution in Portage, Wisconsin.

December 4, 1992: Kathleen Hawk Sawyer is appointed the first female director of the Federal Bureau of Prisons. Starting her career in 1976 as a psychologist at the Federal Correctional Facility in Morgantown, West Virginia, Sawyer moved up and held positions at different prisons across the country. She served as director of the Federal Bureau of Prisons until 2003.

December 13, 2005: Stanley "Tookie" Williams is executed by lethal injection shortly after midnight. Governor Arnold Schwarzenegger of California denied his bid for clemency earlier on December 12, 2005. Williams had been convicted of murder in two separate incidents and is credited with starting the Crips gang. He had spent his last several years on death row writing and trying to persuade youth that gangs and violence are wrong. He had been nominated more than once for the Nobel Peace Prize.

December 31, 2007: Sara Jane Moore, age 77, is released from prison on parole. She served 32 years behind bars for the 1975 assassination attempt on President Gerald Ford. She was released from the federal prison in Dublin, California, east of San Francisco.

Important Court Cases

- *Cooper v. Pate*, **378 U.S. 546 (1964):** An inmate at the Illinois State Penitentiary brought suit, alleging that solely because of his religious beliefs, he was denied permission to purchase certain religious publications and denied other privileges enjoyed by other prisoners. The Court ruled that the inmate, a black Muslim, must be treated equally with other religious groups, unless the prison can demonstrate good reasons to do otherwise.
- *Hudson v. Palmer*, **468 U.S. 517 (1984):** The U.S. Supreme Court decided that prison inmates have many rights, but they do not have a right to privacy in their prison cells that would entitle them to Fourth Amendment protection against unreasonable searches.
- *Sandin v. Conner*, **515 U.S. 472 (1995):** DeMont R. D. Conner, a convicted murderer serving 30 years to life in Hawaii's maximum security correctional facility, brought suit against Cinda Sandin, a manager in the prison. Conner's claim was that Sandin had not allowed Conner to call witnesses before being subjected to punishment for breaking prison rules. Conner argued that Sandin's failure to do so amounted to a violation of procedural due process under the Fourteenth Amendment. The Supreme Court had previously ruled that such due process rights as a hearing and the ability to call witnesses came into play when the state's actions had clearly violated a substantive right of the prisoner. Chief Justice William Rehnquist, writing for the majority, articulated a standard that required a prisoner to demonstrate that authorities had imposed an atypical and significant hardship rather than carrying out the routine, day-by-day business of the prison. The Court rejected Conner's claim.
- *Vitek v. Jones*, **445 U.S. 480 (1980):** A convicted felon was transferred from state prison to a mental hospital pursuant to a Nebraska statute, which provides that if a designated physician or psychologist finds that a prisoner "suffers from a mental disease or defect" that "cannot be given proper treatment" in prison, the director of correctional services may transfer the prisoner to a mental hospital. The Supreme Court stated in its decision that, although the state's interest in segregating and treating mentally ill patients is strong, the prisoner's interest in not being arbitrarily classified as mentally ill and subjected to unwelcome

treatment is also powerful, and the risk of error in making the determinations required by the state statute is substantial enough to warrant appropriate procedural safeguards against error. And the Court said that the medical nature of the inquiry as to whether or not to transfer a prisoner to a mental hospital does not justify dispensing with due process requirements. Furthermore, because prisoners facing involuntary transfer to a mental hospital are threatened with immediate deprivation of liberty interests, and because of the risk of mistaken transfer, certain procedural protections, including notice and an adversary hearing, are appropriate in the circumstances present in this case.

- *Wolff v. McDonnell*, **418 U.S. 539 (1974):** An inmate, on behalf of himself and other prisoners at a Nebraska prison, filed a complaint for damages and injunctive relief, alleging that disciplinary proceedings at the prison violated due process; that the inmate legal assistance program did not meet constitutional standards; and that the regulations governing inmates' mail were unconstitutionally restrictive. The Court declared in its ruling that a prisoner is not wholly stripped of constitutional protections, and though prison disciplinary proceedings do not implicate the full array of rights due a defendant in a criminal prosecution, such proceedings must be governed by a mutual accommodation between institutional needs and generally applicable constitutional requirements. The state may constitutionally require that mail from an attorney to a prisoner be identified as such, and that his name and address appear on the communication, and that—as a protection against contraband—the authorities may open such mail in the inmate's presence.

Websites to Check Out

- *Federal Bureau of Prisons. U.S. Justice Department.* Available at: *http://www.bop.gov/.* The Federal Bureau of Prisons website lists all the federal prisons, shows their security levels, and in addition, gives other information ranging from population statistics at federal facilities, faith-based organizations operating in federal prisons, and other valuable information, such as career opportunities and research.
- *Prisoners' Rights Project. American Civil Liberties Union.* Available at: *http://www.aclu.org/prisoners-rights.* The Prisoners' Rights Project, found within the ACLU's website, is dedicated to ensuring that our nation's prisons, jails, and other places of detention comply with the Constitution, domestic law, and international human rights principles. Thus, it features many articles and videos, as well as special reports related to various aspects of prisoners' rights and inmate issues.
- *Corrections Corporation of America.* Available at: *http://www.cca.com/about/.* Learn more about the largest private corrections company in America, which describes itself as a full-service corrections management provider. CCA, as this website indicates, specializes in the design, construction, expansion and management of prisons, jails, and detention facilities, as well as inmate transportation services through its subsidiary company TransCor America. CCA houses more than 80,000 inmates in more than 60 facilities under contract with the Federal Bureau of Prisons and various states.

Books

- Booth, D. (2007). *Why Are So Many Black Men in Prison: A Comprehensive Account of How and Why the Prison Industry Has Become a Predatory Entity in the Lives of African-American Men.* Memphis, TN: Full Surface Publishing.
- Champion, D. J. (2007). *Probation, Parole, and Community Corrections.* 6th ed. Upper Saddle River, NJ: Prentice Hall.
- Clear, T. D., Cole, G. F., and Reisig, M. D. (2006). *American Corrections.* 7th ed. Belmont, CA: Thomson/Wadsworth.
- Drucker, E. (2011). *A Plague of Prisons: The Epidemiology of Mass Incarceration in America.* New York: New Press.
- Ross, J. I., and Richards, A. C. (2002). *Behind Bars: Surviving Prison.* Royersford, PA: Alpha.

Movies

- *Brubaker:* A 1980 film about a prison in distress and the warden who attempts to reform the system. The screenplay is a fictionalized version of the 1969 book *Accomplices to the Crime: The Arkansas Prison Scandal* by Tom Murton and Joe Hyams. Murton was the warden of Cummins Prison in Arkansas.
- *The Glass House:* A 1972 movie written by Truman Capote. This film is one of the first to give a more gritty view of prison life.
- *The Shawshank Redemption:* A 1994 movie that depicts the struggles that accompany life both in and out of prison.
- *Cool Hand Luke:* Paul Newman starred in this 1967 movie about prison life that was described as brutally realistic.

TV Shows

- *Oz:* A television drama produced on HBO, it aired from July 1997 to February 2003. "Oz" was the nickname for the Oswald State Correctional Facility, a fictional maximum security prison. In an experimental unit of the prison, unit manager Tim McManus works to provide rehabilitation and help inmates learn responsibility during incarceration. The unit is an extremely controlled environment, with a carefully managed number of members of each racial and social group, with the hope of easing tensions among these various groups. The inmates in the unit struggle to fulfill their own needs. Some fight for power—either over the drug trade or over other inmate factions and individuals. The show offers a no-holds-barred account of prison life.

Review for Chapter Fifteen:

Research Paper or Term Paper Topics:

- Rehabilitation in prison
- Prisoners' rights
- Overcrowded jails and prisons

Important Terms to Know

Maximum security prisons:
Prisons designed and organized to minimize the possibility of escape and reduce the incidence of violence. Maximum security prisons feature heavy security and discipline with strict limits on the freedom of inmates.

Supermax prisons: Prisons designed to house the most dangerous and violent prisoners and where inmates are confined to their cells about 23 hours a day.

Minimum security prisons:
These prisons house the least violent offenders. The prisoners have more freedom and privileges, as well as more contact with the outside world.

Solitary confinement: Special cells where inmates are confined when they are unruly and have broken prison rules. Solitary confinement separates inmates from the general population and minimizes most kinds of stimulation. Called punitive segregation by prisons, often inmates refer to solitary confinement as "the hole."

Private prisons: Prisons built and operated by private companies to take inmates from state or federal authorities, often to alleviate overcrowding in state and federal facilities.

Parole: The conditional release of an inmate from incarceration, under supervision, after part of the prison sentence has been served.

Study Guide Questions

True or False:

1. The American correctional system costs the American taxpayers about $50 billion a year.

2. Prisons house offenders who have been sentenced to a year or less of incarceration.

3. There are more than 250 private prisons or facilities that have been contracted by state and federal authorities to house convicted felons.

4. More than 40 percent of all prison inmates are African Americans.

5. Most state or federal correctional facilities are operating at or over capacity.

Multiple Choice Items:

6. Supermax prisons are correctional facilities that are
   a. comfortable with many amenities
   b. medium security prisons
   c. run by trusted inmates
   d. designed to hold the most dangerous and violent prisoners

7. The national average to house one prisoner for a year is
   a. $10,000
   b. $20,000
   c. $30,000
   d. $50,000

8. The U.S. Supreme Court has ruled that prisoners do **not** have the right to
   a. free cable and TV in their cell
   b. practice their religion
   c. have their medical needs met
   d. be safe from brutality

9. One of the special problems in prisons these days is the problem of an aging prison population. Those prisoners aged 55 and older have increased by _____ percent since 1990.
    a. 50
    b. 100
    c. 200
    d. 300

10. The rate of confirmed AIDS cases among prison inmates is about ____ as high as that for the entire U.S. population.
    a. twice
    b. four times
    c. eight times
    d. ten times

References

Abner, C., (2006), "Graying prisons, states face challenges of an aging inmate population," *State News* (November/December), Available at: www.csg.org/knowledgecenter/docs/sn0611GrayingPrisons.pdf.

Alarid, L. F., and Cromwell, P. F., eds. (2002). *Correctional Perspectives: Views From Academics, Practitioners, and Prisoners.* New York: Oxford University Press.

Albanese, J. S. (2013). *Criminal Justice.* 5th ed. Upper Saddle River, NJ: Pearson.

Andersen, H. S., Sestoft, D, and Lillebaek, T. (2003). A longitudinal study of prisoners on remand: Repeated measures of psychopathology in the initial phase of solitary versus non-solitary confinement. *International Journal of Law and Psychiatry* 26:165–177.

Barkan, S. E., and Bryjak, G. J. (2004). *Fundamentals of Criminal Justice.* Boston: Pearson.

Beck, A. J., and Guerino, P., (2011), "Sexual Victimization Reported by Adult Correctional Authorities, 2007–2008," Bureau of Justice Statistics [online], Available at: http://bjs.ojp.usdoj.gov/index.cfm?ty=pbdetail&iid=2204.

Beck, A. J., and Harrison, P. M. (2001). *Bureau of Justice Statistics Bulletin: Prisoners in 2000* (NCJ 188207). Washington, DC: U.S. Department of Justice.

Bohm, R. (2008). *A Concise Guide to Criminal Justice.* New York: McGraw Hill.

Bohm, R. M., and Haley, K. N. (2012). *Introduction to Criminal Justice.* 7th ed. New York: Glencoe/McGraw-Hill Co.

Bureau of Justice Statistics, 2011, http://bjs.ojp.usdoj.gov/index.cfm?ty=pbdetail&iid=2375.

Butterfield, F., (July 12, 1999), "Prisons brim with mentally ill, study finds," *New York Times* [online], Available at: http://www.nytimes.com/1999/07/12/us/prisons-brim-with-mentally-ill-study-finds.html?pagewanted=all&src=pm.

"Civil Commitment of Sex Offenders," (2011), Office of the Legislative Auditor, State of Minnesota. [online], Available at: http://www.auditor.leg.state.mn.us/ped/2011/ccsosum.htm.

Clear, T. R., Cole, G. F., and Reisig, M. D. (2006). *American Corrections.* 7th ed. Belmont, CA: Thomson/Wadsworth.

Cole, G. F., and Smith, C. E. (2007). *The American System of Criminal Justice.* 11th ed. Belmont, CA: Thomson/Wadsworth.

Cooper v. Pate, 378 U.S. 546 (1964),

Dilton, P. M. (1999). *Mental health and treatment of inmates and probationers.* Bureau of Justice Statistics (NCJ-174463). Washington DC: U.S. Department of Justice.

Estelle v. Gamble, 429 U.S. 97 (1976).

Fagin, J. A. (2007). *Criminal Justice: A Brief Introduction*. Boston: Allyn & Bacon.

Fulwood v. Clemmer, 206 F. Supp 370 (1962).

Gaines, L. K., and Miller, R. L. (2007). *Criminal Justice in Action*. 4th ed. Belmont, CA: Thomson/Wadsworth.

Gawande, A., (March 30, 2009), "Hellhole: The United States holds tens of thousands of inmates in long-term solitary confinement. Is this torture?" *New Yorker* [online], Available at: http://www.newyorker.com/reporting/2009/03/30/090330fa_fact_gawande#ixzz23Laryxoj.

Gittlemacker v. Prasse, 428 F.2d 1 4 (3 Cir. [1970]).

Glaze, L. E., and James, D. J., (2006), "Mental health problems of prison and jail inmates," Bureau of Justice Statistics. [online], Available at: http://bjs.ojp.usdoj.gov/index.cfm?ty=pbdetail&iid=789.

Harlow, C. W., (1999), "Prior Abuse Reported by Inmates and Prisoners," Bureau of Justice Statistics. [online], Available at: http://bjs.ojp.usdoj.gov/content/pub/pdf/parip.pdf.

Inciardi, J. A. (2005). *Criminal Justice*. 7th ed. New York: McGraw Hill.

Irwin, J. (1970). *The Felon*. Englewood Cliffs, NJ: Prentice Hall.

Knowles, G. J. (1999). Male prison rape: A search for causation and prevention. *Howard Journal* 38 (3). 267–282.

"Lawmakers Weigh Major Changes to Probation, Parole," (2012), *Corrections.com* [online], Available at: http://www.corrections.com/news/article/30485.

Liptak, A., (May 23, 2011), "Justices, 5–4, tell California to reduce prison population," *New York Times* [online],. Available at: http://www.nytimes.com/2011/05/24/us/24scotus.html?pagewanted=all.

Marx, G. (1992). When the Guards Guard Themselves: Undercover Tactics Turned Inward. *Policing and Society* 2, 151–172.

Masters, R. E., Way, L. B., Gerstenfeld, P. B., Muscat, B. T., Hooper, M., Dussich, J. P. J., Pincu, L., and Skrapec, C.A. (2013). *CJ: Realities and Challenges*. 2nd ed. New York: McGraw-Hill.

McEwen, T., (1995), "NIJ Survey of Wardens and State Commissioners of Corrections," National Institute of Justice [online], Available at: https://www.ncjrs.gov/App/Publications/abstract.aspx?ID=18555.

Mears, D. P., (2006), "Evaluating the Effectiveness of Supermax Prisons," Urban Institute [online], Available at: https://www.ncjrs.gov/pdffiles1/nij/grants/211971.pdf.

Oliver, W. M., and Hilgenberg, J. F. (2006). *A History of Crime and Criminal Justice in America*. Boston: Allyn & Bacon.

Ortmeier, P. J. (2006). *Introduction to Law Enforcement and Criminal Justice*. 2nd ed. Upper Saddle River, NJ: Pearson.

Peters, R. H., Greenbaum, P. E., Edens, J. F., Carter, C. R., and Ortiz, M. M. (1998). Prevalence of DSM-IV substance abuse and dependence disorders among prison inmates. *American Journal of Drug and Alcohol Abuse 24*(4): 573–587.

Procunier v. Martinez, 416 U.S. 396 (1974).

Reid, S. T. (2012). *Crime and Criminology*. 13th ed. New York: Oxford University Press.

Siegel, L. J., and Senna, J. J. (2008). *Introduction to Criminal Justice*. 11th ed. Belmont, CA: Thomson/Wadsworth.

"State and Federal Prison Facility Characteristics," (2012), Bureau of Justice Statistics [online], Available at: http://bjs.ojp.usdoj.gov/index.cfm?ty=tp&tid=133.

Vitek v. Jones, 445 U.S. 480 (1980).

West, H. C., and Sabol, W. J. (2009). *Prison and Jail Inmates at Midyear 2009*. Bureau of Justice Statistics. (No. NCJ 230113). Washington, DC: Bureau of Justice Statistics.

Wolff v. McDonnell, 418 U.S. 539 (1974).

"Women in Prisons," (2010), Corrections.com [online], Available at: http://www.corrections.com/news/article/23873-women-in-prisons.

Part Six

What Happens to Victims
in the Criminal Justice
System?

Chapter Sixteen

Who are the Victims?

Watch a classic whodunit movie or television show, and who gets the most attention?

That question may be easy to answer because of the very term that is used to classify this genre of crime fiction. A crime takes place. Often, it is a murder, and the rest of the plot is designed to lead the viewer—or the reader, say, in a classic Agatha Christie novel or in any number of detective or mystery stories—through a maze of clues in an attempt to figure out "who done it?" The emphasis is not on the victim so much as it is on the person who committed the crime.

It's this kind of focus that keeps us coming back to a variety of TV shows, such as *CSI, Bones, The Closer, Rizzoli and Isles, Unforgettable, Law & Order,* and *Cold Case.* Can we, the viewer, follow the clues to unravel the mystery and figure out who the guilty person is? In TV shows like *Criminal Minds* and *Without a Trace,* the detectives doggedly follow clues or criminal profiles to hunt down the culprit. And in the programs that purport to use the latest crime scene technology, it is presumably science that allows medical examiner's and lab technicians to analyze the clues that help to pinpoint the identity of the guilty party.

Of course, the victim, if still alive, might be questioned and his or her life picked over, or if murdered, the victim's body is scrutinized for subtle clues that shed light on who did it. There may be perfunctory or dutiful reference to the victim and there is frequently a statement of sympathy for the victim. Furthermore, some detectives, prosecutors, or medical examiners say that they want to bring about justice for the victim. However, that's not really

We thus hold that if the State chooses to permit the admission of victim impact evidence and prosecutorial argument on that subject, the Eighth Amendment erects no *per se* bar. A State may legitimately conclude that evidence about the victim and about the impact of the murder on the victim's family is relevant to the jury's decision as to whether or not the death penalty should be imposed. There is no reason to treat such evidence differently than other relevant evidence is treated.

—*Chief Justice William Rehnquist,* Payne v. Tennessee, *501 U.S. 808 (1991)*

what keeps our interest in such fictional or fictionalized shows—it's really the mystery of who is guilty and the process of tracking down and catching the bad guy.

It was not until more recently in criminal justice history that victims of crimes and their survivors have been given attention or been assigned a role in the criminal justice process. Victims were not considered important or given much respect in the adjudication process except, perhaps, as witnesses to their own or their loved ones' victimization. Traditionally, there was a legal reason for this. It is the state, not the individual, who is officially the victim of the crime. When charges are brought against a person, the indictment or the information reads: "*The State of Michigan v. Robert Bashara*" (for instance). It is not the victim versus the offender: It is the state versus the accused.

Beginning in the 1980s, however, because of increased scholarly attention to their plight and a fledgling victims' rights movement, attempts were made to change the situation (Bohm & Haley, 2012). Prior to the early 1980s, only four states had laws that protected the basic rights of crime victims in the criminal justice system. Now, every state has such laws (Bohm & Haley, 2012).

You will remember that it was in the 1970s that the federal government began collecting data about victims on an annual basis. The National Crime Victimization Survey began to ask victims about the crimes they experienced, and what we first learned was that there are many more victims of criminal events than were recorded in the FBI's Uniform Crime Reports. However, that is not all we know about victimization. This chapter will explore several important and critical questions related to the victims of crime:

- Who are the victims of crime?
- What are the effects of crime on victims?
- What are the costs of victimization?
- Who advocates for victims?
- What are the rights afforded to victims?

WHO ARE THE VICTIMS OF CRIME?

Many new terms have evolved in the last few decades related to victims and the study of victims (or *victimology*). For example, the term *crime victimization* itself is a relatively new term, which means the injuring or killing of a human being through behavior that is prohibited by law (Masters et al., 2013). There are also terms such as *primary victim*—referring to the person injured or killed as a result of a criminal act—and *secondary victim*, which refers to any individual who is affected by the primary victim's suffering.

Statistics that come from victimization research indicate that from age 12 , the younger the person the greater the likelihood of being victimized by a violent crime (Albanese, 2013). People who are 65 and older are 12 times less likely to be the victim of a crime, and the group most likely to become a victim of either a violent crime or a property crime contains young people between the ages of 12 to 19 years (Albanese, 2013). The reason for this is fairly easy to understand. Young people are active and mobile and expose themselves to more risks. They visit more dangerous places, at later hours, and take fewer security precautions than do older people (Albanese, 2013).

Except for the crime of rape, women are less likely to be victims of crimes than are men. Women are victimized by violent crime at a rate of 16 per 1,000 people in the population, whereas the rate for men is 18 per 1,000 (Truman, 2010). Violence between intimate partners is a growing problem that disproportionately victimizes women. A National Violence Against Women (NVAW) Survey was conducted in 2000 (Tjaden & Thoennes, 2000). The survey of 8,000 men and 8,000 women concluded that intimate partner violence is "pervasive in U.S. society" (Tjaden & Thoennes, 2000, p. 5).

According to the National Crime Victimization Survey, approximately one million violent crimes are committed annually by current or former intimate partners, about 85 percent of which are against women (Albanese, 2013). These findings suggest that serious crimes are frequently committed by people against other people they know. However, the good news is that based on the NCVS data, over 30 years the number of murders involving intimate partners has been reduced by half (Rennison, 2003).

In America, blacks are victims of violent crime at higher rates than any other race. The African American victimization rate for rape, robbery, and assault is 26 per 1,000, compared to a victimization rate of 21 per 1,000 for whites. Similarly, black households are victimized by property crimes, such as burglary, larceny, and motor vehicle theft, at a rate of 170 per 1,000, while for whites the victimization rate, for the same crimes, is 142 per 1,000 (Truman & Rand, 2011).

There is also an association between income and the risk of victimization. For instance, households with incomes below $15,000 per year are more likely to be burglarized than those with incomes above $15,000. Middle-income households—those with incomes between $25,000 and $75,000—have the lowest crime victimization rates, but the rate increases for those households with incomes more than $75,000 per year (Truman & Rand, 2011). Persons with higher incomes also have the lowest violent crime rates, while those with the lowest incomes experience the highest rates of violence. This may be accounted for by the location of residence, and it may well be that a higher income allows wealthier people to choose to live in low-crime areas (Albanese, 2013).

WHAT ARE THE EFFECTS OF CRIME ON VICTIMS?

All victims suffer. In a violent crime, either the victim is threatened with injury or death, or he or she is injured or killed. But even if the victim is "only" robbed or had his or her house broken into and valuables stolen, the victim still experiences trauma and loss. Different people have different reactions to traumatic events. Some victims experience shock and numbness, intense emotion, fear, distress, guilt, anger, or resentment, as well as depression and isolation. Others may have more physical symptoms, such as anxiety, panic, headaches, gastrointestinal problems, sleeplessness, and loss of appetite (Tjaden & Thoennes, 2000). Persons who have experienced a break-in of their home or apartment with the loss or destruction of their personal property experience a sense of invasion and violation. Individuals who have experienced assault may have all of the symptoms of post-traumatic stress disorder, a psychiatric disorder which often follows a traumatic event.

Symptoms of PTSD fall into three main categories:

- Reliving the event, during which the individual experiences flashback episodes, where the event seems to be happening again and again, repeated upsetting memories of the event, regular nightmares of the event, and strong, uncomfortable reactions to situations that remind him or her of the event.

- Avoidance, in which the victim has emotional "numbing," or feeling as though he or she doesn't care about anything, feeling detached, being unable to remember important aspects of the trauma, having a lack of interest in normal activities, and avoiding places, people, or thoughts that remind him or her of the event.
- Arousal, in which there are difficulties concentrating, being easily startled, feeling more aware (hypervigilance), feeling irritable or having outbursts of anger, and having trouble falling or staying asleep (Post-Traumatic Stress Disorder, 2012).

In the aftermath of victimization, it is expected that society will help the victim cope with his or her misfortune. Victim services are comprised of dedicated activities aimed at helping reduce victims' suffering and to aid their recovery.

The Cost of Crime Victimization

While we will discuss various aspects of victimization in Chapters Sixteen and Seventeen, we have not addressed the issue of what victimization costs the United States each year. While it is difficult to calculate the heavy cost to victims and to our society, the U.S. Department of Justice has estimated that victimization costs $105 billion annually in property and productivity losses and outlays for medical expenses (Extent and Cost of Crime Victimization, 1996). If this amount of money is broken down for every person in this country, it would cost each man, woman, and child $425 a year. However, what this amount of money doesn't include—and really can't include—are the losses associated with pain, emotional trauma, and death or risk of death from victimization.

Who Advocates for Victims?

Several victim special-interest groups have been troubled by the psychological and financial burdens that crime poses on its victims. Women's groups, in particular, are concerned about the double trauma of rape victims, who are first assaulted by the rapist and then are often handled insensitively by the criminal justice system (Territo et al., 2004). In 1975 and 1976, social service providers and criminal justice personnel organized the National Organization for Victim Assistance (NOVA) to promote a victim-oriented perspective in the administration of criminal justice (Territo et al., 2004). The NOVA website proclaims that they champion dignity and compassion for victims of crime and crisis.

Along with NOVA are groups such as Justice Solutions and Mothers Against Drunk Driving (MADD). Justice Solutions is a national non-profit organization dedicated to enhancing rights, resources, and respect for victims and communities hurt by crime. Justice Solutions also tries to enhance governmental and societal responses to crime and its consequences on individuals and communities, as well as strengthening crime prevention initiatives in America (Mission Statement, 2011). Mothers Against Drunk Driving was started in 1980, and its purpose is to aid the victims of crimes performed by individuals driving under the influence of alcohol or drugs and to aid the families of such victims, while increasing public awareness of the problem of drinking and drugged driving (Mission Statement, 2012). These two groups, like many others, are victim oriented and dedicated to working to improve the treatment of victims and witnesses, in order to create a balance between the consideration shown to them and the attention paid to defendants.

According to the Victim Assistance Online website, there are more than 600 victim assistance organizations and programs worldwide (VAOnline.org, 2012). Some of the national victim assistance organizations and programs in the United States that are listed and described on their websites are:

- *EDAN—Everyone Deserves a Name:* This organization provides the voluntary services of 19 certified forensic artists to help law enforcement agencies in identifying John/Jane Does by recreating the face of the deceased. This organization will only accept requests from law enforcement agencies.
- *FBI Office for Victim Assistance:* The mission of the Office for Victim Assistance (OVA) is to ensure that victims of crimes investigated by the FBI are afforded the opportunity to receive the services and notification as required by federal law. The FBI recognizes not only the necessity of providing for the legal rights of victims, but the benefits that effective and timely victim assistance brings to investigations.
- *Joint Center for Violence and Victim Studies:* The JCVVS is an interdisciplinary university affiliation between California State University at Fresno and Washburn University, Kansas. The center's mission is to address issues of violence and victimization through education, research, and public policy initiatives.
- *National Center for Missing Adults:* The National Center for Missing Adults (NCMA) is a non-profit agency providing nationwide assistance to law enforcement and families of missing persons. The group provides a variety of services, including advocacy, search assistance, national distribution of information related to missing persons, and various programs addressing child safety, such as the child ID program. It acts as a clearinghouse of information and does not provide investigative services or employ private investigators.
- *National Center for Victims of Crime:* This website has many links to crime-specific pages and large amounts of resource material on and for victims of crime, victims' rights advocacy and support, as well as national and state laws/programs.
- *National Crime Victim Law Institute:* The National Crime Victim Law Institute, established in 2000, is a non-profit research and educational organization at Lewis & Clark Law School, Portland, Oregon. NCVLI is the only national organization in the country working to assert victims' rights in criminal trial courts. In addition to its teaching mission, NCVLI performs a number of critical functions. It maintains and disseminates a resource bank of crime victim law; it assists attorneys who provide direct legal services to crime victims; it works to establish legal clinics nationwide to represent victims in court; and it files *amicus* briefs advocating for crime victims' rights in the courts
- *Office for Victims of Crime:* Possibly the single best source for information directly relating to victim assistance and the people who work in this field. The Office of Victims of Crime is an Office of Justice Program within the U.S. Department of Justice. It is an outstanding resource for research, articles, grants, funding, and facts related to victims and victims' rights.
- *Parents of Murdered Children:* Parents of Murdered Children is a national organization that provides ongoing emotional support to parents who have lost a child to murder. The organization will offer support in dealing with the criminal justice system; assistance to any survivor, and will, if possible, link that survivor with others in the same vicinity who have survived their loved one's murder; individual assistance, support, and advocacy; training to professionals in such fields as law enforcement, mental health, social work, community services, law, criminal justice, medicine, education, religion, the media, and mortuary science. The

training for professionals is for those professionals who are interested in learning more about survivors of homicide victims and the aftermath of murder.

WHAT ARE THE RIGHTS GRANTED TO VICTIMS?

In the early 1980s, only four states had laws that protected the basic rights of crime victims (Bohm, 2008). Now, every state has such laws. In fact, states have enacted more than 30,000 crime victim-related statutes, and the federal government has passed legislation providing basic rights and services to federal crime victims, such as victim assistance and victim compensation programs (Implementing Victims' Rights: Why Corrections Professionals Should Care, 2011).

The federal government, through its Crime Victims Fund, has made millions of dollars available for crime victims' compensation. In addition, the fund supports a broad array of programs and services that focus on helping victims in the immediate aftermath of crime and continuing to support them as they rebuild their lives (Crime Victims Fund, 2012). Millions of dollars are invested annually in victim compensation and assistance in every U.S. state and territory, as well as for training, technical assistance, and other capacity-building programs designed to enhance service providers' ability to support victims of crime in communities across the nation.

The Crime Victims Fund is derived from fines, forfeited bonds, and penalties paid by federal criminal offenders, as well as gifts, bequests, and donations. Since the fund was established in 1984, billions of dollars have been given out to victims of crime. In the fiscal year 2009/2010, more than $920 million was paid to victims of crime for medical and dental care, economic support, and funeral and burial expenses (Report to the Nation, 2012). In addition, in the same year, more than seven million victims benefited from the Victims of Crime Act (VOCA) states' victim assistance, as almost $776 million was used to:

- Respond to the physical and emotional needs of victims.
- Help victims and their families stabilize their lives after victimization.
- Help victims and families understand and participate in the criminal justice system.
- Provide victims with a measure of safety and security (Report to the Nation, 2012).

In addition to funding from the Office of Victims Assistance and VOCA funds, there are now many rights granted to crime victims—at least in some states and jurisdictions. Among those rights are:

- The right to notice of victims' rights.
- The right to be treated with fairness, dignity, and respect.
- The right to be informed, present, and heard at important criminal justice proceedings.
- The right to confer with the prosecutor.
- The right of sexual assault victims to be paid for forensic exams.
- The right to HIV testing of sex offenders and notice of the results.
- The right to reasonable protection from the accused.
- The right to privacy.
- The right to a speedy resolution of the case.

- The right to a prompt return of the victim's property.
- The right to notice of the offender's release.
- The right to restitution from the offender or compensation from the state (Office for Victims of Crime, 2012).

In the next chapter, we will take a closer look at victim advocates, the process of recovery, and alternative approaches in the criminal justice system that seek to provide for greater involvement of the victim and the community in the justice process.

FOR FURTHER CONSIDERATION

Historical Events Relevant to Chapter Sixteen

January 12, 1968:   AT&T announces its designation of 911 as a universal emergency number.

April 30, 2003:   The Amber Alert program is passed by Congress establishing AMBER, which stands for America's Missing: Broadcast Emergency Response. This alert was the creation of a national network to increase a quick response to kidnapped and abducted children. Awareness is brought to the attention of law enforcement and the community.

September 13, 1994:   The Violence Against Women Act of 1994 (VAWA) is signed by President Bill Clinton on this date. VAWA provides $1.6 billion toward investigation and prosecution of violent crimes against women, imposes automatic and mandatory restitution on those convicted, and allows civil redress in cases prosecutors chose to leave unprosecuted. The act also established the Office on Violence Against Women within the Department of Justice.

October 12, 1984:   Congress passes the Victims of Crime Act (VOCA). Although amended in 1988, this law called for the establishment of the Office for Victims of Crime (OVC) and created the Crime Victims Fund. The Crime Victims Fund provides funds to states for victim assistance and compensation programs that offer support and services to those affected by violent crimes.

October 27, 1998:   Congress creates the Crime Victims with Disabilities Awareness Act. This act is the first attempt to gather information regarding victims with disabilities.

November 4, 2008:   The Victims' Bill of Rights Act of 2008, referred to as Marsy's Law, in honor of Marsalee "Marsy" Nicholas, a University of California–Santa Barbara student. In 1983, Marsy was stalked and killed by her ex-boyfriend. He was released from jail a week later. This law provides more protection to crime victims and increases the length of parole denials to seven, 10, and 15 years.

December 31, 1965:   California creates the first crime victim compensation program in the United States.

December 31, 1974:   The Federal Law Enforcement Assistance Administration (LEAA) funded the first victim/witness programs in Brooklyn and Milwaukee. The National District Attorneys Association provided a grant to several district attorneys' offices in the hopes that victims would cooperate and improve prosecution outcomes.

December 31, 1983: The U.S. Department of Justice establishes the Office for Victims of Crime (OVC) to implement President Ronald Reagan's task force recommendations. The OVC created a national resource center, provided trainings for professionals, and became a model for laws protecting victims.

December 31, 1984: The Victims of Crime Act (VOCA) is passed by Congress. At the same time, the Crime Victims Fund is created to help fund state victim compensation and services. Millions of dollars are collected each year to help fund victim services. The funds come from offenders convicted of federal crimes, such as criminal fines, forfeited bail bonds, and penalties.

December 31, 2002: By the end of 2002, all 50 states, the District of Columbia, U.S. Virgin Islands, Puerto Rico, and Guam have established crime victim compensation programs.

Important Court Cases

- ***Booth v. Maryland*, 482 U.S. 496 (1987):** After having found Mr. Booth guilty of two counts of first degree murder and related crimes, the jury sentenced him to death after considering a presentence report prepared by the state of Maryland. The report included a victim impact statement, as required by state statute. The victim impact statement was based on interviews with the family of the two victims, and it provided the jury with two types of information. First, it described the severe emotional impact of the crimes on the family and the personal characteristics of the victims. Second, it set forth the family members' opinions and characterizations of the crimes and of Mr. Booth. The U.S. Supreme Court concluded that the introduction of a victim impact statement at the sentencing phase of a capital murder trial violates the Eighth Amendment, and therefore the Maryland statute is invalid to the extent it requires consideration of this information. The Court said that this kind of information is irrelevant to a capital sentencing decision, and its admission creates a constitutionally unacceptable risk that the jury may impose the death penalty in an arbitrary and capricious manner.
- ***Payne v. Tennessee*, 501 U.S. 808 (1991):** During the penalty phase of Mr. Payne's capital trial, the state presented the grandmother of a surviving victim, who stated that her grandson missed his mother and sister, both of whom were killed in Payne's attack. The prosecutor also referred to the effects of the crimes on the victims' family in his closing arguments. The U.S. Supreme Court ruled that the Eighth Amendment does not prohibit a capital-sentencing jury from considering "victim impact" evidence.

Websites to Check Out

- *U.S. Office for Victims of Crime Directory of Crime Victim Services.* Available at: *http://ovc.ncjrs.gov/findvictimservices.* The OVC's new online Directory of Crime Victim Services is designed to help victim service providers and individuals locate assistance quickly and easily. Visitors to this website can find crime victim services in their state, across the country, or around the globe.

- *Federal Bureau of Investigation. Victims' Assistance Office.* Available at: *http://www.fbi.gov/stats-services/ victim_assistance/.* The FBI has a Victims' Assistance Office, and on the FBI's website there is a Victims' Assistance page, which provides information, news, brochures, and resources related to victims and victim services.
- *National Organization for Victim Assistance (NOVA).* Available at: *http://www.trynova.org/* The National Organization for Victim Assistance is the oldest victim assistance organization. Its website provides information and services for crime victims and assistance providers.

Books

- Doerner, W. G., and Lab, S. P. (2011). *Victimology.* 6th ed. New York: Anderson.
- Karmen, A. (2009). *Crime Victims: An Introduction to Victimology.* Belmont, CA: Wadsworth.
- Waller, I. (2011). *Rights for Victims of Crime: Rebalancing Justice.* Lanham, MD: Rowman and Littlefield.

Movies

- *The Accused:* A 1988 film starring Jodie Foster as the victim of a gang rape by several drunk bar patrons with many also inebriated bar patrons cheering on the perpetrators. A district attorney is assigned to the case and wants to drop it. Her supervisor in the DA's office wants her to reach a plea bargain requiring some jail time. Sarah, the rape victim, is enraged by the deal, mostly because she did not get to tell her story in court. Later, Sarah decides to prosecute the men who cheered on the rape for criminal solicitation. After deliberation, the jury finds the three men guilty.
- *Erin Brockovich:* This 2000 movie, starring Julia Roberts as Erin Brockovich, is a biographical film about Ms. Brockovich, who fought against the West Coast energy corporation Pacific Gas & Electric Company. The movie depicts her fight to prove that the Pacific Gas & Energy Company knew it contaminated water with chemicals and that this led to serious illnesses in many people.
- *Heaven's Rain: Heaven's Rain* is a 2000 feature film based on the true story of the lifelong quest of Brooks Douglas, who would later become an Oklahoma state legislator, to bring his parents' killers and his sister's rapists to justice.

TV Shows

- *Law & Order: Special Victims Unit:* A television drama that was a spin-off from the original *Law & Order, Law & Order: SVU* premiered in 1999 and is still running. The show centers around sex crimes and is mainly a police procedural, with the most time spent on investigating the case and finding the culprit. Victims are mostly treated with respect, although they are usually not the focus in the episodes.

- *Final Witness:* A crime series that debuted on June 27, 2012 on ABC, this series combines documentary and drama while focusing on a different real-life murder each week from the victim's point of view. Each episode includes interviews with the victim's family and friends, real witnesses, prosecutors, and law enforcement officers, as well as scripted scenes with actors.

Review for Chapter Sixteen:

Research Paper or Term Paper Topics:

- Victimology
- Victims' rights

Important Terms to Know

Crime victimization:	The injury or killing of a human being through behavior that is prohibited by law.
Post-traumatic stress disorder:	
	A psychiatric disorder which often follows a traumatic event.
Primary victim:	The individual who is injured or killed as a result of a criminal act.
Secondary victim:	Any person who is affected by the primary victim's suffering.
Victim assistance:	Individuals or organizations that offer support and other services to victims of crimes.
Victimology:	The scientific study of victims, including their behaviors, injuries, recovery, legal rights, and needed assistance.

Study Guide Questions

True or False:

1. Traditionally, the criminal justice system has not paid much attention to victims.

2. In general, the younger the person (over the age of 12), the more likely the person is to be a crime victim.

3. There is an association between income and the risk of victimization.

4. There are more than 600 victim assistance organizations.

Multiple Choice Items:

5. Despite how it may seem on TV and in the movies, the person most likely to be a crime victim is
   a. a young woman
   b. a woman over the age of 65
   c. a man over the age of 65
   d. a male between ages 12 and 19

6. It is estimated that victimization costs for all victims in the United States is
   a. $105 billion annually
   b. $10 million annually
   c. $50 million annually
   d. $100,000 million annually

7. This government agency has an office for victim assistance:
   a. the Department of Defense
   b. the Commerce Department
   c. the FBI
   d. the Auditor General's Office

8. Victims these days have many rights. Among these rights are
   a. the right to reasonable protection from the accused
   b. the right to choose the criminal charge against the accused
   c. the right to inject lethal drugs into the convicted felon
   d. the right to damages for emotional pain and suffering

References

Albanese, J. S. (2013). *Criminal Justice.* 5th ed. Upper Saddle River, NJ: Pearson.

Bohm, R. (2008). *A Concise Guide to Criminal Justice.* New York: McGraw Hill.

Bohm, R. M., and Haley, K. N. (2012). *Introduction to Criminal Justice.* 7th ed. New York: Glencoe/McGraw-Hill Co.

"Crime Victims' Fund," (2012), Office for Victims of Crime.org, Available at: http://www.ojp.usdoj.gov/ovc/about/victimsfund.html.

"The Extent and Cost of Crime Victimization: A New Look," (1996), National Institute of Justice [online], Available at: http://www.nij.gov/pubs-sum/184372.htm.

"Implementing Victims' Rights: Why Corrections Professionals Should Care," (2011), Justice Solutions.org [online], Available at: http://www.justicesolutions.org/art_pub_ACAVictimRightsArticle.htm.

"Mission Statement," (2011), Justice Solutions, Available at: Mission Statement (2012), Mothers Against Drunk Driving, http://www.madd.org/about-us/mission/.

Masters, R. E., Way, L. B., Gerstenfeld, P. B., Muscat, B. T., Hooper, M., Dussich, J. P. J., Pincu, L., and Skrapec, C.A. (2013). *CJ: Realities and Challenges*. 2nd ed. New York: McGraw-Hill.

Office for Victims of Crime, (2012), Available at: https://www.victimlaw.org/.

"Post-Traumatic Stress Disorder," (2012),National Center for Biotechnology Information, U.S. National Library of Medicine, Available at: http://www.ncbi.nlm.nih.gov/pubmedhealth/PMH0001923/.

Rennison, C. M. (2003), "Intimate Partner Violence, 1993–2001," (NCJ 197838), Bureau of Justice Statistics Crime Data Brief [online], Available at: http://bjs.ojp.usdoj.gov/index.cfm?ty=pbdetail&iid=1001.

"Report to the Nation," (2012), Office for Victims of Crime, Available at: http://www.ojp.usdoj.gov/ovc/pubs/reporttonation2011/index.html.

Territo, L., Halsted, J. B., and Bromley, M. L. (2004). *Crime and Justice in America: A Human Perspective*. Upper Saddle River, NJ: Pearson.

Tjaden, P., and Thoennes, N., (2000), "Nature, extent, and consequences of intimate partner violence," U.S. Department of Justice, National Institute of Justice [online], Available at: http://bjs.ojp.usdoj.gov/index.cfm?ty=pbdetail&iid=2217.

Truman, J. L., (2011), "Crime Victimization 2010," Bureau of Justice Statistics [online], Available: http://www.bjs.gov/content/pub/pdf/cv10.pdf.

Truman, J. L. and Rand, M. R., (2010), "Crime Victimization 2009," Bureau of Justice Statistics [online], Available at: http://bjs.ojp.usdoj.gov/content/pub/pdf/cv09.pdf.

VAOnline.org, (2012), Available at: http://www.vaonline.org/index.html.

Chapter Seventeen

Victimization and Recovery

Being a crime victim can be frightening and confusing. A victim may be in a panic and want to flee, or a victim may be in shock, showing signs of numbness and passivity. Many just do not know where to go or what to do. Until the 1970s, victims had few options. They could contact the police, go to a doctor's office, or go to a local emergency room and request help. Today, however, there are many programs, services, and resources that can help victims repair their lives and property, obtain mental health treatment, find shelter, or obtain their rights while seeking justice.

Some of the most important services available today for victims include:

- *Crisis intervention:* Immediate assistance after a traumatic event.
- *Hotlines:* A telephone crisis line that anyone can call at any time to get information and resources.
- *Shelters and transitional housing:* Temporary housing for victims, especially those who have experienced physical abuse in an intimate relationship.
- *Sexual assault resource centers:* Rape and sexual assault crisis centers provide health services, counseling, community education, and advocacy for victims of sexual assault.
- *Community education and outreach:* Programs and organizations that provide information about services, or help to raise awareness about problems or about the resources available in the community.

Crime is a violation of people and relationships. It creates obligations to make things right. Justice involves the victim, the offender, and the community in a search for solutions which promote repair, reconciliation, and reassurance.

—*Howard Zehr, Professor of Restorative Justice at Eastern Mennonite University's Center for Justice and Peacebuilding in Harrisonburg, Virginia*

CHANGES IN THE CRIMINAL JUSTICE SYSTEM THAT INCREASE THE ROLES OF VICTIMS

Thanks to a growing concern for victims in the 1970s, things began to change in the criminal justice system, as it became more widely acknowledged that victims were often forgotten. At times prior to this, the concerns of victims were neglected—except insofar as they could assist the prosecution by testifying in court. That suddenly changed, though, when the President's Task Force on Victims of Crime in 1982 gave focus to a burgeoning victims' rights movement and urged the expansion of victim-assistance programs (Schmalleger, 2003).

In the 1990s, the National Institute of Justice conducted a survey of 319 full-service victim assistance programs based in law enforcement agencies and prosecutors' offices. The survey found that the majority of people seeking services from victim assistance offices were victims of domestic assault. The most common assistance they received was information about legal rights (Victims' Assistance Programs, 1995). At about the same time, voters in California approved Proposition 8, a resolution that called for changes in the state's constitution to reflect concern for victims.

Although there have been efforts to bring about a new amendment to the U.S. Constitution related to victims' rights, such an amendment has never made it through Congress (Schmalleger, 2003). However, 32 states have passed their own victims' rights amendments, and significant federal legislation has already been adopted (Schmalleger, 2003). A Victim and Witness Protection Act was passed by the federal government in 1982. This act requires judges to consider victim impact statements at federal sentencing hearings and places responsibility for their creation on federal probation officers (Schmalleger, 2003).

In more states, victims have been allowed not only to give victim-impact statements at sentencing, but they have also been permitted to participate in negotiation proceedings with prosecutors and defense attorneys (Reid, 2009). Many jurisdictions have instituted special training programs to increase the understanding that law enforcement officers, prosecutors, judges, and others have of the needs of victims and witnesses. Today, problems such as domestic violence and child abuse are more often treated by law enforcement as criminal acts—not as domestic problems to be shuttled off to other agencies.

In 1991, the U.S. Supreme Court, in *Payne v. Tennessee*, ruled that victim impact statements may be used at capital sentencing hearings (*Payne v. Tennessee*, 501 U.S. 808 [1991]). The Court stated in the majority opinion in this case that a state may legitimately conclude that evidence about the victim and about the impact of the murder on the victim's family is relevant to the jury's decision as to whether or not the death penalty should be imposed.

Another change in the criminal justice system is the development of victims' compensation programs. In many cases, what victims need most is financial compensation for the property losses they have incurred, medical expenses, or both (Reid, 2009). This need was recognized by California, where the state constitution's Victims' Bill of Rights recognizes a right of restitution for "all persons who suffer losses as a result of criminal activity" (California Constitution, 2007, Art. 1, Sec. 28, b). However, all 50 states have enacted victims' compensation legislation (Reid, 2009). While enforcement has been a problem, there has also been a problem in funding of these compensation programs, although the Office of Crime Victims through the U.S. Department of Justice grants funds in the millions of dollars each year to every state.

The changes in the criminal justice system to better accommodate victims have been important, but perhaps even more important are direct services which help victims navigate the criminal justice process and also help them to recover from the trauma of victimization.

Victim Advocates

A victim advocate is a person who directly provides victim services. Victim advocates may work in a domestic violence program, a rape crisis center, a district attorney's office, a police department, Child Protective Services, or Adult Protective Services. Victim advocates assist victims with obtaining community services such as health care, housing, education, and employment. They usually offer support services for every phase of the criminal justice process.

Furthermore, victim advocates provide crisis intervention and usually accompany victims to the hospital or to court. They may help victims to navigate the sometimes confusing criminal justice system by explaining court procedures and ensuring victims' rights.

Following a traumatic victimization, one of the first official personnel to be notified are usually victim advocates (Masters et al., 2013). It is their responsibility to give victims at least three kinds of help: psychological first aid, survivor support, and treatment interventions to facilitate recovery (Masters et al., 2013). Recovery is perhaps the most important goal of victim services. For the victim, going through a recovery process will, hopefully, help the victim find meaning from the traumatic experience and integrate what has been learned so that he or she can resume a functional life (Masters et al., 2013). For many victims, that may mean that the victim advocate makes a referral for mental health services, which may lead to short-term or long-term counseling or therapy, which may be required for recovery to take place.

Victim Protection and Assistance

The U.S. Victims of Crime Act, passed by Congress in 1984, created a $100 million crime victims' fund drawn from criminal fines in federal offenses (Crime Victims' Fund, 2012). The money in this fund supports state victim compensation and other programs to assist victims.

Many states have also passed laws to assist crime victims. Most of the state statutes are designed to compensate violent crime victims who report crimes and cooperate with the investigation and prosecution. Compensation to victims can help with medical expenses, funeral expenses, lost wages, and the support of deceased victims' dependents (Samaha, 2006). However, in many instances, the limit on the amount of compensation available to individuals or families is too low to be truly meaningful.

Some states have established victim-witness assistance programs, which are often supervised by prosecutors. These programs provide services such as:

- *Personal advocacy:* Helping victims receive all the services to which they are entitled.
- *Referral:* Recommending or helping victims obtain other needed assistance.
- *Restitution assistance:* Making sure judges order restitution and encouraging probation officers to collect restitution, and also helping violent crime victims to properly fill out restitution claim forms.
- *Court orientation:* Explaining the criminal justice system and their role in it.
- *Transportation:* Taking victims and witnesses to and from court, to social service agencies, and even, at times, to shelters.

- *Escort services:* Escorting witnesses to court and staying with them during court proceedings.
- *Emotional support:* Giving victims support during their ordeals with crime and with the criminal justice proceedings following it (Samaha, 2006).

Thirty-two states have written victims' rights provisions into their constitutions (About Victims' Rights, 2012). Typical provisions require the criminal justice system to treat victims with compassion and respect, inform victims of critical stages in the trial process, and invite victims to attend and comment on trial proceedings (Samaha, 2006).

Justice and Social Justice

Bringing victims into the criminal justice process is viewed by some as an effort to promote justice for crime victims. However, many criminologists believe that the criminal justice system should always and more consistently strive toward social justice. But what do the terms *justice* and *social justice* really mean?

If we talk about the criminal *justice* system, it is important to make some effort to define what justice means. However, that's easier said than done. If you review the criminal justice literature looking for a clear definition of justice, you're likely to be disappointed. There are, in fact, many possible definitions—each one somewhat different and often with different meanings.

For example, here is the way Dean Champion, author of *The American Dictionary of Criminal Justice* (2001) defines justice: "An ideal concerning the maintenance of right and the correction of wrong in the relations of human beings" (p. 76). *Black's Law Dictionary* (Garner, 2000) defines it this way: "The fair and proper administration of laws" (p. 697). And Jack G. Handler, in *Ballentine's Law Dictionary* (1994), defines it as: "The goal of a society which demands that its courts diligently apply its laws to the facts of each case, in every case" (p. 287). As you can see in these definitions, different experts have different ideas about the exact meaning of justice. However, the last definition (from *Ballentine's Law Dictionary*) suggests that justice has to do with the way that the criminal justice system carries out trials. Crank (2003) suggests that justice practices—in trials as well as in other aspects of the criminal justice system—are embodied in the criminal justice system.

Way back in Chapter One of this book, in the lengthy report of the Commission on Law Enforcement and the Administration of Justice brought about by President Lyndon Baines Johnson in 1968, the commission defined the criminal justice system as an apparatus that society uses to "enforce the standards of conduct necessary to protect individuals and the community." While it was said in that chapter that experts may find fault with this definition, still it is a useful tool that helps us to better understand the nature of the criminal justice system.

When we think about enforcing the standards of conduct and morality in our society, we also have to keep in mind that the principal players in the criminal justice system tend to view their work as "doing justice" (Manning, 1999, p. 31). Doing justice means that justice is carried out by believing in and carrying out the laws, policies, and procedures of the criminal justice system efficiently and effectively (Crank, 2003).

According to J.P. Crank in his book *Imaging Justice*, this idea of achieving justice daily through living up to the standards of right and wrong in the work of the players in the criminal justice system makes this a normative idea of justice (2003). Thus, there is a powerful moral component which permeates many aspects of criminal justice work. But strong beliefs in doing justice, the moral notions of helping society by putting away the bad guys, and the intense emotions that become very personal when the players on the justice side view themselves in a struggle with the evil forces of the world brings about another idea of justice, which is referred to as social justice.

If it is difficult to define justice, it is also confusing to try to pin down a meaning for social justice. Sister Helen Prejean, the author of *Dead Man Walking*, travels the country talking about social justice and the death penalty. In her work with poor people in New Orleans, she wasn't concerned about crime and the death penalty until she began her work as a spiritual adviser to death row inmates. That enabled her to make the connection to social justice.

"I don't see capital punishment as a peripheral issue about some criminals at the edge of society that people want to execute. I see the death penalty connected to the three deepest wounds of our society: racism, poverty, and violence" (Prejean, 1997).

Lynch and Stretsky (1999) define social justice in this way: A society exhibits social justice when it promotes the needs of the members of society and when it treats its people in an equal manner. Some critics of the traditional criminal justice system argue that the system, as it is usually applied in the United States, is inconsistent with the principles of social justice. That is, these critics say, the criminal justice system does not promote socially just outcomes or practices. That is the point that Prejean tries to make: Our society is not a socially just society if the people who are on death row and the people who get executed are the poor, the disadvantaged, and the minority members of society. Criminal justice policies—such as the death penalty and the war on drugs—reflect prejudices within the system, resulting in unequal treatment.

According to John Rawls, a political philosopher and a social justice theorist, and David Miller, also a social justice theorist, justice is based on two supposedly equal conceptions. First, guilty offenders are held accountable for their actions, and second, that criminal justice processes are implemented fairly, without being affected by personal bias.

Social justice, then, places emphasis on providing equality to all members of society. Social justice not only involves criminal offenders, but it includes all members of society in a much broader sense. For example, many people of lower status, as well as minorities, have been victimized simply because of their social standing. This is not the type of victimization that has been committed by one person but by the social structure and culture of our society. Those with more money and wealth also possess the most power. Rich, older, white men make the laws that everyone must obey; therefore, some would argue, law is biased in their favor. In order to achieve social justice, Rawls and Miller contend, we must become aware of our natural biases and take steps to correct them (Miller, 2001; Rawls & Kelly, 2001).

In order to achieve justice in America, we must punish the guilty while also preserving people's rights as human beings. When we know someone is guilty, some people begin to believe that they are no longer entitled to human rights. This is especially the case when it involves a criminal offender who has allegedly killed, raped, or abused a child. This brings us to the grueling question of which is more important: due process or crime control?

The two conceptions of justice, punishing the guilty and ensuring fairness and equal rights for offenders, often conflict with one another. Ideally, the United States justice system would seek to achieve a balance between these two conceptions.

PEACEMAKING CRIMINOLOGY

There is a branch of criminology which is concerned with social justice. It is called peacemaking criminology. This is a theoretical perspective that focuses on non-violence, social justice, and reducing the suffering of both the victim and the offender (Fuller, 2010). Some of the principles of peacemaking are embodied in the restorative justice movement, but both are aimed at easing the increasing pressures on the criminal justice system by employing alternative mechanisms for resolving social conflict. These two philosophical approaches suggest the criminal justice system should be the institution of last resort for resolving social problems, and the peacemaking and restorative justice movements provide the intermediary processes that can resolve issues in ways that do not require the expense and resources of the traditional criminal justice process (Fuller, 2010).

According to the principles of restorative justice, the criminal justice system is just a small part of society's response to crime. Restorative justice practices involve the community—and most importantly—establish and strengthen programs within the community to respond, not only to crime but also to some of the underlying conditions that contribute to crime (Bazemore & Schiff, 2001). The main principles of restorative justice can be summarized as follows:

- Crime is primarily an offense against human relationships and secondarily a violation of the law.
- Restorative justice recognizes that crime is wrong and should not occur and also recognizes that after it does, there are dangers and opportunities. The danger is that the community, the offender, and/or the victim will emerge from the criminal justice system response further alienated, more damaged, disrespected, disempowered, feeling less safe, and less cooperative with society. The opportunity is that injustice is recognized; equity is restored; the future is clarified so that participants are safer, more respectful, and more empowered and cooperative with society.
- Restorative justice is a process to make things "as right as possible," which includes: Attending to needs created by the offense, such as safety and repair of injuries to relationships and physical damage resulting from the offense; and attending to needs related to the cause of the offense (addictions, lack of social or employment skills, lack of moral or ethical base, etc.).
- The primary victims of an offense are the ones most impacted by the crime. The secondary victims are others impacted by the crime and might include family members, witnesses, criminal justice officials, community, etc.
- As soon as immediate victim, community, and offender safety concerns are satisfied, restorative justice views the situation as an opportunity to teach the offender and an opportunity to encourage the offender to learn new ways of acting and being in the community.
- Restorative justice prefers responding to the crime as early as possible and with the maximum amount of voluntary cooperation and minimum coercion, since healing in relationships and new learning are voluntary and cooperative processes.
- Restorative justice prefers that most crimes are handled using a cooperative structure, including those impacted by the offense, to provide support and accountability. This might include primary and secondary victims and family, the offender and family, community representatives, government representatives, faith representatives, school representatives, etc.
- Restorative justice recognizes that not all offenders will be cooperative. Therefore, an outside authority must make decisions for uncooperative offenders. The actions of the authorities and the consequences

imposed should be tested by whether they are reasonable, restorative, and respectful for victim, offender, and the community.

- Restorative justice prefers that offenders who pose significant safety risks and are uncooperative be placed in settings where the emphasis is on safety, values, ethics, responsibility, accountability, and civility. They should be exposed to the impact of their offense on victims, invited to learn empathy, and offered learning opportunities to become better equipped with skills to be a productive member of society. They should continually be invited—not coerced—to become cooperative with the community and be given the opportunity to demonstrate this in appropriate settings.
- Restorative justice requires follow-up and accountability structures utilizing the natural community as much as possible, since keeping agreements is the key to building a trustful community.
- Restorative justice recognizes and encourages the role of community institutions, including the religious/faith community, in teaching and establishing the moral and ethical standards that build up the community (Fuller, 2010).

Perhaps the most distinguishing aspect of restorative justice is its goal of widening the response to crime to include the community. Restorative justice establishes programs that connect the government with community programs to provide alternative mechanisms to respond to crime. Programs such as neighborhood justice centers, victim compensation agencies, rape crisis centers, and juvenile court conferencing circles all seek to provide ways to reduce the harms caused by crime and to heal the rift between offenders and victims (Fuller, 2010). Restorative justice programs include the following:

- *Victim-offender reconciliation programs:* These programs place offenders and victims together with a trained mediator who facilitates an interaction that allows for a more satisfying result than in the traditional courtroom or criminal justice process. Such programs allow victims to put a human face on their losses and suffering. Offenders are given an opportunity to explain their motivations. Each side can learn more about the humaneness and circumstances of the other.
- *Family group conferencing:* These programs use a mediator to enable everyone connected to an offense to develop a solution that is acceptable to all. Offenders are not simply sentenced; they are included in a process that determines an equitable solution.
- *Victim-offender panels:* If the victim cannot (because the offender is incarcerated or because the offender chooses not to meet with the victim) or will not meet with the offender, then the victim can meet with a panel of offenders who committed similar crimes. The idea is to let a victim explain how he or she has suffered so the offender can appreciate the suffering experienced by victims.

Restorative justice programs in the United States are mainly available to juvenile offenders and victims (Masters et al., 2013). However, restorative justice has been used in a variety of cases involving adult offenders and victims—often with satisfying results. For example, in the book *In the Shadow of Death*, Beck, Britto, and Andrews (2007) describe efforts to integrate offenders' families into the process of transforming conflict and promoting justice and healing. Based on hundreds of hours of in-depth interviews with family members of offenders and victims, legal teams, and leaders in the abolition and restorative justice movements, the authors present a vision of justice strongly rooted in the social fabric of communities. They suggest that forgiveness and recovery are possible in the wake of even the most heinous crimes.

But restorative justice is controversial and has both its critics and proponents. Critics argue that the victim's safety is a concern in cases where a violent crime was committed and the potential for the offender to pressure, coerce, or manipulate the victim into accepting certain outcomes. On the other hand, restorative justice advocates cite the failures of the traditional criminal justice process and the need to find alternatives to the usual criminal justice response of excluding the victim and the community and continuing to impose harsh sentences on offenders who are removed to faraway prisons for long periods of time.

Given the efforts to balance the criminal justice system with the principles of social justice and reparative justice, many criminologists are dedicated to improving our justice system—which many would agree is flawed. But what is the future of our criminal justice system? That question will be explored in our last chapter, Chapter Eighteen.

FOR FURTHER CONSIDERATION

Historical Events Relevant to Chapter Seventeen

January 1, 1983: The Victim and Witness Protection Act of 1982 goes into effect. This is legislation designed to protect and assist victims and witnesses of federal crimes. The law permits victim impact statements in sentencing hearings to provide judges with information concerning financial, psychological, or physical harm suffered by victims. The law also provides for restitution for victims and prevents victims and/or witnesses from being intimidated by threatening verbal harassment. The law establishes penalties for acts of retaliation by defendants against those who testify against them.

April 23, 1982: President Ronald Reagan appoints the Task Force on Victims of Violence.

May 17, 1996: President Bill Clinton signs the federal Megan's Law. This law provides for the public dissemination of information from states' sex offender registries. It also provides that information collected under state registration programs could be disclosed for any purpose permitted under a state law. And it requires that state and local law enforcement agencies release relevant information necessary to protect the public about persons registered under a state registration program established under the Jacob Wetterling Crimes Against Children and Sexually Violent Offender Registration Act.

June 8, 1982: Proposition 8 (or the Victims' Bill of Rights) is a law enacted by California voters. The law restricts the rights of convicts and those suspected of crimes, and extends the rights of victims. To do this, it amended both the constitution of California and ordinary statutes.

November 29, 1990: The Victims' Rights and Restitution Act of 1990 is passed by Congress. This act incorporates a Bill of Rights for federal crime victims and codifies services that should be available to victims of crime.

December 20, 1982: The Final Report of the President's Task Force on Victims of Violence is issued. The report confirmed what many knew: The innocent victims of crime have been overlooked, their pleas for justice have gone unheeded, and their wounds—personal, emotional, and financial—have gone unattended.

Important Court Cases

- ***Hagen v. Commonwealth*, 437 Mass. 374b (2002):** The defendant in *Hagen v. Commonwealth* was convicted of rape in 1987, but the execution of his sentence was stayed until early 2001, when the prosecution finally requested revocation of the stay. Citing the victim's right to a prompt disposition, the victim's attorney also requested revocation of the stay. The defendant objected, but the Massachusetts court ruled that victims have a right to a speedy resolution of cases.
- **In re *Amy Unknown*, 591 F.3d 792 (2009):** "Amy," the victim of childhood sexual abuse and of a widely broadcast set of photos depicting her abuse, pursued restitution under the Crime Victims' Rights Act, against defendants who viewed her photos on the Internet. The U.S. Court of Appeals for the 5th circuit ruled that a victim of child pornography should not receive court-ordered payments from those who possessed the images but had no hand in creating them. In this case, the images were created by her uncle, who was convicted and imprisoned on child pornography charges, but the images continued to be widely circulated and downloaded.

Websites to Check Out

- *Office of Crime Victims Advocacy. U.S. Department of Commerce.* Available at: *http://www.commerce.wa.gov/ portal/alias__CTED/lang__en/tabID__244/DesktopDefault.aspx.* The U.S. Commerce Department has an Office of Crime Victims Advocacy website, with a page containing considerable information about victim services.
- *Peacemaking Criminology. The National Social Science Association.* Available at: http://www.nssa.us/journals/2007-29-1/2007-29-1-05.htm. The National Social Science Association's website has a lengthy article with references on peacemaking criminology.
- *Restorative Justice Online.* Available at: *http://www.restorativejustice.org/.* There are many websites devoted to articles and information about restorative justice. However, Restorative Justice Online is a clearinghouse for a wealth of information about restorative justice.

Books

- Miller, D. (2001). *The Principles of Social Justice.* Cambridge, MA: Harvard University Press.
- Miller, S. L. (2011). *After the Crime: The Power of Restorative Justice Dialogues between Victims and Violent Offenders.* New York: New York University Press.
- Pepinsky, H. E., and Quinney, R. (1991). *Criminology as Peacemaking.* Bloomington: Indiana University Press.
- Voth, D. L. (2010). *Quality Victim Advocacy: A Field Guide.* Bluffton, OH: Workplay Publishing.
- Zehr, H. (2002). *The Little Book of Restorative Justice.* New York: Good Books.

Movies

- *Victims for Victims: The Theresa Saldana Story:* A made-for-television film released in 1984, it features the story of actress Theresa Saldana, who was stabbed and nearly killed by a deranged fan. Following her long recovery, Saldana founded the Victims for Victims organization and participated in lobbying for the 1990 anti-stalking law.
- *Take:* This 1998 film stars Minnie Driver (Ana) and Jeremy Renner (Saul) as two people whose lives cross and are bound together during a bungled robbery by Saul, in which Ana's son is killed. The action of the movie moves back and forth between two days: the day of the crime and the day of Saul's execution many years later. As a result, the human side of crime is reflected and the viewer begins to understand how the crime affected both Ana and Saul since that day the murder took place. The climax of the movie comes in an unplanned meeting between Ana and Saul just before his execution. Although the circumstances of the meeting are far from reflecting best restorative justice practices, the effect on the characters and the viewers is powerful.

Review for Chapter Seventeen:

Research Paper or Term Paper Topics:

- Victim advocacy
- Peacemaking criminology
- Social justice and the criminal justice system
- Restorative justice

Important Terms to Know

Justice: A difficult-to-define term that may relate to the overall purpose of the criminal justice system.

Peacemaking criminology: A theoretical perspective that focuses on non-violence, social justice, and reducing the suffering of both victim and offender.

Restorative justice: An approach to criminal justice that views crime as harm to the community and which emphasizes that the appropriate response to crime is to bring together victims, offenders, and the community to promote healing.

Social justice: Fairness and equality in providing services to the people in a society.

Victim advocate: An individual who may provide a variety of direct services to victims.

Victim compensation: Crime victim compensation is a direct reimbursement to or on behalf of a crime victim for a wide variety of crime-related expenses, including medical costs, funeral and burial costs, expenses for mental health counseling, and lost wages or loss of support.

Victim-offender reconciliation programs:
Programs that bring together offenders and victims so that each can learn more about the other side and develop greater understanding.

Study Guide Questions

True or False:

1. By Supreme Court ruling, victim impact statements cannot be used in a trial.

2. All 50 states have enacted victim compensation laws.

3. Victim compensation funds can help victims with funeral expenses.

4. Justice is a word and a concept that has only one definition.

5. Peacemaking criminology is a criminal justice perspective that focuses on non-violence and social justice.

Multiple Choice Items:

6. Victim advocates provide direct services to victims, and these direct services may include
   a. reassurance that they do not have to testify as a witness
   b. help with housing
   c. taking the victim on vacation
   d. appearing in court in place of the victim

7. Victim-witness assistance programs may provide services, but **not** this service:
   a. referral for professional help
   b. restitution assistance
   c. escort services
   d. private massage sessions

8. Social justice refers to the idea of
    a. groups of people being just
    b. a justice system favoring the rich and powerful
    c. a society that gives individuals and groups fair treatment
    d. a justice system that ignores victims

9. Restorative justice is a criminal justice practice that views crime as
    a. an opportunity to teach the victim a lesson
    b. a way to heal the community
    c. a chance to isolate and punish offenders
    d. an offense against human relationships first

References

"About Victims' Rights," (2012), Office for Victims of Crime [online], Available at: http://www.ojp.usdoj.gov/ovc/.

Bazemore, G., and Schiff, M. (2001). *Restorative Community Justice: Repairing Harm and Transforming Communities*. Cincinnati: Anderson.

Beck, E., Britto, S., and Andrews, A. (2007). *In the Shadow of Death: Restorative Justice and Death Row Families*. New York: Oxford University Press.

"California Constitution," (2007), Available at: http://en.wikisource.org/wiki/California_Constitution/ARTICLE_I.

Champion, D. J. (2001). *The American Dictionary of Criminal Justice*. 2nd ed. Los Angeles: Roxbury Publishing Co.

Crank, J. P. (2003). *Imagining Justice*. Cincinnati: Anderson Publishing.

"Crime Victims' Fund," (2012), Office for Victims of Crime.org, Available at: http://www.ojp.usdoj.gov/ovc/about/victimsfund.html.

Fuller, J. R. (2010). *Criminal Justice: Mainstream and Crosscurrents*. Upper Saddle River, NJ: Prentice Hall.

Garner, B. A. (2000). *Black's Law Dictionary*. 7th ed. St. Paul, MN: West Group.

Handler, J. G. (1994). *Ballentine's Law Dictionary*. Albany, NY: West Publishing.

Lynch, M., and Stretsky, P. (1999). Marxism and social justice: Thinking about social justice, eclipsing criminal justice. In B. Arrigo, ed. *Social Justice, Criminal Justice: The Maturation of Critical Theory in Law, Crime, and Deviance*. Belmont, CA: West/Wadsworth.

Manning, P. (1999). "Semiotics and justice: Justice, justice, and justice." In B. Arrigo, ed. *Social Justice, Criminal Justice: The Maturation of Critical Theory in Law, Crime, and Deviance*. Belmont, CA: West/Wadsworth.

Masters, R. E., Way, L. B., Gerstenfeld, P. B., Muscat, B. T., Hooper, M., Dussich, J. P. J., Pincu, L., and Skrapec, C. A. (2013). *CJ: Realities and Challenges*. 2nd ed. New York: McGraw-Hill.

Miller, D. (2001). *Principles of Social Justice*. Cambridge, MA: Harvard University Press.

"Office for Victims of Crime," (2012), Available at: http://www.victimlaw.org/.

Payne v. Tennessee, 501 U.S. 808 (1991)

Prejean, H., (1997, "Would Jesus Pull the Switch?" Claretian Publications [online], Available at: http://salt.claretianpubs.org/issues/deathp/prejean.html.

Rawls, J., and Kelly, E. (2004). *Justice as Fairness: A Restatement*. Cambridge, MA: Belknap Press.

Reid, S. T. (2009). *Crime and Criminology*. 12th ed. New York: Oxford University Press.

Samaha, J. (2006). *Criminal Justice*. 7th ed. Belmont, CA: Thomson/Wadsworth.

Schmalleger, F. (2003). *Criminal Justice Today: An Introductory Text for the 21st Century.* 7th ed. Upper Saddle River, NJ: Prentice Hall.

"Victim Assistance Programs: Whom They Service, What They Offer," (1995), Office of Justice Programs. National Institute of Justice [online], Available at: http://www.nij.gov/pubs-sum/184412.htm.

Part Seven

The Future of Criminal Justice

Chapter Eighteen

How Bright is the Future of Our Criminal Justice System?

Judges and other members of the American criminal justice system like to say that the American system of justice is the best in the world. If it is, then some criminologists would contend that we are in deep trouble. Others might simply say that while it might be a system with a great many problems, this should just motivate us to work toward improving it.

As new problems arise, equity and justice will direct the mind to solutions which will be found, when they are scrutinized, to be consistent with symmetry and order ...

—Benjamin N. Cardozo, The Growth of the Law, *1924*

DOES THE CRIMINAL JUSTICE SYSTEM NEED REFORMING?

In some respects, the criminal justice system seems to be functioning quite adequately. Research continues to point to continuing evidence that the crime rate—for both violent crime and property crime—has been steadily declining for almost 20 years. Advances in technology have improved the ability of detectives to investigate crime scenes. DNA testing has helped to exonerate the innocently convicted. And computer technology has brought about changes in spotting and reacting to hot spots of crime, better crime statistics, and revolutions in court rooms.

But there is room for pessimism, too. For example, some of the major problems in the criminal justice system are glaring areas of concern:

- High rates of incarceration over the past two decades or more have not succeeded in contributing to lowered recidivism rates or to lower crime rates.
- The glowing promise of forensic science has turned out—in some important respects—to be a hoax and a sham.
- The number of exonerations related to the employment of DNA testing has served to highlight one important fact: Too many people have been wrongfully convicted.
- Related to wrongful convictions is the whole rotten underside of police investigations and shabby prosecutions, both of which point to serious problems in ethics and morality in law enforcement and prosecutions, underlining the inability of both the police and prosecutors to adequately supervise themselves.
- Despite the steadily falling crime rate, there is still far too much crime—both violent crime and property crime.
- Terrorism looms as a dark cloud over our society, and many people wonder if our criminal justice system can prevent the kind of terrorism that befell us on September 11, 2001.
- The number of gangs in this country is growing rather than declining. The justice system cannot seemingly do anything about gangs.
- The war on drugs has been a colossal failure, but we have yet to come up with a better answer to the problems of drug addiction in our country.
- Racial disparities are very evident in both stop and frisks, arrests, and sentencing. Our justice system is supposed to be color-blind—but it is not.
- The United States not only incarcerates more people than any other country, but we are also a leader among nations in the number of people we execute. We cannot—seemingly—find a solution to the long-standing controversy over the death penalty.

In the last chapter, Chapter Seventeen, we addressed the concept of social justice. If we want our country to be a socially just nation, then we must bring about a number of reforms reflected in the above list of problems and concerns in our criminal justice system. Essentially, we cannot say we are a just society if there is a different form of justice for the poor and minorities than there is for the wealthy and the white. Nor can we proclaim ourselves to be a just society if racial profiling determines who gets stopped and searched on our highways, if a disproportionate number of African Americans and Hispanics are incarcerated, and if a third of all young, black males are under the supervision of the criminal justice system (Masters et al., 2013).

That is one way of looking at the challenges facing us in the 21st century: Can we reform our criminal justice system so it is, in fact, a just system? But more importantly, can we construct a criminal justice system that removes some of the concerns and flaws listed above, and in addition, becomes a system in which every citizen has the same rights, opportunities, and equality in the eyes of the law?

The Top Challenges to the Criminal Justice System

No. 1: Incarceration Rates

What is the problem?

One in 33 adults in the United States is under some form of correctional supervision, such as probation, jail, prison, or parole (Guerino, Harrison, & Sabol, 2011). Less than three decades ago, that number was one in 77 adults. The United States incarcerates about half the world's penal population as one of every 136 adults is in a jail or prison (Masters et al., 2013). Nearly 2.3 million people are currently housed in federal or state prisons or in jails (Guerino, Harrison, & Sabol, 2011).

The total U.S. prison population fell to 1.6 million at the end of 2010, and this represented a decline of 0.6 percent since 2009. However, that was the first decline in the prison population in almost four decades (Guerino, Harrison, & Sabol, 2011).

The high incarceration rate would be understandable if the crime rate for violent crime was increasing every year—or even if it was staying steady. But that is not the case. During 2010, there was a double-digit drop (down 13 percent) in the rate of violent victimization, according to the Bureau of Justice Statistics (Truman, 2011). Violent crime includes rape or sexual assault, robbery, aggravated assault, and simple assault. The drop in violent victimization went from about 17 victimizations per 1,000 residents in 2009 to 15 per 1,000 in 2010. During the ten-year period from 2001 to 2010, the overall violent victimization rate decreased by 40 percent and the property victimization rate fell by 28 percent (Truman, 2011).

Furthermore, the declines that were seen in 2010 and in the decade leading up to 2010 reflected a larger trend of annual decreasing criminal victimization. In 2010, violent and property victimization rates fell to their lowest levels since the early 1990s. From 1993 to 2010, the violent crime victimization rate decreased 70 percent, dropping steadily from about 50 victimizations per 1,000 persons age 12 or older in 1993 to about 15 per 1,000 in 2010.

So, if there are fewer crimes and fewer arrests, why has the incarceration rate increased over the past 20 years?

According to Ruth Masters and her colleagues (Masters et al., 2013), the increase in the prison population from the 1970s to the present time largely reflects changes in public policy and that those changes have been driven by public fears. What are the public fears? Masters and her cohorts suggest that when the media focuses on and sensationalizes cases of violent crime and at the same time portrays judges and parole authorities as too lenient, then the media and the politicians—backed by the public's fears—advocate a tough-on-crime approach. The tough-on-crime approach calls for more punitive and longer sentences, and this reinforces the widespread belief that harsh punishment will reduce crime. The public believes this, the judges believe this, and parole boards believe this. When judges sense increased pressure to order longer jail and prison terms, presumably this reassures the public that the criminal justice system is tough and is protecting them from crime.

With get-tough-on-crime approaches across the board, legislatures, including the federal government, have adopted mandatory minimum sentences, which usually feature fixed sentences that judges are unable to reduce. In addition, parole boards, also feeling the pressures, have been reluctant to grant paroles, even to prisoners eligible for parole. The bottom line result is that prisons (including federal prisons) and jails in every state are overcrowded.

But there is no evidence that incarcerating offenders for long sentences reduces recidivism and makes them less likely to commit new crimes if and when they are released.

Is anything currently being done about it?

Thanks to the recession throughout most of the first decade of the 21st century, states and state departments of correction have had no choice. They could not sustain high levels of incarcerations. As a consequence, many states have had to parole more offenders and reduce their prison populations. California, for example, was forced to reduce its high prison population (which reached a peak of 170,794 in 2006), not only because of a huge financial deficit in that state, but also because in 2011, the U.S. Supreme Court upheld an order demanding California drastically reduce its prison population or else build more prisons to relieve overcrowding. That led to changes to the state's parole system and prison realignment, which have both reduced the influx of inmates to California's state prison system (Palta, 2012). Other states, faced with similar budget woes, have had to parole more inmates.

What still needs to be done?

Several things need to be done to reduce the prison population in the United States:

- There must be a greater recognition in each state that incarceration is not the answer to solving any concerns. Higher rates of incarceration will not lead to further declines in crime, it will not reduce the recidivism rate, nor will it lead to a more just society.
- Since people of color are disproportionately represented in our jails and prisons, this problem must be effectively addressed. Thirty-eight percent of sentenced prisoners are black, 34 percent white, and 20 percent Hispanic (Masters et al., 2013). Black males are six times more likely than whites to be incarcerated in jail or prison (West, 2010). This strongly suggests that incarceration may often be based on the race of the offender. This is a problem that states need to address.
- Legislative bodies need to take a look at the reason why prisons and jails are overcrowded and make smart decisions about how to address the problem. In the past, the problem has been dealt with by building new and bigger prisons, but this answer is no longer feasible because states cannot afford to entertain this kind of response. A better approach might be to start with changes in mandatory minimum sentences and reworking laws that specify long sentences.
- Finally, the justice system must look at alternatives to jails and prisons and make better use of approaches that keep offenders in the community.

No. 2: Forensic Science

What is the problem?

We are all used to televisions shows such as *CSI, Bones, Body of Proof,* and similar shows demonstrating the cutting-edge technology available to law enforcement in order to identify victims and also to identify culprits. On TV, the lab technicians and medical examiners are highly skilled and knowledgeable scientists who aid law enforcement in capturing the guilty. As a result, many attorneys have indicated the presence of the so-called "*CSI* Effect," which leads jurors to expect that there will be scientific proof positively linking a defendant to a crime (Heinrick, 2006).

However, in real life, the technicians are not always well trained, they may frequently be overworked and constantly battling an overload of evidence that needs to be analyzed, and the scientific techniques they use may not be science at all.

We have come to expect that when an expert witness testifies in a trial that he or she will present evidence based on infallible science. This is particularly true if the scientist comes from the FBI's forensic crime lab. However, that expectation that people—even those in the criminal justice system—have had has been shattered by growing evidence that the forensic science system is seriously flawed.

A 2009 National Academy of Sciences report on forensic science has called into question most of the "science" that has been used for decades in criminal justice—including fingerprint identification, hair analysis, comparison of bullets, bite marks, arson investigations, handwriting analysis, shoe and tire prints, and hair analysis (Edwards, 2012). The report indicates that there is a lack of scientific research to confirm the validity and reliability of forensic disciplines, that there is a lack of standards for training and certifying forensic practitioners, and a general failure to adhere to performance standards (Edwards, 2012).

In 2012, the American Bar Association has reinforced what was stated in the 2009 report (Gertner, 2012). The errors in all areas of forensic science have been accumulating for years and has, it is suggested, helped lead to wrongful convictions. FBI examiners claimed until recently that they could match fingerprints to the exclusion of any other person in the world with 100 percent certainty using a method with an error rate of essentially zero. The academy found that assertion to be "not scientifically plausible," and this has led to virtually no research on the validity of fingerprint identification (Hsu, 2012).

Is anything currently being done about it?

It was certainly a step in the right direction to have the National Academy of Sciences study the problem and submit an important report in 2009. Congress and the Obama administration in 2012 began trying to regulate forensic science to help establish standards. There is at this writing a bill before the U.S. Senate to create a new office of forensic science in the Justice Department. And Commerce, Science, and Transportation Committee Chairman John D. Rockefeller IV, from West Virginia, is preparing legislation to expand the role of the National Science Foundation and the National Institute of Standards and Technology in setting scientific standards and research goals related to forensics (Hsu, 2012).

During July 2012, the Justice Department and the FBI announced that they have jointly launched a review of thousands of criminal cases to determine whether any defendants were wrongfully convicted or deserve a new trial because of flawed forensic evidence (Hsu, 2012). It is the largest post-conviction review ever done by the FBI, and it will include cases conducted by FBI laboratory hair and fiber examiners since at least 1986. The review comes after the *Washington Post* reported in April 2012 that Justice Department officials had known for years that flawed forensic work might have led to the convictions of potentially innocent people but had not performed a thorough review of the cases (Hsu, 2012).

What still needs to be done?

What the Department of Justice and the FBI are doing is a start, but there is more that must be accomplished to establish greater trust in forensic work. Some recommendations are that:

- Congress establish a forensic department in the Department of Justice.
- Standards be established for training and certification of forensic scientists.
- Rigorous and meticulous research be carried out in all forensic areas to provide the science that is needed to make forensic analysis a real science.
- All forensic laboratories be removed from the control and supervision of police departments to create independent analysis of evidence.

No. 3: Wrongful Conviction

What is the problem?

Advances in DNA testing are exposing errors made in trials and convictions at what some see as an alarming rate (Hsu, 2012). In 2012, researchers with the Urban Institute reported that new DNA testing appeared to clear convicted defendants in 16 percent of Virginia criminal convictions between 1973 and 1988 in which evidence was available for retesting (Roman et al., 2012). A 2009 study of post-conviction DNA exonerations—now at this time up to 289 nationwide—found invalid testimony in more than half the cases (Garrett & Neufeld, 2009).

The same problems are seen over and over in exoneration cases: Faulty eye-witness identification, flawed forensic science, coerced confessions, the manufacture of evidence by police officers, the withholding of exculpatory evidence from the defense by prosecutors, prosecutors suborning perjured testimony, shoddy police work, and various other problems that lead to the conviction of the innocent. The number of exonerations related to the use of DNA testing has served to highlight one essential fact: Too many people have been wrongfully convicted.

What is currently being done about it?

Of course, there are programs like the Innocence Project, Centurion Ministries, and the Center for Wrongful Convictions at Northwestern University, but these programs only scratch the surface of the problem. These kinds of programs and centers are aimed at exonerating the innocent and they do call attention to the problem.

However, more has to be done—not to undo the conviction and sentence when the innocent are convicted, but to prevent wrongful convictions in the first place.

In North Carolina, the Innocence Inquiry Commission, the first of its kind in the country, was created in 2006 after several high-profile cases of wrongful convictions raised questions about the criminal justice system (North Carolina Innocence Inquiry Commission, 2006). The wrongfully convicted can appeal their verdicts to the Innocence Inquiry Commission, which is a state agency, but their claims generally are limited to technical problems at the trial level, not simply claims of innocence. The commission has legal authority and powers to delve into such claims and then put them before a panel of judges who can grant immediate freedom.

North Carolina's innocence commission was established as an independent state agency to give it more power. It has the legal authority to subpoena information that other innocence projects cannot always get (About Us, 2006). Other states are looking at North Carolina's fledgling commission as a model. In Florida, some high-profile lawyers are working to set up an Actual Innocence Commission. Lawyers in Chicago and California also have been interested in the commission (Blythe, 2010).

The California State Senate in 2004 created the California Commission on the Fair Administration of Justice (California Commission, 2008). The purpose of this commission was to investigate problems inherent in the criminal justice system and make recommendations for change (Final Report, 2008). This commission issued its report in 2008 and recommended sweeping changes by the state legislature, the police, judges, prosecutors, and defense attorneys in various areas, including eyewitness identification, confessions, informant testimony, and forensic evidence.

What still needs to be done?

Few other states so far have established commissions on the order of California's Commission on the Fair Administration of Justice. However, North Carolina is not the only state to take steps to prevent and address wrongful convictions and grant greater access to biological evidence. In fact, eight other states have established criminal justice reform commissions (Ostendorff, 2011). For instance, Connecticut has its Advisory Commission on Wrongful Convictions, which was created in 2003, and which reviews wrongful convictions and recommends changes to prevent similar mistakes. And Florida has an Innocence Commission composed of attorneys, lawmakers, judges, prosecutors, and police who examine common errors in wrongful convictions.

However, all states should have such commissions. Such commissions should be brought into existence by the state and funded by the state so that they are not dependent on private donations, as are such programs as the Innocence Project.

Furthermore, more states should do what Wisconsin did after a state task force examined causes of wrongful convictions beginning in 2003. Lawmakers in that state two years later passed laws to better preserve biological evidence, improve eyewitness identification procedures, and require interrogation recordings (Ostendorff, 2011). It is one thing for a commission to recommend changes to reduce the possibility of wrongful convictions, but it is quite another to have the state legislature actually pass new laws bringing about reforms.

No. 4: Police Investigations and Prosecutions

What is the problem?

A significant number of wrongful convictions came about because of serious problems involving misconduct and inadequate police work on the part of the police. In addition, prosecutors share blame for prosecuting cases that contain errors and police misconduct, and prosecutors also have their own share of ethical violations and misconduct.

One of the reasons for wrongful convictions starts with an inadequate police investigation. Inadequate police investigation would mean that the detective work was sloppy or incompetent. Often, this means that certain tests were not conducted, that certain police procedures were not followed, or that certain information known to the police about another suspect (other than the one charged) was not investigated. Furthermore, the police role in a criminal case may go well beyond simply inadequate work or incompetence. Sometimes the police investigation might involve misconduct, which would include inducing false confessions, planting evidence, overlooking evidence that would clear a suspect, manufacturing evidence, or perjury.

According to the Innocence Project, cases of wrongful convictions uncovered by DNA testing are filled with evidence of negligence, fraud, or misconduct by both police officers and police departments and by prosecutors (Understand the Causes, 2012). Investigations into wrongful convictions have exposed official misconduct at every level and stage of a criminal investigation (Understand the Causes, 2012). Some of the common forms of misconduct by law enforcement officials include:

- employing suggestion when conducting identification procedures.
- coercing false confessions.
- lying or intentionally misleading jurors about their observations.
- failing to turn over exculpatory evidence to prosecutors.
- providing incentives to secure unreliable evidence from informants.

There are also common forms of misconduct by prosecutors, which include:

- withholding exculpatory evidence from the defense.
- deliberately mishandling, mistreating, or destroying evidence.
- allowing witnesses they know or should know are not truthful to testify.
- pressuring defense witnesses not to testify.
- relying on fraudulent forensic experts.
- making misleading arguments that overstate the probative value of testimony.

Prosecutorial misconduct is a leading cause of wrongful conviction, and a recent Innocence Project report provides evidence that appeals courts in the United States do not effectively identify and overturn these injustices (West, 2010).

Although countless instances of misconduct never come to light, the Innocence Project review found that with 65 of the first 255 DNA individuals exonerated, there were issues related to allegations of prosecutorial misconduct in their appeals or in civil suits filed after exoneration. In about half of those cases, courts found either error or misconduct by prosecutors, but judges only found "harmful error"—enough to overturn a conviction—in 12 cases (West, 2010).

The rate of harmful error findings (18 percent) in wrongful conviction cases is nearly identical to the rate found in a much broader universe of cases examined in a 2003 study by the Center for Public Integrity. These cases weren't innocence cases (meaning they hadn't been overturned based on evidence of innocence), but the courts found harmful error by prosecutors in 17.6 percent of cases (Williams, 2003).

Many experts find that things can go wrong in prosecutions as prosecutors collaborate year in and year out with the same group of police officers, forensic scientists, expert witnesses, and judges. They come to trust each other, developing bonds that sometimes lead to shortcuts. If the evidence is weak, it becomes easier to ignore those weaknesses or paper them over. At each step, errors are ratified rather than exposed.

What is currently being done about it?

The Innocence Project, along with other organizations concerned with wrongful convictions, are working diligently at making the legal community, as well as the general public, more aware of the problem. Likewise, watchdog agencies and investigative journalism organizations, such as the Center for Public Integrity, attempt to reveal abuses of power, corruption, and dereliction of duty by public institutions in order to try to cause them to operate with honesty, integrity, and accountability while putting the public interest first.

What still needs to be done?

A lot more needs to be done. The risk of disciplinary action may be greater for police officers as their misconduct may go before a police review board. However, there are few sanctions for the discretion afforded to prosecutors. In light of this, the following recommendations should be considered:

- District attorneys and prosecuting attorneys should be elected by the public based on their integrity.
- Elected district attorneys and prosecuting attorneys need to work at changing the culture of misconduct if they find it exists in their office.
- There should be more and more rigorous training for both police officers and prosecutors in ethics and integrity.
- Judges and state bar associations need to pursue more sanctions for prosecutors who engage in misconduct.

No. 5: Crime

What is the problem?

On the day this chapter was written, 24-year-old James Holmes, an Aurora, Colorado, man, went to a crowded movie theater at midnight and opened fire on the people watching a Batman movie. Twelve people were killed and 58 were wounded (Frosch & Johnson, 2012).

While mass murders like the shootings by James Holmes, or the shooting of Congresswoman Gabriel Gifford and several other people in Phoenix, Arizona, in January 2011, are relatively rare, still we can watch TV news every night and hear about a terrible, violent crime. In this country, every year in recent years there are about 14,000 murders. In 1980, there were more than 23,000 murders in the United States (Fox, 2010). As we learned in Chapter Three, both violent crime—like murder—and property crime have been declining since 1993, with crime in general lower than at any time in the past several decades.

The fact is that even if crime is declining, there is still far too much crime that takes place. For instance, if you compare the number of homicides in America with the rates for other countries, you'll see that more murders take place in this country than in any other Western country. Murder rates are a fraction of what they are in the United States in such countries as England, Germany, France, and the Netherlands.

What is currently being done about it?

That crime is declining is a fact. What we don't know is why. Books (such as Franklin Zimring's *The Great American Crime Decline*, 2007) have been written on the subject, but no one can really explain why we have had a decreasing crime rate for almost 20 years. Various hypotheses have been advanced, but no single theory is accepted by all sociologists and criminal justice experts. However, some believe the crime decline might be related to the combined roles of the police and citizens in crime prevention.

For instance, many neighborhoods and communities have gone back to an original idea in law enforcement and that involves neighborhood watches. Neighborhood watches, once referred to as peacekeeping, were common more than a thousand years ago when citizens banded together for mutual responsibility to ward off criminal behavior. In today's typical neighborhood watch program, citizens combat crime by increasing surveillance of public areas, promoting the behavior of residents that increases citizens' safety, and reporting suspicious behavior to the police (Territo et al., 2004).

Environmental approaches to crime prevention and security were made popular by Oscar Newman in his book *Defensible Space* (1973). The concept of crime prevention through environmental design is that proper design and effective use of the physical environment can produce behavioral effects that will reduce the incidence and fear of crime (Territo et al., 2004). Florida is one state that has pioneered the use of design to reduce crime, and they have done this primarily through the Convenience Business Security Act and the Safe Neighborhoods program.

The Convenience Business Security Act was passed by the Florida legislature. It requires every convenience business to provide employee training, adequate lighting, cash management procedures, unobstructed views, security cameras, and other measures that result in a safe environment and a reduction in robberies (Territo et al., 2004). The Florida legislature also brought about the Safe Neighborhoods Program, which is designed to reduce opportunities for crime by coordinating crime prevention activities (Territo et al., 2004).

One of the major innovations in organizing the police during the past three decades is referred to as community policing. Community policing, again, harkens back to a concept promoted by Sir Robert Peel in the 1820s, and that is that the police cannot be responsible for preventing crime. Instead, community policing—bringing the citizen back into the equation as an active participant—is required (Fuller, 2010).

The term community policing covers a wide range of police activities and programs, but underlying all of the various activities and programs involves enlisting citizens to help solve law-and-order problems in their own communities (Fuller, 2010). In 2003, almost 60 percent of police departments in this country had community policing officers or departments (Fuller, 2010). In some cities, community policing involves bringing together citizens to participate in what Wilson and Kelling promoted in their landmark 1982 article "Broken Windows," by cleaning up parks, boarding up old buildings, painting over graffiti, and making neighborhoods and business districts look more presentable and less inviting to criminal elements. Another strategy of community policing, also advocated by Wilson and Kelling (1982), is to return the police to a close relationship with the public by having them patrol on foot or on bicycles, rather than in patrol cars.

Another strategy related to community-oriented policing is problem-oriented policing. Problem-oriented policing is focused—much like community-oriented policing—on prevention instead of just reacting to a crime that has already been committed. Problem-oriented policing strategies require police departments to identify long-term community problems—such as street-level drug dealers, prostitution rings, gang hangouts, or a series of rapes—and to develop strategies to eliminate them (Siegel & Worrall, 2012). Problem-oriented policing models are supported by the fact that a great deal of urban crime is concentrated in a few hot spots (Siegel & Worrall, 2013). Directing police resources to these hot spots can appreciably reduce crime. However, being problem solvers requires that police departments rely on local residents and private resources (Siegel & Worrall, 2012).

What still needs to be done?

Obviously, with something over 13 million arrests by law enforcement each year, there is still plenty to be done. Community-oriented policing programs should be expanded, and problem-oriented policing strategies need to be continued with a greater use of current technology.

More programs like the Weed and Seed program must be funded and used in more communities. Weed and Seed is a federal program that provides funds to cities to help prevent and control crime and to improve the quality of life in high-crime neighborhoods (Albanese, 2013). Combining law enforcement with community activities, Weed and Seed programs concentrate on law enforcement by coordinating the efforts of police and prosecutors to identify, arrest, and prosecute violent offenders and drug traffickers in targeted areas (Albanese, 2013). At the same time, the program coordinates neighborhood revitalization efforts designed to prevent future crimes. Weed and Seed activities typically involve after-school activities for youth, adult literacy classes, and parental counseling. Recently, well over 300 cities in the United States were using Weed and Seed programs (Albanese, 2013).

It is apparent that successful crime control and prevention programs must involve law enforcement and citizens working together in a collaborative partnership.

No. 6: Terrorism

What is the problem?

As Americans, we had always believed we were immune from terrorist attacks. But that all changed on September 11, 2001, when we discovered just how vulnerable we could be to terrorist attacks by foreigners.

Of course, the previous belief of immunity from terrorism was in itself a false belief, as we have experienced violence throughout our history. Instead, we deluded ourselves with what historian Richard E. Rubenstein (1970) calls "the myth of peaceful progress." This myth alleges that the United States was different from other countries, in that we had learned to settle differences peacefully. Yet, this belied what happened in the 1860s during the Civil War and the violence we experienced in the 1960s associated with racial protests and antiwar riots, not to mention other outbreaks of vigilantism and violence that have accompanied unrest and rebellion related to labor, race and segregation, abortion, and other controversial issues.

However, the terrorism that is of most concern to the criminal justice system today has to do with foreign terrorists holding radical political agendas. The problem for the justice system is to find and arrest people who are intent on carrying out terrorist activities while keeping our citizens safe and at the same time preserving individual civil and human rights.

What is currently being done about it?

Following the 2001 attacks on the World Trade Center and on the Pentagon, Congress enacted and the President signed the USA PATRIOT ACT. The act created a number of new crimes, such as terrorist attacks against mass transportation and harboring or concealing terrorists (Schmalleger, 2003). But the first U.S. response was to declare a war on terror to fight against radical Islamic terrorist groups who wish to destroy this country and its allies (Regali & Hewitt, 2008). The Department of Justice took some of the initial steps at about the same time in this war by designating key terrorist organizations, dismantling terrorist threats and cells, freezing terrorist assets around the world, and killing, capturing, or trying to otherwise incapacitate terrorist operatives (Regali & Hewitt, 2008).

The Department of Justice used the federal criminal justice system to apprehend, prosecute, convict, and incarcerate terrorists. The FBI moved terrorism up to the highest priority in its national security mission. However, one of the central problems that enabled the attacks of September 11 was the lack of information sharing between intelligence and criminal justice agencies. Following the attacks, President George W. Bush proposed the creation of the Department of Homeland Security, a new Cabinet-level federal unit whose primary purpose is to protect the United States by coordinating intelligence efforts and communication with law enforcement (Regali & Hewitt, 2008).

Local law enforcement agencies have also played a role in protecting the country from terrorism by intelligence gathering and sharing of information. Training programs in intelligence gathering have been helpful to local police departments, and some community training programs have been put into place to help empower citizens to play their part in preventing terrorism (Masters et al., 2013).

What still needs to be done?

Law enforcement in every city needs to help create a hostile environment that frustrates or thwarts terrorists from carrying out terrorist activities. Randomly deploying massive numbers of police officers in areas that might be targets of terrorists can be an effective strategy to prevent terrorists from carrying out planned activities (Masters et al., 2013).

Police officers and police departments need to be ever vigilant for what are referred to as precursor crimes. These are offenses committed for the purpose of enabling acts of terrorism. For example, ATM fraud, money laundering, and staged accidents might be precursor crimes (Masters et al., 20913).

Furthermore, the police and the community can work together. The police can offer tips and instructions to the community about suspicious activity that could help to identify suspects. At the same time, citizens can be tolerant of the procedures put into place—for instance, security scanners and safety techniques used at airports—that are necessary to spot would-be terrorists.

No. 7: Gangs and Gang Violence

What is the problem?

Gangs remain a substantial problem in this country. The 1998 National Youth Gang Survey estimated that there was a total of 4,463 active gangs in the United States, with 852 of them operating in large cities. In fact, every city with a population over 250,000 reported some level of gang activity (Peak & Griffin, 2005).

In 2012, the National Gang Center reported that gangs across the country were involved in various crimes, especially drug sales, firearm use, aggravated assault, and burglary, robbery, and breaking and entering (National Gang Center, 2012). While homicides characterize serious gang problems in many cities, gang homicides tend to be heavily concentrated geographically in the United States. Most cities have no gang homicides, and those that do usually report very few of them from year to year (Egley et al., 2006). Research has shown that gang homicides tend to occur in spurts, governed by episodic gang conflicts that wax and wane and sometimes extend over a number of years (Block & Block, 1993; Howell & Moore, 2010; Papachristos, 2009).

The use of firearms in assaults, of course, increases the likelihood of these events resulting in lethal violence in contrast to non-lethal injury. Beginning in the 1980s, youth gangs were reported to have more weapons of greater lethality (Block & Block, 1993; Tita & Abrahamse, 2004). Cities experiencing higher levels of gang violence—evidenced by reports of multiple gang-related homicides over survey years—were significantly more likely than those experiencing no gang homicides to report more pervasive and frequent firearm use by gang members in assault crimes (47 percent versus 4 percent of the jurisdictions, respectively) (Egley et al., 2006).

What is currently being done about it?

Today, about two thirds of all large cities have a specialized gang unit, while about half of all other cities have such a unit (Weisel & Painter, 1997). Most cities seem to respond to gang problems by forming a special unit, and over time these gang units not only do investigative activities, but also work at prevention and enforcement as well (Peak & Griffin, 2005).

An increasingly well-known police response to gangs is the GREAT program (Gang Resistance Education and Training), which originated in 1991 in Phoenix, Arizona. GREAT emphasizes the acquisition of information and skills needed by students to resist peer pressure and gang influences (Peak & Griffin, 2005). A national evaluation of GREAT in 11 cities found that students who participated in GREAT programs reported lower levels of delinquency, impulsive behavior, risk-taking behavior, and approval of fighting, along with higher levels of self-esteem, parental monitoring and attachment, commitment to positive peers, and antigang attitudes (Esbensen, 1996). A more recent evaluation of students' responses to the GREAT curriculum showed that youth had improved attitudes toward law enforcement, more positive peer influences, and a reduction in risk-taking behavior (Esbensen, Osgood, Taylor, Peterson, & Freng, 2001).

Community-oriented policing and problem-solving approaches to gangs are more frequent. Cities that employ this approach work to identify and work with problem neighborhoods, raid drug houses, and mobilize the communities to keep crime out of their areas (Peak & Griffin, 2005).

What is there still to do?

As Peak and Griffin (2005) point out, more needs to be done than police work in order to break the cycle of gang delinquency in this country. Often, there has been a lack of community support for programs aimed at gangs (Peak & Griffin, 2005). However, without community support, the cycle of youth gang violence will continue. In general, street gang membership, gang violence, and other crimes committed by gangs must be understood—and responded to—in light of chronic social patterns and problems.

Gangs are associated with poverty, racial tensions, educational disparities, family instability, weapon availability, drug markets, and housing patterns (Peak & Griffin, 2005). The ultimate solution to gang problems, then, rests in changing social and economic conditions in neighborhoods and cities. That means increasing educational opportunities, improving racial and ethnic attitudes, increasing employment opportunities, and involving communities in working together with the criminal justice system to provide positive alternatives to gang activities.

No. 8: Drugs, Drug Dealing, and Addiction

What is the problem?

America has a long history of trying to deal with the negative effects of drug abuse. Throughout the 20th century, federal laws have been passed numerous times to regulate narcotics, dangerous drugs, and controlled substances.

Acts passed by Congress, such as the Comprehensive Drug Abuse and Prevention and Control Act (1970) and the Omnibus Drug Act (1980), were seen to increase government control and involvement in what became known as "the war on drugs." The Omnibus Drug Act created a U.S. "drug czar," and while each succeeding law was aimed at toughening the approaches to drug users, drug manufacturers, and drug distributors, people in this country continue to use illegal drugs (Masters et al., 2013). Despite the war on drugs, which has featured tough laws and strict sentences, enforcement of drug laws remains a difficult and costly problem.

There is a connection between drugs and crime, as many drug users are addicted to or abuse alcohol or other drugs, and some addicts' need for drugs leads them to commit crimes (Masters et al., 2013). But just the use of drugs leads to arrests. In fact, in this country, arrests for drug abuse violations have increased steadily since 1970 (Masters et al., 2013). And the cost to our society for attempting to enforce drug laws?

By some estimates, the war on drugs has so far cost close to a trillion dollars (Debusmann, 2012). What has that vast expenditure bought? Very little. According to the government's latest "Survey on Drug Use and Health," more than 22 million Americans—nearly 9 percent of the U.S. population—used illegal drugs in 2010, up from 8 percent in 2008 (Results from the 2010 National Survey on Drug Use and Health, 2011). That demand, and the vast profits derived from it, has prompted violence on a mind-boggling scale south of the U.S. border. In Mexico alone, around 50,000 people have died in the past six years as drug cartels fight each other—for access to supply lines to the U.S. market—and the Mexican state (Debusmann, 2012).

What are we currently doing about it?

The strategies put in place to try to solve the drug problem in the United States have apparently been failures. The strategies used over the past few decades have included imposing harsher punishments, decriminalizing drug use and abuse, legalizing certain types of illegal drugs, enhancing law enforcement control efforts, and focusing on medical solutions to drug problems (Masters et al., 2013).

Even if law enforcement agencies had unlimited resources—which, obviously, they don't—there would be no more success than we've seen in the past. In short, as many people are coming to believe—and say publicly (including Barack Obama, when he was running for senator)—the war on drugs has failed (Debusmann, 2012; Obama, 2004).

Despite a lack of success in enforcing drug laws, there have been promising approaches to dealing with individual drug users. Gerstein and Harwood (1990) found that therapeutic community programs, when closely linked to community-based supervision and treatment programs, can significantly reduce rearrest rates. A therapeutic community is a residential treatment environment that provides a constant learning experience, in which the drug user's changes in conduct, attitudes, values, and emotions are implemented, monitored, and reinforced on a daily basis (McNeece et al., 2005).

Also, drug courts have been found to be a promising alternative. Drug courts have been shown to be successful in reducing or eliminating substance abuse while cutting down on criminal behavior.

What still needs to be done?

It may be that enforcement of drug laws is impossible. However, if any progress is to be made, many experts say that the United States must experience a paradigm shift away from its usual way of dealing with the drug problem (McNeece et al., 2005). As long as the approach to drug abuse is to treat the drug user as a criminal and apply severe sanctions, then nothing will change.

Perhaps America should take a close look at the approach being implemented in several western European nations. This approach is called harm reduction and it promotes a public health perspective rather than a criminal justice one. The harm reduction philosophy takes the position that the use of drugs is inevitable and trying to achieve a drug-free society is doomed to failure (McNeece et al., 2005). A second feature of this approach is to treat all drug use as problematic and to make no distinction between legal and illegal drug use or abuse. And finally, this philosophy suggests that all drug problems should be seen as basically public health rather than criminal justice concerns.

Countries that have implemented harm reduction approaches report significant success in terms of involving drug users in treatment. Since they do not have a goal of eliminating drug use, their aims are remarkably different from those in the United States (McNeece et al., 2005). By considering this approach, drug users would no longer be brought into the criminal justice system, and all of the law enforcement resources could be focused on preventing illegal drugs from entering the country.

No. 9: Racial Bias

What is the problem?

Justice is supposed to be color-blind. But is it in the United States?

Throughout the American criminal justice system, it appears that race is a factor. It is a factor in who gets stopped and frisked, who gets arrested, who has charges filed against him, and the kinds of sentences that are imposed.

A number of empirical studies have found that state and local police officers routinely stop and/or search African American motorists at a rate far greater than their representation in the driving pool (Siegel & Worrall, 2012). There are more minorities in prison per capita than whites, which suggests to many that there is racial bias in sentencing (Siegel & Worrall, 2012). This is disturbing to sociologists and criminal justice experts because of the impact it has on the minority community. Western (2006) points out that by the time they reach their mid-thirties, 60 percent of black high school dropouts are either prisoners or ex-cons. This has resulted in a collective experience for young black men that is far different from the rest of American society (Western, 2006).

A number of research studies find that racial bias still exists in the judicial process. In one recent study of federal sentencing, it was discovered that Hispanics and blacks receive harsher sentences than white defendants (Siegel & Worrall, 2012). Furthermore, studies show that African Americans are more likely to be detained before trial than whites; that prosecutors are less likely to divert minorities from the legal system than whites; that minorities live in poor communities, and people living in poor areas get harsher sentences, regardless of their race; and African Americans receive longer sentences for drug crimes than whites (Siegel & Worrall, 2012).

African Americans are incarcerated at a rate of nearly 6 (5.6) times the rate of whites (Uneven Justice: State Rates of Incarceration, 2007). One in three (32 percent) black males can expect to serve time in prison at some time in their lives, Hispanic males have a 17 percent chance, and white males have a six percent chance. Thus, incarceration in America is concentrated among African American men. While one in 87 white males between the ages of 18 to 64 is incarcerated and the figure for similarly situated Hispanic males is one in 36, in black males it is one in 12. More than one third (37 percent) of black male dropouts between the ages of 20 and 34 are behind bars (Collateral Cost: Incarceration Effects on Economic Mobility, 2010).

What is currently being done?

In August 2004, the American Bar Association Justice Kennedy Commission issued a report describing criminal justice racial disparities in detail and recommended measures to eliminate or reduce such disparities. While the commission expressed some uncertainty as to the exact causes of the disparities, it was certain about two things: (1) Racial disparity must be recognized as a serious problem; and (2) the problem must be addressed in a serious way (Report to the House of Delegates, 2004). The commission went on to say that it was important to encourage responsible officials to identify racial disparities in the criminal justice process, whether intentional or unintentional, that result in the dissimilar treatment of similarly situated individuals. Once identified, officials can develop policy and practices to reduce or eliminate the problem. Another recommendation of the commission was the creation of criminal justice procedure and ethnic task forces to, among other things:

- design and conduct studies to determine the extent of racial and ethnic disparity in the initial stages of criminal investigations, prosecutions, dispositions and sentencing.
- make public reports of the results of their studies; and make specific recommendations intended to eliminate racial and ethnic discrimination and unjustified social and ethnic disparities.

What still needs to be done?

What can these results teach us about how state-level anti-disparity processes can more effectively combat racial disparities? The first four recommendations for action involve the nature of the anti-disparities processes, while the final two relate to the participation of attorneys and other citizens. To summarize, anti-disparities processes should be

- comprehensive in scope;
- sponsored, at least in part, by institutional actors outside of the court system;
- governed in a transparent, participatory, and systematic fashion; and
- committed to accomplishing their major objective at a rapid pace.

Attorneys, criminal justice professionals, and concerned citizens should

- stimulate criminal justice reform by personal initiative and public activism, rather than expecting high-level processes to effectively combat disparities alone; and
- recognize their ethical responsibility to act with the utmost urgency to eliminate all racial and ethnic disparities given the country's long history of malign neglect.

No. 10: Death penalty

What is the problem?

The Gallup Poll has surveyed the country about the death penalty since the 1930s. Public support for the death penalty shifts constantly, as during some decades—such as during the mid-1960s—support dropped to below 50 percent of citizens supporting capital punishment (Public Opinion, 2012). However, there have been other decades—such as during the late 1980s and early 1990s—when support reached as high as 80 percent (Public Opinion, 2012). Today, support for the death penalty is above 50 percent, but when adults polled are asked, "If you could choose between the following two approaches, which do you think is the better penalty for murder: the death penalty [or] life imprisonment with absolutely no possibility of parole?" support drops to about 50 percent (Polling Report.com, 2004).

Support for the death penalty, according to Gallup Polls, has been very high (81 percent) when people were asked if they supported the death penalty for Timothy McVeigh. But given the number of exonerations of innocent people who were given the death penalty, support has waned in recent years (Public Opinion, 2012).

For years, people assumed that the death penalty saved money (Samaha, 2006). But not anymore. Many people are becoming more aware of the expenses associated with executing inmates. The costs associated with death penalty cases far exceed the cost of life imprisonment (Siegel & Worrall, 2012). Because of numerous appeals, the median time between conviction by a jury, sentencing by a judge, and execution averages 14 years in California, and California spends more than $5 million per year on death row appeals (Siegel & Worrall, 2012).

But opposition to the death penalty has been growing for reasons other than the great expense associated with it and the increasing awareness that innocent people are often condemned to die. In addition, many people believe the death penalty is unfairly applied (Masters et al., 2013). Research continues to show that people of color are disproportionately represented on death row. While blacks make up 35 percent of death row inmates, they only make up 13 percent of the U.S. population (Masters et al., 2013).

Another reason for opposition to the death penalty is the lack of evidence demonstrating that it has a deterrent effect. Using various methods of investigating whether capital punishment has a deterrent effect, researchers over the past 60 years have failed to show any deterrent effect (Siegel & Worrall, 2012).

Also, there are death penalty opponents who argue that capital punishment is morally wrong. The Catholic Church, for instance, has taken a stand against it; others simply see it as brutal and demeaning (Siegel & Worrall, 2012).

Finally, the United States remains the only Western industrialized nation to use capital punishment. Moreover, it is one of only six countries known to have executed juveniles since 1995 (Masters et al., 2013).

Yet the death penalty remains a controversial topic, with proponents as well as opponents taking very emotional stands. Thirty-three states in this country still have capital punishment laws on their books, with 17 states having abolished the practice (Masters et al., 2013).

What is currently being done about it?

As innocence projects and innocence inquiry commissions continue to expose the wrongfully convicted, as disparities of race and class in the implementation of capital punishment become more widely apparent, and as the expense of condemning people to die continues to mount and become more of a concern, the popularity of the death penalty seems to be waning (Masters et al., 2013).

The innocence projects and inquiry commissions will continue their work, and when innocent people who have spent long years in prison have been freed, this is often front page news. This is likely to continue to erode public support of the death penalty.

In 2010, the United Nations General Assembly adopted its third resolution calling for the end of the death penalty (Masters et al., 2013). Each time such resolutions come up for a vote in the United Nations, more countries support the resolution.

What still needs to be done?

In general, the United States perhaps needs to follow the lead of other civilized societies and eliminate the death penalty. While that might be very difficult for states such as Texas, Arizona, and Florida, still, there are enough doubts about the efficacy, the fairness, and the humaneness of the death penalty to justify the end of capital punishment.

If it is not abolished by law, then most other states can do what North Carolina did in 2009 and that is to pass a racial justice act. Called the North Carolina Racial Justice Act (RJA), this law allows capital defendants, for the first time, to use statistical evidence to show systemic bias in the death penalty (Racial Justice Act, 2012). If a defendant successfully proves that race was a significant factor in decisions to seek or impose the death penalty at the time of his or her trial, the court is required to convert that sentence to life in prison. This kind of legislation helps correct some of the discrimination and racial bias that take place in sentencing.

Reinventing the Criminal Justice System

There are plenty of problems and challenges in the criminal justice system. However, as is apparent in this chapter, there are many individuals, communities, organizations, states, and departments of the federal government that are well aware of what needs to be addressed and changed in the justice system. While many successful efforts are being made, much more still needs to be accomplished in order for our criminal justice system to be productive, effective, just, and fair to all citizens.

Although America has many shortcomings and presents many challenges, it is also a resourceful country that has the unique ability to pull together resources, innovative thinking, and ideas to meet its problems. Perhaps the criminal justice system doesn't have to be reinvented as much as it needs constant critical examination and continual revision. By recognizing the significant challenges facing the criminal justice system, there is considerable hope that changes will continue to be made and that the criminal justice system of the future will more fully live up to one of the basic tenets of our democracy: a society in which there is liberty and justice for all.

FOR FURTHER CONSIDERATION

Historical Events relevant to Chapter Eighteen

February 8, 2011: Virginia senator Jim Webb reintroduces the National Criminal Justice Commission Act (Senate Bill 306), which will create a blue-ribbon commission to look at every aspect of our criminal justice system, with an eye toward reshaping the criminal justice system from top to bottom. Webb believes it is time to analyze the criminal justice system in its entirety, to examine its interlocking parts, to learn what works and what does not, and make recommendations for reform.

February 16, 1967: President Lyndon Baines Johnson receives the report from a commission he appointed. The report is called *The Challenge of Crime in a Free Society.* This report makes more than 200 recommendations as part of a comprehensive approach toward the prevention and fighting of crime. Some of these recommendations would find their way into the Omnibus Crime Control and Safe Streets Act of 1968. In its report, the crime commission advocates a "systems" approach to criminal justice, with improved coordination among law enforcement, courts, and correctional agencies.

March 7, 1876: August Vollmer is born. He becomes known as the "father of modern law enforcement." He was the first chief of police to require that police officers obtain college degrees, and he persuaded the University of California to allow him to teach criminal justice courses in 1916. He then established a criminal justice program at the University of California–Berkeley. Vollmer was the first police chief to create a motorized force, placing officers on motorcycles and in cars so they could patrol a broader area with greater efficiency. Radios were included in patrol cars. He was also the first to use the lie detector in police work.

May 20, 1929: President Herbert Hoover establishes the Wickersham Commission, which was officially called the National Commission on Law Observance and Enforcement, on this date. Former U.S. Attorney General George W. Wickersham headed the 11-member group charged with identifying the causes of criminal activity and to make recommendations for appropriate public policy. The commission also noted that additional problems were created by uneven enforcement by the various states and recommended that that role be assigned exclusively to the federal government. The commission also recommended the removal of the corrupting influence of politics from police departments. Further, it recommended that police recruits and officers already serving as police officers be given adequate training.

Important Court Cases

- ***Whren v. United States*, 517 U.S. 806 (1996):** In this 1996 Supreme Court case, the High Court ruled that law enforcement could stop drivers for any traffic violation regardless of the true intent behind the officer's decision to stop the driver. The defendants, who were both black, contended that police officers might decide which motorists to stop based on decidedly impermissible factors, such as the race of the car's occupants. But the Court ruled that a traffic stop is permissible as long as a reasonable officer in the same circumstances could have stopped the car for the suspected traffic violation.
- ***Williams v. Illinois*, 132 U.S. 1976 (2012):** The Supreme Court retreated somewhat from a groundbreaking decision in 2009, which said that crime lab reports may not be used in criminal trials unless the analysts responsible for creating them provide live testimony. That decision in 2009 in *Melendez-Diaz v. Massachusetts* was reaffirmed two years later in a second decision in the case of *Bullcoming v. New Mexico* (2011), and the Court ruled that only the analyst who did the work, rather than a colleague or supervisor, would do. These decisions are based on the Sixth Amendment's confrontation clause, which gives a criminal defendant the right "to be confronted with the witnesses against him." In this case, the Court said its earlier rulings did not apply to all technicians.

Websites to Check Out

- *The Sentencing Project.* Available at: *http://www.sentencingproject.org/template/index.cfm.* This website is dedicated to working for a fair and effective U.S. criminal justice system by promoting reforms in sentencing policy, addressing unjust racial disparities and practices, and advocating for alternatives to incarceration.
- *Death Penalty Information Center.* Available at: *http://www.deathpenaltyinfo.org/.* The Death Penalty Information Center is a website that provides analysis and information on issues concerning capital punishment. Founded in 1990, the center promotes informed discussion of the death penalty by preparing in-depth reports, conducting briefings for journalists, and serving as a resource to those working on this issue.
- *Citizens United for Rehabilitation of Errants (CURE).* Available at: *http://www.curenational.org/.* The CURE website is sponsored by the CURE organization, which was begun in 1985. The organization believes that prisons should be reserved only for those who truly need to be incarcerated and that prisons should provide rehabilitation services for prisoners to help them turn their lives around. The organization uses its website to provide information to help bring about reform in the criminal justice system.
- *The Innocence Project.* Available at: *http://www.innocenceproject.org/.* The Innocence Project was founded in 1992 by Barry C. Scheck and Peter J. Neufeld at the Benjamin N. Cardozo School of Law at Yeshiva University to assist prisoners who could be proven innocent through DNA testing. To date, 297 people in the United States have been exonerated by DNA testing, including 17 who served time on death row. The Innocence Project's staff of attorneys and law students provides direct representation or critical assistance in most of these cases. The Innocence Project's mission is to free innocent people who remain incarcerated and to bring substantive reform to the system responsible for their unjust imprisonment.

Books

- Berman, G., and Fox, A. (2010). *Trial and Error in Criminal Justice Reform: Learning from Failure.* Baltimore: Urban Institute Press.
- Muraskin, R., and Roberts, A. R. (2005). *Visions for Change: Crime and Justice in the Twenty-First Century.* Upper Saddle River, NJ: Pearson.
- Stuntz, W. J (2011). *The Collapse of American Criminal Justice.* Cambridge, MA: Belknap Press.

Movies

- *Crash:* A 2004 dramatic movie, it depicts the lives of various people, both in and out of the criminal justice system, who engage in racism and racial profiling.
- *Flying While Muslim:* A 2010 movie about the intolerance and racial profiling that occurs post-2001.
- *Deadline:* This 2004 documentary details the last few months of Governor George Ryan's term as governor of Illinois. Concerned about the number of innocent people on death row in Illinois, he must decide what to do about the 168 people on death row in that state.
- *The Thin Blue Line:* An Errol Morris film from 2003, this tells the story of an innocent man condemned to die in Texas for the murder of a police officer.

TV Shows

- *The Shield:* A television drama that ran from 2002 until 2008, it featured police corruption as a main plot in the series.

Review for Chapter Eighteen:

Research Paper or Term Paper Topics:

- The death penalty
- The war on drugs
- Criminal justice reform
- Problem-oriented policing
- Broken windows concept

Important Terms to Know

Broken windows theory: A theory proposing that disorder leads to crime because criminals assume a neighborhood that tolerates disorder will also ignore criminal acts.

Community-oriented policing:
A policing strategy that depends on getting community members to address the problems that occur in their neighborhoods.

CSI **effect:** This term most often refers to the belief that jurors have come to demand more forensic evidence in criminal trials based on their familiarity with TV shows such as the *CSI* franchise.

Exoneration: The word exonerate means to free someone from blame or responsibility. An exoneration often means that a person is found to be not guilty (frequently through use of DNA evidence) of the crime for which he or she was previously convicted.

Incarceration rate: In order to compare rates of incarceration, the number of people imprisoned from year to year, state to state, or country to country, the rate of incarceration is usually expressed in terms of the number of people placed in prison per 100,000 people.

Problem-oriented policing:
A policing strategy based on conducting specific and detailed research on a community's problems to discover the underlying dynamics of crime.

Wrongful conviction: The conviction of a person for a crime that later proves to be erroneous, and the person is actually innocent.

Study Guide Questions

True or False:

1. One of the primary challenges to the criminal justice system is a high rate of incarceration.

2. It is because of a steadily increasing amount of crime that we have overcrowded prisons and jails.

3. The same problems are seen over and over again and account for wrongful convictions and subsequent exonerations and include faulty eyewitness identification, flawed forensic science, coerced confessions, and shoddy police work.

4. Community-oriented policing is viewed as one of the major problems in the criminal justice system.

5. Gangs and gang violence remain a substantial problem in this country.

Multiple Choice Items:

6. In general, it is now becoming evident that there is a lack of scientific research to confirm the reliability of such forensic areas as
   a. hair analysis
   b. bite marks
   c. arson investigation
   d. bullet comparison
   e. all of the above

7. It is generally agreed that the war on drugs has
   a. been a colossal failure
   b. been the best thing that ever happened in this country
   c. solved the drug problem
   d. cost the United States very little money

8. Prosecutorial misconduct has been found to be present in about 18 percent of
   a. convictions
   b. wrongful convictions
   c. drug convictions
   d. misdemeanor convictions

9. A number of empirical studies has found that state and local police officers routinely stop and/or search African American motorists
   a. at a far lower proportional rate than white drivers
   b. at about the same rate as for white drivers
   c. at a much higher rate than for white drivers
   d. at a far lower rate than for Asian drivers

References

"About us," (2006), North Carolina Innocence Inquiry Commission [online], Available at: www.innocencecommission-nc.gov/.

Albanese, J. S. (2013). *Criminal Justice*. 5th ed. Upper Saddle River, NJ: Pearson.

Block, C. R., and Block, R. (1993). *Street Gang Crime in Chicago*. Washington, DC: National Institute of Justice.

Blythe, A., (Feb. 22, 2010), "Taylor case brings commission renown," *Raleigh News Observer* [online], Available at: http://www.newsobserver.com/2010/02/22/351527/taylor-case-brings-commission.html.

California Commission on the Fair Administration of Justice, (2008), "Final Report" [online], Available at: www.ccfaj.org/.

"Collateral Cost: Incarceration Effects on Economic Mobility," (2010), The Pew Charitable Trust [online],. Available at: www.pewstates.org/uploadedFiles/PCS.../Collateral_Costs(1).pdf.

Debusmann, B., (April 16, 2012), "Obama and the failed war on drugs," *Reuters* [online], http//blogs.reuters.com.

Edwards, H. T., (April 17, 2012), "How Reliable Is Forensic Evidence in Court?" Frontline, PBS-TV, Available at: http://www.pbs.org/wgbh/pages/frontline/criminal-justice/real-csi/judge-harry-t-edwards- how-reliable-is-forensic-evidence-in-court/.

Egley, A. Jr., Howell, J. C., and Major, A. K. (2006). *National Youth Gang Survey: 1999–2001*. Washington, DC: U.S. Department of Justice, Office of Juvenile Justice and Delinquency Prevention.

Esbensen, F. A. (1996). Gang resistance education and training: The national evaluation. *Police Chief*, September, 34–38.

Esbensen, F. A., Osgood, D. W., Taylor, T. J., Peterson, D., and Freng, A. 2001. How great is G.R.E.A.T.? Results from a longitudinal quasi-experimental design. *Criminology and Public Policy* 1 (1), 87–118.

"Final Report," (2008), California Commission on the Fair Administration of Justice [online], Available at: www.ccfaj.org/.

Fox, J. A., (2010), "Homicide Trends in the U.S. Bureau of Justice Statistics," Available at: bjs.ojp.usdoj.gov/content/pub/pdf/htius.pdf.

Frosch, D., and Johnson, D., (2012), "Gunman kills 12 in Colorado, reviving gun debate," *New York Times* [online], Available at: http://www.nytimes.com/2012/07/21/us/shooting-at-colorado-theater-showing-batman-movie.html?pagewanted=all.

Fuller, J. R. (2010). *Criminal Justice: Mainstream and Crosscurrents*. Upper Saddle River, NJ: Prentice Hall.

Garrett, B. L., and Neufeld, P. J., (2009), "Invalid forensic science testimony and wrongful conviction," *Virginia Law Review* [online], Available at: virginialawreview.org/content/pdfs/95/1.pdf.

Gerstein, D. R., and Harwood, H. J., eds. (1990. *Treating Drug Problems*. vol. 1. Washington, DC: National Academy Press.

Gertner, N., (2012), "National academy of sciences report: A challenge to the courts," In *Criminal Justice* [online], Available at: http://www.google.com/#hl=en&rlz=1R2ADRA_enUS476&sclient=psy-ab&q=Gertner+2012+A+challenge+to+the+courts+Criminal+Justice&oq=Gertner+2012+A+challenge+to+the+courts+Criminal+Justice&gs_l=serp.12...52070.55746.1.59206.17.17.0.0.0.0.133.1829.5j12.17.0.les%3B..0.0...1c.0wwWN6N_gXs&pbx=1&bav=on.2,or.r_gc.r_pw.r_qf.&fp=bb1985a4b0dff75f&biw=1280&bih=558.

Guerino, P., Harrison, P. M., and Sabol, W. J., (2011), "Prisoners in 2010," Bureau of Justice Statistics [online],. Available at: http://www.google.com/#hl=en&rlz=1R2ADRA_enUS476&sclient=psy-ab&q=bureau+of+justice+statistics+prisoners+in+2011&rlz=1R2ADRA_enUS476&oq=prison+Bureau+of+Justice+Statistics+2011&gs_l=hp.1.1.0i8j0i22.7411.20286.0.26346.45.40.2.3.3.0.374.4434.17j22j0j1.40.0.les%3B..0.0...1c.IGUx803oTkQ&pbx=1&bav=on.2,or.r_gc.r_pw.r_qf.&fp=bb1985a4b0dff75f&biw=1280&bih=558.

Heinrick, J. (2006). Everyone's an expert: The CSI effect's negative impact on juries. *Triple Helix* Fall, 2006, 59–61.

Howell, J. C., and Moore, J. P. (2010). *History of Street Gangs in the United States*. National Gang Center Bulletin No. 4. Tallahassee, FL: Institute for Intergovernmental Research, National Gang Center.

Hsu, S. S., (April 16, 2012), "Convicted defendants left uninformed of forensic flaws found by Justice Department," *Washington Post* [online], Available at: http://www.washingtonpost.com/local/crime/convicted-defendants-left-uninformed-of-forensic-flaws-found-by-justice-dept/2012/04/16/gIQAWTcgMT_story.html.

Kingsbury, A., (February 27, 2009), "Under Obama, drug war tactics poised to shift," *USA Today* [online], Available at: http://www.usnews.com/news/national/articles/2009/02/27/under-obama-drug-war-tactics-poised-to-shift.

Masters, R. E., Way, L. B., Gerstenfeld, P. B., Muscat, B. T., Hooper, M., Dussich, J. P. J., Pincu, L., and Skrapec, C. A. (2013). *CJ: Realities and Challenges.* 2nd ed. New York: McGraw-Hill.

McNeece, C. A., Bullington, B., Arnold, E. A., and Springer, D. W. (2005). "The war on drugs: Treatment, research, and substance abuse intervention in the twenty-first century." In Muraskin, R., & Roberts, A. R. *Visions for Change: Crime and Justice in the Twenty-First Century.* pp. 88–120. Upper Saddle River, NJ: Pearson.

National Gang Center, (2012), Available at: www.nationalgangcenter.gov/.

Newman, O. (1973). *Defensible Space: Crime Prevention through Urban Design.* New York: Macmillan Publishing Co.

North Carolina Innocence Inquiry Commission, (2012), Available at: http://www.innocencecommission-nc.gov/.

Ostendorff, J., (July 18, 2011), "States look to right wrong convictions," *USA Today* [online], Available at: http://www.usatoday.com/news/nation/2011-07-17-dna-evidence-exonerates-innocent-prisoners-wrongful-convictions_n.htm.

Paltra, R., (June 13, 2012), "California's Prison Population Drops Dramatically." Southern California Public Radio, Available at: Scpr.org.

Papachristos, A. V. (2009). Murder by structure: Dominance relations and the social structure of gang homicide. *American Journal of Sociology* 115, 74–128.

Peak, K. J., and Griffin, T. (2005). "Gangs: Origin, status, community response, and policy implications." In Muraskin, R., & Roberts, A. R. *Visions for Change: Crime and Justice in the Twenty-First century.* pp. 43–59. Upper Saddle River, NJ: Pearson.

Public Opinion, (2012), "Gallup Poll Reports Lowest Support for Death Penalty in Nearly 40 Years." Death Penalty Information Center. Available at: http://www.deathpenaltyinfo.org/category/categories/resources/public-opinion.

"Racial Justice Act," (2012), ACLU website [online], Available at: http://www.aclu.org/capital-punishment/north-carolina-racial-justice-act.

Regali, R. M., and Hewitt, J. D. (2008). *Exploring Criminal Justice.* Sudbury, MA: Jones and Bartlett Publishers.

"Report to the House of Delegates," (2004), American Bar Association Justice Kennedy Commission [online], Available at: http://www.google.com/#hl=en&rlz=1R2ADRA_enUS476&sclient=psy-ab&q=Report+to+the+House+of+delegates.+ABA+2004&oq=Report+to+the+House+of+delegates.+ABA+2004&gs_l=serp.12...2857.20403.0.22908.80.57.1.0.0.11.188.5257.37j18.57.0.les%3Beghsbq..0.0...1.oTWntY3P7DE&pbx=1&bav=on.2,or.r_gc.r_pw.r_qf.&fp=bb1985a4b0dff75f&biw=1280&bih=558.

Results from the 2010 National Survey on Drug Use and Health: Summary of National Findings. (2011). Substance Abuse and Mental Health Services Administration. NSDUH Series H-41, HHS Publication No. (SMA) 11-4658. Rockville, MD: Substance Abuse and Mental Health Services Administration.

Roman, J., Walsh, K., Lachman, P., and Yahner, J., (2012), "Post-Conviction DNA Testing and Wrongful Conviction," Urban Institute [online], Available at: www2.timesdispatch.com/mgmedia/file/796/urban-institute-report/.

Rubenstein, R. E. (1970). *Rebels in Eden: Mass Political Violence in the United States.* New York: Little, Brown.

Samaha, J. (2006). *Criminal Justice.* 7th ed. Belmont, CA: Thomson/Wadsworth.

Schmalleger, F. (2003). *Criminal Justice Today: An Introductory Text for the 21st Century.* 7th ed. Upper Saddle River, NJ: Prentice Hall.

Siegel, L. J., and Worrall, J. L. (2012). *Introduction to Criminal Justice.* 13th ed. Belmont, CA: Wadsworth/Cengage.

"Support for Death Penalty," (2004), Pollingreport.com [online], Available at: Pollingreport.com.

Territo, L., Halstead, J. B., and Bromley, M. L. (2004). *Crime and Justice in America: A Human Perspective.* Upper Saddle River, NJ: Pearson.

Tita, G. E., and Abrahamse, A. (2004). Gang homicide in LA, 1981–2001. *Perspectives on Violence Prevention* 3, 1–18.

"Uneven Justice: State Rates of Incarceration by Race and Ethnicity," (2007), The Sentencing Project [online], Available at: http://www.sentencingproject.org/detail/publication.cfm?publication_id=167.